The Global Currency Power of the US Dollar

Anthony Elson

The Global Currency Power of the US Dollar

Problems and Prospects

palgrave
macmillan

Anthony Elson
School of Advanced International Studies
Johns Hopkins University
Washington, DC, USA

ISBN 978-3-030-83518-7 ISBN 978-3-030-83519-4 (eBook)
https://doi.org/10.1007/978-3-030-83519-4

This Palgrave Macmillan imprint is published by the registered company Springer Nature Switzerland AG
The registered company address is: Gewerbestrasse 11, 6330 Cham, Switzerland

To Queenie

For her True Love and Friendship,
her Indomitably Positive and Generous Spirit,
and
her Unhalting Support of my Professional Work

Preface

This is the fifth book with a focus on a different aspect of globalization that I have written over the last 12 years. The work "global" or "globalization" appears in the title for all of them. In one sense, this output is a natural reflection of my interests in various themes of international economics that I have developed over a long career beginning with my graduate training in international affairs and economics at Columbia University, many years of service on the professional staff of the IMF, work as a consultant with the World Bank, and teaching at Duke, Johns Hopkins and Yale Universities.

In another sense, each of these books has a link with one of its predecessors, as in the preparation of each of them I discovered that there was a topic that I touched on in each one that I wanted to explore in more depth in a subsequent book. In my third book on the global financial crisis, I wanted to examine in much more detail, and with the benefit of time and further knowledge, a topic that I examined more briefly in 2009–2010 in the immediate wake of the crisis, when I was writing my first book. In this particular book, the key role of the US dollar as the de facto currency for the global economy was a topic that I touched on briefly in my previous book on the role of the United States in the global economy.

The subject of the dollar as a global currency is a fascinating topic, as our understanding of its role continues to evolve and the future prospects for its duration are often questioned. This book hopefully contributes in a useful, interesting and significant manner to this important topic. Since the early 1970s when the Bretton Woods system of the early post-World War II era broke down, the dollar has served as the main currency of the global economic and financial system by fiat, i.e., without any basis in treaty, as a reflection of the hegemonic role of the United States in that system and the convenience that private traders and institutions have found in using the dollar for cross-border transactions. This special role of the dollar has intensified with the expansion of economic and financial globalization in the last few decades. This book attempts to explain how this situation developed and the factors that have helped to keep it in place. The book also examines a number of defects and potential threats to the stability of the global financial system that can be associated with the current dollar-based reserve currency system. It then examines three different scenarios that could deal with those threats; the prospects for each of these should become clearer during the remainder of the current decade.

As much as possible, I have tried to make this book a self-contained exposition, where technical terms are spelled out rather than included with an assumption that they are familiar to the reader. As a result, I am hopeful that the book will appeal to a wide range of readers from students of public policy to a general audience with an interest in the role of the United States in the global economy, as well as to practitioners in the fields of foreign affairs and business who are not specialists in international economics and finance.

Washington, USA — Anthony Elson

Previous Titles by This Author

Governing Global Finance: The Evolution and Reform of the International Financial Architecture (2011)

Globalization and Development: Why East Asia Surged Ahead and Latin America Fell Behind (2014)

The Global Financial Crisis in Retrospect: Evolution, Resolution and Lessons for Prevention (2017)

The United States in the World Economy: Making Sense of Globalization (2019)

Contents

1 The US Dollar as a Global Currency 1

2 The Origins of the Global Currency Power of the US Dollar 15

3 The Growth in the Role of the Dollar as a Global Currency Power 31

4 The Benefits of the Dollar System to the United States and the Rest of the World 53

5 The Defects of the Dollar-Centered Global Financial System 73

6 Prospects for the Dollar 95

7 Possible Reforms of the Dollar-Centered Reserve System 121

8 The IMF and Reform of the Dollar-Centered Reserve System 139

9 The Dollar and Digital Currencies 159

10 Conclusions 181

Index 199

Glossary

BIS	Bank for International Settlements
CBDCs	central bank digital currencies
CDOs	collateralized debt obligations
CFETS	China Foreign Exchange Trade System
CHIPS	Clearinghouse Int'l Payments System (USA)
CIPS	Cross-border Interbank Payments System (China)
DCEP	Digital Currency/Electronic Payment (China)
ECB	European Central Bank
EMDEs	emerging and developing economies
EMU	European Economic and Monetary Union (eurozone)
EPU	European Payments Union
FSB	Financial Stability Board
G7/G10/G20	Group of 7/10/20 nations
GATT	General Agreement on Tariffs and Trade
GFSN	Global Financial Safety Net
GVCs	global value chains
ICU	International Credit Union
ILOLR	international lender of last resort
IMF	International Monetary Fund
INSTEX	Instrument in Support of Trade Exchanges
MBS	mortgage-backed securities
MMT	Modern Monetary Theory
NIIP	net international investment position
PBOC	Peoples Bank of China
RCEP	Regional Comprehensive Economic Partnership
REPO	repurchase agreement

SDRs	Special Drawing Rights (IMF)
SIFMA	Securities Industry and Financial Markets Association
SWIFT	Society for Worldwide Interbank Financial Telecommunication
TAA	Trade Adjustment Assistance
TPP	Trans Pacific Partnership
WHO	World Health Organization
WTO	World Trade Organization

List of Tables

Table 1.1	Relative currency shares for 2020	2
Table 7.1	Global indicators for major economic zones 2019	128

CHAPTER 1

The US Dollar as a Global Currency

The dollar is the domestic currency of the United States, but it is also the dominant currency in the global economy that is used in the trade and financial transactions of many other countries throughout the world. Consider the following facts: the United States accounts for 4% of the world's population, 11% of global trade and around 16% of global GDP (on a purchasing power parity basis), but the dollar currency zone comprised of countries, whose currencies are closely tied to the US dollar and where the dollar dominates most cross-border transactions and the currency shares of their foreign reserves, accounts for roughly two-thirds of the global economy. This basic asymmetry between the size of the US economy and the scope of its currency in the world economy is the fundamental fact underlying the global currency power of the US dollar.

Normally, it is assumed that countries convert their own currency into the currency of other countries with which they wish to carry out trade and financial transactions. However, in reality, the dollar is the main currency used in these foreign exchange operations and, in some cases, it is the only currency used in these transactions, even though the countries carrying out the transactions have their own currencies. Currencies of other advanced countries or regions, such as the pound, the euro and the yen, also are used beyond their territorial domain, but on a much smaller scale than the dollar. Like the dollar, these currencies are so-called reserve currencies that countries use for the composition of their official foreign

A. Elson, *The Global Currency Power of the US Dollar*,
https://doi.org/10.1007/978-3-030-83519-4_1

Table 1.1 Relative currency shares for 2020

	Dollar	*Euro*	*Yen*	*Pound*	*Yuan*
Official reserves	59.0	21.2	6.0	4.7	2.2
Global payments	42.6	37.5	4.3	3.8	1.9
International banking positions	50.3	32.1	5.3	5.1	n.a
International debt securities	45.1	40.0	1.7	7.8	n.a
Foreign exchange transactions (April 2019)	88.3	32.2	16.8	12.8	4.3

Sources BIS, IMF and SWIFT

reserves, but the dollar is by far the most important one. At the end of 2020, the dollar accounted for nearly 60% of global reserves reported to the IMF, compared with 21% for the euro, 6% for the Japanese yen, 4.7% for the British pound and 2.2% for the Chinese renminbi.[1] The dollar also dominated these other currencies in terms of its share of global payments, the international banking positions, international debt securities and foreign exchange transactions, as reported in Table 1.1.

This book attempts to explain how the US dollar has become the dominant currency of the global economic and financial system. It also examines the various dimensions of the global currency power of the US dollar and assesses its benefits and costs for the stability of that system. These costs have risen in recent years, while the United States' traditional hegemonic role in maintaining the stability of the system has been weakened. In this light, the book considers various arrangements that could replace it, in the context of a reform of the international monetary system, in which the US dollar has played a central role throughout the post-World War II (WW2) era.

For purposes of this book, the international monetary system is defined to cover (a) the rules and procedures for the exchange rate arrangements that individual countries maintain for their cross-border trade and financial transactions; (b) the role of reserve currencies held by central banks for their operations; and (c) the work of the International Monetary Fund (IMF), which is the central inter-governmental organization charged with oversight of the system. The global financial system includes the international monetary system, as well as international financial transactions involving equity, debt and direct investment, portfolio management, and the borrowing and lending of banks and non-banks. These transactions would not be possible without the architecture provided by the international monetary system.

The economic effects of the current Covid-19 crisis have highlighted the dominant currency role of the US dollar, as well as the potential problems that could arise in the future. Accordingly, the contents of this book should be seen as directly relevant to post-crisis international policy debate. Some of the concerns about the dollar's role in the international monetary system discussed in this book were also raised in the wake of the global financial crisis of 2008–2009, but they were not pursued at the official level in the years following that crisis because of the intense focus of the advanced countries on global economic recovery and a reform of international financial regulation. However, since that crisis, much more has been learned about the global dollar system and the risks and defects associated with what is a largely unregulated system of dollar liquidity and credit, which are reflected in this book.

The Global Currency Power of the US Dollar

During 2019 and 2020, the dollar-based global banking system was about the same size as the domestic banking system within the United States (around US$30 trillion or one-third of global GDP, which is the twice the share of the US economy), when measured by the value of dollar-denominated assets and liabilities of non-resident banks, according to data collected by the Bank for International Settlements (BIS). (The dimensions of the dollar-based global financial system are examined in more detail in Chapter 3.) These dollar-denominated assets and liabilities circulating outside the United States grew relatively slowly during the first period of unrestricted capital flows (1975–1995), but then expanded sharply thereafter as more countries removed long-held restrictions on capital account transactions and financial institutions in the advanced countries became more active in international financial operations. The period since the turn of the century has been one of particularly strong growth in cross-border capital flows, associated with the sharp expansion in financial globalization.

From the early days of the post-WW2 era, the US dollar was in wider circulation overseas than any other currency because of its central role under the Bretton Woods system as the anchor for other currencies and its widespread use by central banks in their purchases and sales of foreign exchange under a system of fixed exchange rates. With the breakdown of this system in the early 1970s and the shift to more flexible exchange rate arrangements, along with more freedom in capital account transactions, the dollar continued to function as the main international reserve currency. This historical background to the development of the global dollar system is examined in more detail in Chapter 2.

The US dollar fulfills the same functions in the global dollar system that it does in the US economy as regards its use as a unit of account, a medium of exchange and a store of value. As a unit of account, the dollar is the main currency used in the invoicing and settlement of foreign trade, the denomination of securities in international financial transactions and as a peg or anchor for other exchange rates. As a medium of exchange, the dollar is the main currency used in foreign exchange transactions with other currencies and as an intervention currency by central banks in maintaining the value of their currencies. As a store of value, the dollar is the main currency in which foreign reserves held by central banks and "safe" assets maintained by financial market participants are denominated.

These choices involving the dollar reflect the cumulative effect of decisions by a country's private market participants as regards, for example, the currency to be used in trade, foreign exchange and financial transactions, and by that country's official agencies as regards, for example, the currency to be used as an anchor or intervention currency for a country's exchange rate and the currency in which its official foreign reserves are to be held. There are also strong complementarities in these choices with regard to trade and financial transactions, on the one hand, and between these transactions and the currency denomination of official reserves, on the other. Over time, there has been an historical tendency for decisions on currency choice to follow a sequence beginning with trade, followed by financial transactions and then official reserves. The unique features of the global currency power of the US dollar raised in this paragraph are explored in more detail in Chapter 3.

What are the main determinants of the global currency power of the US dollar? The dominant role of the dollar in the global financial system is fully consistent with the dominant economic, political and military roles that the United States has played in the global system since the end of World War II. In fact, it can be argued that the primacy of the dollar in international economic relations has been viewed by many American political leaders as an important instrument or expression of that power, even though it is not commonly discussed in those terms. One recent example of how that power has been expressed is the frequent use of financial sanctions by the US government. These sanctions typically involve restrictions on access by foreign governments, business firms and/or individuals to the international payments system that is based largely on the US dollar and operates mainly through global American banks.

In linking the global currency power of the dollar to the dominant role of the United States in the global system, one must also recognize the hegemonic role that the United States has played in promoting the stability of the international financial system by means of its efforts to maintain a sound macroeconomic policy and a strong regulatory framework for its domestic financial system, as well as its leadership role in a number of international organizations (such as the IMF and World Bank) and policy groups (such as the G7 and G20). These institutions and groups were created to sustain the liberal international economic order that emerged in the early post-WW2 years.

More specifically, the global currency power of the dollar would not exist without its links to the domestic capital markets of the United States, which are unparalleled for their breadth and depth and freedom of access for non-residents, in particular for the purchase and sale of US government securities that function as the primary "safe haven" asset for public and private investors throughout the global financial system. The global currency power of the dollar is also sustained by the strong rule of law and the protection of property rights that exists in the United States, as well as the credibility of its monetary and fiscal policy institutions.

The determinants of the global currency power of the dollar raised above are discussed in more detail in Chapters 3 and 4.

The Special Role of the Dollar in Crisis Times

The global financial crisis of 2008–2009 and the Covid-19 crisis of 2020 highlighted a number of unique features of the global dollar system, even though the origins of these crises were completely different. In the wake of each of these crises, (a) there was sudden and substantial capital flight from many countries, mainly emerging and developing economies (EMDEs), to the United States as a "safe haven" for assets; (b) the foreign exchange value of the US dollar sharply appreciated in response to these inflows; (c) most of these inflows were directed by investors to the safety and liquidity of US government debt (so-called "safe haven" or "safe" assets), which experienced a sharp increase in their price and decline in their relative yield compared with other financial assets, or to different forms of cash holdings; and (d) the Federal Reserve functioned as an unofficial, international lender of last resort by establishing a number of special credit facilities for both domestic bank and non-bank borrowers and swap lines of credit with a number of other central banks that were essential for the global dollar system to continue to operate effectively.

These responses reflect many aspects of the global dollar system that have evolved over a number of years, which have not been formalized in any collective agreement, but reflect the outcome of cumulative market behavior of private agents and cooperative arrangements and decisions among central banks. These responses to the crisis were unique to the role of the dollar as the dominant currency of the global economy and the role of the United States as the hegemonic power within the global dollar system.

The first common feature of the global financial and Covid-19 crises (point "a" above) was a massive shift of capital to the United States from countries in the rest of the world, representing both a "sudden stop" of the these flows to these countries and a reversal of these capital flows to the United States. The size of the shift in the current Covid-19 crisis from the EMDEs amounted to around US$80 billion during the period from March to June 2020 which was more than double the flows into the EMDEs during all of 2019. Similarly, during the second half of 2008, when the global financial crisis erupted, net capital outflows amounted to US$54 billion, compared with net inflows of US$45 billion during all of 2007.[2] Most of these flows were denominated in US dollars, given the predominance of the United States in the international investment positions of various countries across the globe. Both the size of these flows and their volatility represent a key feature of the global financial system that has grown substantially during the last few decades. Theses flows now far exceed the size of trade flows that were the main component of international transactions during the first half of the post-WW2 era. More recently, capital flows into or out of the United States have also been triggered by shifts in the monetary policy of the Federal Reserve with corresponding changes in dollar-based short-term interest rates in the United States, as well as other rates along the yield curve. Both the dominant size and openness of US capital markets and the strong role of the dollar in the valuation of international capital flows account for the strong extra-territorial effects of Federal Reserve monetary policy changes.

The recent capital outflows in early 2020 posed a difficult policy choice to the EMDEs, as would any tightening of monetary policy by the Fed to a much less dramatic extent, in regard to their inflation-output trade-off. The capital outflows would lead to pressures for a depreciation of the currency in the originating country with likely inflationary effects in that country in the absence of any offsetting monetary policy adjustment by its central bank. However, any tightening of monetary policy to counteract these inflationary effects would have an adverse effect on output and the rate of economic growth of that country. This potential cost to output is augmented by the dominant role that the dollar plays in the invoicing and settlement of trade. Under such a system, any depreciation of the country's currency vis-à-vis the dollar would mainly increase the cost of imports without any significant benefit to exporters if they price most of their traded goods in dollars. The volatility of capital flows has been a principal motivating factor in the decision of EMDEs to significantly increase their holdings of foreign reserves as a safeguard or self-insurance mechanism against sudden stops in capital inflows.

The sharp appreciation of the US dollar associated with the capital inflows (point "b" above) also occurred in a relatively brief period of time and represented a significant break from its prior trend. The exchange rate for the US dollar is the most freely flexible of all exchange rates in the international monetary system in that the Federal Reserve, acting in consultation with the US Treasury Department (which has legal responsibility for the government's exchange rate policy), does not intervene in foreign exchange markets on a regular basis with a view to influencing the basic value of the dollar. Such intervention has only occurred on a few isolated occasions in the past when the US government was concerned about a significant misalignment of currencies among its major trading partners and agreed with them on a joint pattern of intervention to bring about an adjustment in relative currency values. As in the case of capital flows, exchange rates for these countries are subject to a significant degree of volatility, which is another hallmark of the international monetary system. This degree of risk in currency trading is normally minimized by means of swaps and futures trading, but it is also one factor that has fostered the expansion of a global dollar system where such risk would be absent.

The conversion of dollar and non-dollar assets held abroad into US government securities traded in financial markets of the United States (point "c" above) reflects two other important features of the global dollar system. One is the unfettered access by foreign official and private operators to the financial markets of the United States, which are free of capital controls for legitimate international financial transactions and are unmatched in terms of their breadth, depth and liquidity. According to the McKinsey Global Institute, the value of assets and liabilities recorded in the financial markets of the United States (mainly located in New York City) are more than two times larger than that of the next two largest global financial centers (London and Luxembourg).

The other important feature of financial transactions taking place in the United States is the role that US government securities play as a global "safe" asset for both private and public agents and institutions abroad. A "safe" asset is one that is held for temporary investment or precautionary purposes and can be converted into liquid form quickly, with little or no change in value. A number of different assets may satisfy these criteria to varying degrees, but US government debt securities have been preeminent in that they are the most widely held and pursued in times of crisis. This judgement of safety reflects widespread confidence among market participants in the debt management capacity and commitment of the United States to a sound fiscal position. As a result, around 40% of all debt securities issued by the US government were held by non-residents prior to the Covid pandemic. This confidence in the safety of US government debt has been translated into a lower interest cost (which can be called a liquidity premium or convenience yield) than that paid by other governments on their debt, as well as a significant spread in favor of the United States with respect to the yield that it earns on its investments and assets held abroad. The size and openness of US financial markets and the special role of US government securities as a global safe asset are two factors that have promoted the widespread use of the dollar in the valuation of global debt securities and capital flows.

The final important feature of the international financial flows associated with the two crises (point "d" above) is the extraordinary role played by the Federal Reserve (the Fed) as an unofficial, international lender of last resort. Early on in both crises, the Fed activated a swap network or a set of reciprocal credit arrangements with 14 other central banks from selected advanced and emerging market countries as a direct response to funding problems that arose within the global dollar system. In certain cases, foreign banks that had raised dollar financing on a short-term basis in the United States for credit operations abroad encountered difficulties in rolling over these liabilities as the holders of these claims sought safer investments in cash or government securities because of the uncertainty created by the crises. In these circumstances, central banks in the countries of the involved banks approached the Fed for temporary dollar lines of credits that they could use for lending to those banks until they could repay their creditors or secure new funding for their operations as other actions taken by the Fed helped to normalize such funding arrangements. These exceptional foreign lending operations of the Fed are unique to its role as an unofficial international lender of last resort, given the large size of the global dollar system and the dominant role of the dollar as a reserve currency. These operations were essential for maintaining stability of the global financial system at a time of significant stress in the system.

The Fed also sharply increased its balance sheet at the outbreak of each crisis by establishing special short-term lines of credit for domestic financial institutions in need of liquidity and by purchasing various forms of US-based government and private sector debt in order to maintain the liquid market value of these debts in cases where a temporary freeze in market conditions had arisen. These operations fall within the Fed's traditional role as a domestic lender of last resort geared to easing or removing liquidity constraints faced by otherwise solvent financial institutions in carrying out their borrowing or lending operations. It also engaged in large purchases of US government debt of various maturities in order to maintain domestic interest rates along the yield curve at very low levels (following significant cuts in its policy rate) in order to ease the burden of the crises and promote economy recovery.

The four features of the global dollar system discussed in the preceding paragraphs are examined in more detail in Chapters 3 and 4.

The Benefits and Costs of the Global Dollar System

The onset of the global financial crisis in 2008–2009 raised important questions about the long-run stability of the dollar-centered international monetary system and the global dollar system. Even though the revised Bretton Woods Agreement of 1978 established the objective of having the reserve asset created by the IMF (i.e., SDRs or Special Drawing Rights) become the principal reserve asset of the system to replace the dollar as the center of the international monetary system, the dollar has continued to play that role. Broadly speaking, as a matter of convenience, the dollar system has provided certain benefits to its participants that can help to explain its continued dominance. However, over time, a number of costs, some of which were demonstrated in the global financial crisis, can be associated with the dominant currency status of the dollar that represent a growing threat to the stability of the global financial system.

For the United States, one of the most important benefits has been the "exorbitant privilege" it has enjoyed from the fact that its government debt is considered a safe asset for which there is growing demand on the part of the rest of the world. This fact has meant, in effect, that there has not been any limiting budget constraint on the United States, with the result that it has been able to maintain a government budget deficit and an external current account deficit for most of the last 40 years. No other country has enjoyed such an extended period of autonomy in the conduct of its fiscal and monetary policies and the power to delay indefinitely any adjustment of its financial imbalances. On a smaller scale, the United States has also derived a certain amount of "seigniorage" (or hidden/implicit revenue) from the role that its government debt plays as an international safe asset and the use of its currency in international transactions.

For private traders and investors in the United States, the global currency power of the US dollar has eliminated exchange rate risk for many of their international transactions (both trade and financial), while lowering the settlement costs for these transactions. It has also broadened the scope and opportunities for these transactions globally given the widespread use of the dollar throughout the rest of the world.

Governments in the rest of the world have generally benefitted from the dominant currency arrangement of the United States within the global economy, as it has maintained a reasonably stable conduct of its macroeconomic policy over the long term that has avoided excessive inflation and maintained a relatively stable rate of economic growth. The United States has also been the primary supporter for the liberal international economic order of the post-WW2 era that has promoted economic prosperity among the advanced and EMDE countries. By foregoing the use of capital controls, the United States has allowed foreign countries to benefit from free and unfettered access to its domestic financial markets that are unparalleled for their breadth, depth and liquidity. In times of financial stress, as noted earlier, the Federal Reserve has reliably functioned as an international lender of last resort ensuring the liquidity of dollar safe assets and the availability of dollar liquidity for the conduct of international transactions. In carrying out these functions, the United

States has fulfilled the role of a hegemonic power that is needed to maintain the system in good times and bad. The benefits of the global dollar system summarized above are examined in more detail in Chapter 4.

It is also important to recognize that there are a number of costs or defects related to the global dollar system and dominant currency status of the dollar that have been building over time in terms of the burden they have imposed on certain countries, the distortions they have created for the international adjustment process, and the potential threats they represent for the stability of the global financial system. Even though these elements are understood in official circles, it is striking that little systematic attempt has been made since the global financial crisis to address them in fora such as the G20, the IMF, the Financial Stability Board or the OECD. A great deal of official effort has been given to improving the statistical framework for understanding the scope of international financial transactions and to strengthening the focus of regulatory regimes on financial system stability (as captured by the term "macroprudential regulation"), as distinct from the soundness of individual banks. This work has been extremely important and can be seen as a pre-requisite for effective policy debate on the broader issue of international monetary reform.

The defects of the global dollar system, in general terms, arise from the adverse spillover effects of monetary policy decisions of the Federal Reserve on capital flow volatility and the impact of the global financial cycle that is influenced by monetary developments in the United States. In addition, one can observe a significant pattern of self-insurance by the EMDEs in their large accumulation of dollar-denominated foreign reserves (or "uphill" capital flows) that has imposed significant costs on these countries and reflects the inadequacy of the Global Financial Safety Net (i.e., central bank swap networks, regional financial arrangements and IMF financing) within the international monetary system to deal with liquidity shortages during crises, notwithstanding the exceptional role that has been played by the Federal Reserve.

A further defect of the system relates to the safe asset quality of the bonds provided by the US government for global liquidity and the potential limits on its ability to maintain a growing supply in a global economy in which the relative share of the United States has been declining, and will continue to do so. There are also problems related to the asymmetric adjustment process associated with the persistence of large current account imbalances (so-called global imbalances) among the United States (a persistent large deficit country), and a number of surplus countries. These imbalances have been a factor driving some of the volume and volatility of international capital flows and the incidence of financial crises in the global financial system. These defects have been exacerbated by recent actions of the US government that have signaled some withdrawal from the traditional hegemonic role it has played in the global dollar system. These defects have also been compounded by the sharp deterioration in the debt position and prospects of the US government as a result of its response to the Covid-19 crisis that will need to be addressed over the medium to long term. The issues raised in this and the previous paragraph regarding the growing costs of the global dollar system are examined in more detail in Chapters 5 and 6.

Possible Reforms of the International Monetary System

A number of proposals have been advanced in recent years for improving the stability of the international monetary and financial system that have the common goals of limiting the incidence of financial crisis and ensuring that the system is supportive of long term, sustainable global economic growth and low inflation. Some of these involve improving the operations of the IMF and strengthening its oversight of financial systems, both at the national and global levels, as it continues to be the main forum for inter-governmental cooperation on international monetary and financial affairs. Three particular avenues of reform are presented in this book to deal with the defects of the current dollar-dominated global reserve system.

One reform would be to promote more actively the transition from a dollar-centered international monetary system to a multipolar one involving the dollar, euro and renminbi which, among other things, would ease the problem in the supply of safe assets. To some extent, this transition has already been under way given the existence of the euro since 1999 and the growing sizes of euro and renminbi currency zones. However, there are still significant limitations in the ability of these currencies to extend their role as global reserve currencies that need to be evaluated. Careful consideration would have to be given to the process for managing a transition to a multipolar reserve currency system and the possible disruptive effects of international capital flows. These issues are examined in more detail in Chapter 7.

A second reform would be to strengthen the role of the IMF as an international lender of last resort for the international monetary system, among other things, in order to eliminate much of the need for self-insurance on the part of the EMDEs. This change would require a substantial increase in the financial resources of the IMF and a strengthening in its surveillance function with respect to the macroeconomic policy management of its member countries and its formal oversight of the international financial system. Further changes in the governance structure of the institution would also be required in order to secure the full support of all of its members.

A more far-reaching reform of the Fund would be to focus on achieving the objective of making the SDR the principal reserve asset of the international monetary system, as specified in the revised Fund Agreement of 1978. Such a reform would take time as certain changes would need to be made in the Agreement in order for this objective to be achieved, as regards, for example, the removal of current limitations on the use of SDRs in private market transactions. However, a number of other steps can be taken now to promote its more active use in official transactions and to increase the global supply of SDRs on a regular basis, while creating a Substitution Account to foster conversion of dollar reserves into SDRs. Possible reforms of the IMF along these lines are discussed in more detail in Chapter 8.

A third avenue of significant change of the dollar-based international monetary system can possibly be associated with the rise of digital currencies. In recent years, there has been an explosion of interest in the potential benefits of digital currencies (or cryptocurrencies), in both private and official form. The creation of Bitcoin and the prospective launch of the Libra stablecoin (now called Diem) are only the two best-known, private digital currency ventures among thousands that have been created in the last few years. Global stablecoins such as Diem, in particular, could pose a potential threat to the global currency power of the dollar, if allowed to expand nationally and internationally with appropriate regulatory oversight. At the same time, in the public sphere, a number of central banks are examining the possibility of issuing central bank digital currencies (CBDCs) as a means of improving payments systems at both the national and global levels. The central banks of China and Sweden are prominently in the lead in the development of CBDCs. The arrival of CBDCs may also have implications for the global currency power of the dollar, in particular as regards the proposal to establish a "Synthetic

Hegemonic Currency" to replace the dollar. The role of digital currencies in the evolution of the international monetary system and the role of dollar are examined in more detail in Chapter 9.

* * *

A concluding Chapter 10 highlights the main lessons and conclusions of the book and summarizes the outlook for the global currency power of the dollar over the medium to long term, both from the perspective of the challenges facing the United States in maintaining its global safe asset status and the possible changes and reforms that may occur within the international monetary system.

Notes

1. These data are based on the currency shares of allocated reserves for the fourth quarter of 2020, as reported in the IMF's Composition of Foreign Exchange Reserves (COFER) database, which is available at www.imf.org.
2. These data for the two crises are based on portfolio flows of bonds and equity calculated by the IMF for its World Economic Outlook exercises of October 2020 (Fig. 1.10) and of April 2009 (Fig. 4.1).

CHAPTER 2

The Origins of the Global Currency Power of the US Dollar

Introduction

As noted in Chapter 1, the global currency power of the dollar is a result of both official action and the effect of market decisions by private trades and investors. The major official action that accounts for the dominant currency status of the dollar stems from the Bretton Woods Agreement of 1944 that created the International Monetary Fund (IMF). This Agreement (as amended in 1969 and 1978) established the basic framework and rules for the post-World War II (WW2) international monetary system that remain in effect today, even though there have been a number of important changes in the system as it has evolved over time. This chapter explains the major role for the dollar embodied in the Bretton Woods Agreement and briefly highlights the significant changes that have occurred since then.

In some respects, the Bretton Woods Agreement and design for the IMF were built on certain features of the currency arrangements that existed in the period between WW1 and WW2, and in particular the 1920s. In the wake of WW1, the gold standard to which most countries adhered was abandoned, having been the organizing arrangement for the international monetary system during the period 1880–1913. After the war, various attempts were made to resurrect the gold standard through a series of international conferences that culminated in its re-establishment in the mid-1920s. These efforts were facilitated by

A. Elson, *The Global Currency Power of the US Dollar*,
https://doi.org/10.1007/978-3-030-83519-4_2

the Financial Committee of the League of Nations and its Economic and Financial Section, which in certain respects were precursors for the IMF. This connection was reflected in their work in organizing post-War monetary conferences, in assisting countries in re-establishing the links of their currencies to the gold standard, and in collecting and disseminating economic and financial statistics on member countries and preparing reports on the world economy.[1] This period was also important in making more widespread a modification to the rules of the gold standard that was in limited use in the pre-War period by which countries could maintain as official reserves not only gold, but also the convertible currencies of other gold standard participants as backing for their currency and for balance of payments adjustment. This modification was captured by use of the term, "gold exchange standard".

This period in history was also important for the recognition gained by the US dollar as a major reserve currency in preference to the pound sterling that had been the dominant currency within the international monetary system throughout the gold standard era. Up until 1925, the pound had been the pre-eminent international currency in regard to the pricing of trade (e.g., commodities) and the denomination of international bank loans and bond issuance. These characteristics of the currency were intimately related to the dominant role played by Great Britain in international trade and finance in the late nineteenth and early twentieth centuries. However, by the late 1920s, the United States had also gained prominence as an international financial center, as 55% of all foreign bond issues were denominated in US dollars and launched in its New York financial district.[2] In addition, with the advent of the gold exchange standard and countries' selection of reserve currencies to supplement their holdings of gold, the dollar was recognized at least on a par with the pound. While gold holdings continued to account for around 80% of official reserves during the second half of the 1920s, the dollar represented slightly more than one-half of the reserve currency component of official reserves, with British pounds covering most of the rest.[3]

This choice of the dollar as a reserve currency by countries participating in the gold exchange standard was a recognition of the growing importance of the United States as a global power, not only in economic and financial affairs, but also in international politico-military affairs. This stature was also reflected in the fact that the United States possessed, on average, around 40% of the stock of gold reserves held by governments around the world during the inter-war period, far more than any other country.[4]

The Bretton Woods System

The gold exchange standard collapsed in the wake of the Great Depression as countries abandoned its rules for fixing their currencies to a price for gold and for adjusting international payments imbalances in an effort to reverse the catastrophic decline in output and employment that occurred in 1930–1931. A period of exchange rate volatility and intensified trade and exchange restrictions ensued that resulted in a major deterioration in international trade and a virtual suspension of international capital flows in the period leading up to WW2.

The Bretton Woods Conference of 1944 was a landmark event in international monetary relations in terms of its success in establishing a viable framework for the management of exchange rate systems among the member countries of the IMF during the initial decades of the post-WW2 era. This achievement, together with the reduction in trade barriers brought about by successive rounds of trade liberalization under the General Agreement on Tariffs and Trade (GATT), laid the groundwork for the post-war recovery and sustained growth of the global economy during the second half of the twentieth century.[5]

In some respects, the Bretton Woods Agreement built on the gold exchange standard of the 1920s in its recognition of gold as the ultimate anchor for the system supplemented by the use of reserve currencies. However, unlike pre-war arrangements, the dollar was recognized as the principal reserve currency because of the size of the gold holdings by the United States and the relative strength of its economic and financial position at the end of the war. The Bretton Woods framework also differed from previous monetary regimes in that it established rules for a system of adjustable, fixed exchange rates. In principle, the exchange rate for each member country of the Fund (or so-called "par value") was to be pegged to gold or dollars at an agreed rate and made convertible into dollars for current account transactions. However, since the United States held 70% of the monetary gold stock at the end of the war, it was not feasible to implement a link of par values to gold for all countries other than the United States, and as a result each country established fixed exchange rates with respect to the dollar for their future transactions. In effect, the United States remained on the gold standard, while all other countries participated in a new, adjustable fixed exchange rate system with their currencies pegged to the dollar. This practice effectively recognized the dominant status of the dollar in the post-war international monetary system and the transfer of global currency power from the pound sterling to the dollar.

This two-tiered system of exchange rates was seen as providing two anchors for the stability of the international monetary system. One was the provision of fixed exchange rates maintained by a fixed (but adjustable) peg to the dollar that was understood to operate as a brake on excessively expansionary policies by each member country of the IMF. The other was the link of the US dollar to a fixed price of gold that was expected to operate as a similar constraint on the United States. If, for example, the United States pursued an excessively expansionary monetary policy, then dollar liabilities would accumulate among its trading partners, which could then convert them into gold held by the United States, as intended under the Agreement. In these circumstances, the United States would be expected to take corrective policy measures to reduce its payments imbalance and prevent a decline in its gold stock.

There were also two other unique features of the arrangement. One was that the currency system of each member country was to be monitored by the IMF with the understanding that any decision of a country to allow its exchange rate to move beyond a band of 1% had to be approved by the Fund. The other unique feature of the Agreement was that the Fund could make available some of its financial resources through short-term loans to assist member countries in meeting temporary balance of payments obligations or in adjusting their exchange rate to a new value.

Consistent with these provisions, member countries also agreed to work with the Fund towards the removal of all restrictions on their current account balance of payments transactions in order to establish full convertibility of currencies for the settlement of any imbalances in respect of international trade in goods and services. This condition was an essential counterpart to the trade liberalization objectives of the GATT. These features of the Bretton Woods Agreement represented a major expansion in the role of an international organization in the international monetary system with respect to that played by the League of Nations and its Financial Committee and Economic and Financial Section following WW1. It also represented the first permanent arrangement for central bank and finance ministry cooperation on issues of international monetary relations that has remained viable and in place up until the present day.

Notably, the Bretton Woods Agreement did not commit its signatories to the freedom of capital movements and the removal of restrictions on capital flows, as such restrictions were considered necessary to allow for the domestic control of monetary and fiscal policies by each member of the Fund under a regime of fixed exchange rates and to prevent speculative currency attacks. Curiously, this provision (embodied in Article VI of the Fund Agreement) still remains in effect, notwithstanding the widespread liberalization of capital flows among the advanced countries and many emerging market economies and the enormous expansion in international financial transactions that has occurred since the early 1980s. In the late 1990s, a proposal was advanced to establish capital account liberalization as an objective of Fund membership similar to that for current account convertibility, but this proposal did not receive sufficient support from members and was abandoned. It remains relevant today as the use of capital controls to deal with problems of capital flow volatility is an active topic of debate in both official and academic circles (see Chapters 5 and 8).

In highlighting the key features of the Bretton Woods Agreement, it is useful to consider the main alternative to the American proposal for the international monetary system that came from the British delegation and its chief advisor (JM Keynes), as this proposal is often mentioned as the precedent or inspiration for more recent proposals for international monetary reform.[6] Under Keynes' plan for an International Clearing Union (ICU), a new international currency (Bancor) would have been created to replace the use of gold in the settlement of international payments imbalances. The envisaged process of adjustment would have been symmetrical for both surplus and deficit countries in that there would have been limits on the debtor and creditor positions of participating countries in their Bancor accounts at the ICU that would have triggered domestic economic adjustments and changes in the value of their currencies that were pegged to Bancor at fixed rates. The lack of symmetry between surplus and deficit countries in respect of current account imbalances has continued to be a concern under the global dollar system that is discussed in Chapter 5.

Keynes' proposal was far too radical a change for the United States to accept, given its leadership position in the post-war global economy and the dominant role of the dollar at the end of World War II. More directly, the White Plan for the IMF (named after Harry Dexter White, Keynes' counterpart from the US Treasury Department), which became the basis for negotiations with the British prior to the Conference, was a statement of the global currency power of the dollar and reflected US national interests in its acceptance of lead responsibility for maintaining the stability of the international monetary system. Among other things, the White Plan expressed strong opposition to the creation of a new international currency, as the Keynes Plan had proposed.

The primary role of the United States and the dollar in the Fund was reflected in a number of features of the final agreement. Voting and borrowing were based on the size of "quotas" or financial shares in the Fund, which were determined according to certain economic criteria, such as GDP, trade openness and official reserves. One-quarter of each member's quota was to be paid in gold and dollars, with the remainder in its own currency. The institution was headquartered in the United States (the country with the largest quota, as specified in the Fund Agreement) and its operations were denominated in dollars. Certain decisions of the Fund require a supermajority of 85% of the voting power of members, which has given the United States an effective veto power on these matters, as its quota has always been set at more than 15% of total quotas. The initial share of the United States was set at 25% and has been reduced over time with the expanding shares of other countries in the global economy. While the IMF Agreement was a strong statement of international monetary cooperation, it also institutionalized for the first time in the twentieth century the dominant role of the dollar in the international monetary system that has been maintained up to the present day.

One key feature of the institution where the United States yielded to the European countries was in the designation of the Fund's leading position, or Managing Director. Although this arrangement was not specified in the Articles of Agreement, by convention it was agreed among the major shareholders that the Managing Director would be from a European country, while the Deputy Managing Director (now First DMD) would be chosen by the US government (i.e., Treasury Department). This convention has been maintained up until the present day and has become an important issue in proposals of governance reform, in particular among the growing majority of the Fund members representing emerging market and developing economies.[7] An additional understanding in the "gentlemen's agreement" on leadership positions noted above was that the President of the World Bank, which was created by a separate treaty at the same Bretton Woods conference in 1944, would be an American citizen. This arrangement was seen as particularly important in the early years of the Bank, as it had to raise most of the financial resources for its lending operations in the financial markets of the United States, given the post-war problems of economic recovery facing Europe. The selection of an American with some background in the US-based financial industry was seen as critical in helping to establish the credibility and authority of the Bank. Even though these initial concerns are no longer as important for the Bank as they used to be, the informal understanding on leadership selection among the major shareholders has remained in place.

The End of the Bretton Woods System

The Bretton Woods system had one inherent weakness, or dynamic instability, that led to its demise in 1971 and was captured by reference to the so-called Triffin Dilemma.[8] (A "new Triffin Dilemma" is commonly cited as a problem of the current dollar system that is examined in Chapter 5, so it is useful to discuss its original formulation at this juncture.) As noted earlier, the stability of the Bretton Woods system was premised on the notion that the United States would manage its domestic macroeconomic policies in such a way that its dollar liabilities to other countries would remain below the value of its gold reserves, so that, in principle, it could meet any demand for their conversion into gold. In order to maintain its holdings of gold in tact then, the United States would have to maintain over time a stable macroeconomic policy framework in order to prevent its foreign dollar liabilities from reaching a level that could ultimately exceed the value of its gold holdings. In the event that this expectation was not fulfilled, the other major shareholders in the Fund were faced with a dilemma. They could pressure the United States for corrective policy action, but that would deflate the US economy and reduce its demand for European exports and weaken its foreign direct investment, both of which were vital to the recovery of Western Europe, or they could present their dollar liabilities to the United States for conversion into gold, with the risk that the system would break down. It was also clear that an increase in the official price of gold, and in effect a devaluation of the dollar, would not be a satisfactory solution. Such action would bring about a capital loss for the dollar reserves of European countries and undermine confidence in the system, while failing to act over time as a binding constraint on the United States.

The source of this dynamic instability was based on the fact that the Bretton Woods system required an expansion in dollar liabilities to provide the liquidity for countries to settle their international payment obligations and to serve as their primary reserve asset. This basic dependence of the system on dollar liabilities was first reflected in the creation of the Marshall Plan by the United States in 1948 to promote the post-war recovery of Western Europe. The size of the Marshall Plan was larger than the combined resources of the IMF and World Bank at the time and initiated the widespread use of the dollar for international trade and finance, while the European countries began the process of dismantling wartime controls and restrictions on their currencies in an effort to establish current account convertibility, as called for under the Fund Agreement. In order to facilitate this process, the main European countries created the European Payments Union (EPU) in 1950 to manage the regional clearing and settlement of payments imbalances, in which the US dollar served as the unit of account and medium of exchange, further enhancing its global currency status. The work of establishing current account convertibility of the European currencies took much longer than was expected by the Bretton Woods creators and was only completed in 1958. It was from this date that one can assume that the Bretton Woods system began to operate fully.

This period in the 1950s was also notable in that the operations of an offshore euro-dollar market began in 1957, which reflected the large amount of dollar liquidity circulating among international banks in the London financial center. This development was the result of private market activity that was endorsed by the UK regulatory authorities as a means of enhancing the status of London as an international financial center. From the perspective of American banks, the creation of this market was a means of bypassing a number of regulatory restrictions that applied to their on-shore banking operations. These included reserve requirements against bank deposits, the cost of deposit insurance and limits on the level of interest rates payable on bank deposits (Regulation Q). The creation of the market was also a response to the widespread application of capital controls among the Fund membership.

The emergence of the euro-dollar bank market was also important as a signal of the new post-war role of the dollar as a unit of account and means of payment for international commodity transactions, in particular oil. Sales of oil, for example, between importers in Brazil and oil producers in the Middle East, would be negotiated and paid for in dollars and the payments received would be transferred by the producing country's central bank as a reserve asset to the London financial market where it would circulate among the banks there. These developments were clear evidence of the growing role of the dollar in private market activity, apart from its dominant role as an official reserve currency. They were also clearly linked to the dominant role of the United States within the global economy as a trading nation and financial center. Once established, private market decisions on the role of the dollar would have expanded with the advantages of scale. In this respect, the dominance of the dollar was established in international transactions of both the official and private sectors under the Bretton Woods system, which solidified the global currency power that the dollar has maintained up until the present day.

The euro-dollar financial market was the beginning of offshore dollar-based banking that has been in existence since the late 1950s and has grown to an enormous scale, as discussed in Chapter 3. Its growth also became the focus of increasing official concern, as it was seen as a manifestation of the problem of the "dynamic instability" inherent in the Bretton Woods system noted above. During the 1960s, as the foreign dollar liabilities of the United States continued to expand, mainly as a result of its sustained, expansionary monetary policy, in part related to the growing war effort in Vietnam and domestic social programs, a number of collaborative steps were taken by the major shareholders in the Fund to deal with this problem. The French government was particularly concerned about the special role that dollar liabilities played in international monetary relations and complained about the "exorbitant privilege" of the dollar. The use of this term was meant to convey the idea that the United States could maintain a persistent balance of payments deficit unlike other countries, because the circulation of dollar liabilities to cover that deficit was needed for global liquidity and served as their principal reserve asset.[9]

The discussions on remedial actions among the United States and its European allies was largely managed outside the IMF in the so-called Group of 10 (G10) finance ministers and central bank governors, under the umbrella of the Bank for International Settlements (BIS). One of the G10 decisions involved the creation of a "gold pool" in 1961 among its members to coordinate official sales in the London gold market with a view to stabilizing the private market price of gold and keeping it in line with the official price of US$35 per ounce set in the Bretton Woods Agreement. This action was seen as critical for maintaining confidence in the official exchange rate for the dollar as the anchor of the system. The "gold pool" operations were moderately successful, even though the United States sold more gold outside the market to other members of the "pool" than it did in the market. In 1968, a "gentlemen's agreement" was set by the members not to purchase gold from the United States with their accumulated dollar liabilities.[10] In 1970, however, some of the European countries began to purchase gold from the United States with new reserve liabilities, and in August 1971 the United States suspended any further sales of gold given its reduced gold holdings, at which point the private price of gold was allowed to rise above the official price. This date is also significant as it effectively ended the gold exchange system of Bretton Woods and converted it to a pure dollar standard.

The creation of the "gold pool" was supplemented by the creation in 1962 of a network of swap arrangements among the central banks of the United States and a number of key currency countries of Western Europe (mostly G10 members) together with the BIS. This network was a precursor of the swap networks that were created at the time of the global financial crisis and the Covid-19 crisis noted in Chapter 1. The purpose of the swap network during the Bretton Woods system served a number of different purposes, one of which was to make short-term loans of convertible currencies available to the Federal Reserve and its counterparts for purposes of defending the official exchange rate parities established under the Fund Agreement. In certain cases, they were mobilized in concert with IMF stabilization loans for one of the European members. The swap network also was used to intervene in the Eurodollar market for purposes of eliminating funding gaps in the market and preventing offshore interest rates from diverging sharply from the US domestic bank market. By 1972, the total value of the network had grown to US$11.7 billion (its peak year), which was largely on a par with the total value of Fund resources and equivalent to 40% of the official reserves of participating members.[11] The Federal Reserve's swap network continued to be used after 1972 until the end of the century, but without a fixed set of countries.

The United States also took unilateral actions in the 1960s to deal with the growth of the euro-dollar market, one of which was the imposition of an Interest Equalization Tax that was intended to strengthen the US balance of payments by taxing capital outflows. Instead, however, this measure gave multinational firms an incentive to borrow from foreign banks and issue dollar bonds abroad. Another measure was the issue of medium-term bonds by the US Treasury Department denominated in foreign currency (so-called "Roosa bonds", named after their creator, Treasury Secretary Robert Roosa) in order to attract foreign investment as a hedge against the risk of dollar devaluation. In addition, the US government established voluntary guidelines for the growth of foreign assets by domestic banks and foreign direct investment by multinational corporations. Each of these actions tended to have unintended effects on the growth of the Eurodollar market and further encouraged its expansion.

One final collaborative measure proposed by the G10 and adopted by the IMF membership to deal with the "dynamic instability" problem of the Bretton Woods system was the creation of SDRs (Special Drawing Rights) for the IMF in 1969. This action was unique on the annals of international monetary relations, as it was the first attempt by international agreement to create a global reserve asset to supplement the use of reserve currencies and gold as official reserve assets. Even though it has not fulfilled the expectations formed at the time of its creation, the SDR continues to be the subject of international reform proposals, and features prominently in a proposed reform of the dollar-centered reserve system in Chapter 8.

SDRs are created by an 85% majority decision of the IMF membership and are distributed to each member in proportion to its quota size, thus giving the United States and other major shareholders the largest shares. SDRs are treated as both a foreign reserve asset and foreign liability for each member holding them, with interest earned on a country's holdings and paid on its cumulative allocations at money market rates set according to the weighted average of the countries whose currencies have been used to value the SDR. The value of the SDR initially was determined as a weighted value of the currencies of the 16 largest shareholders, adjusted daily, with the weights reviewed every five years. Today, the currency composition of the SDR has been greatly simplified and includes the dollar, euro, pound, yen and renminbi. Members are obligated to accept SDRs in exchange for convertible currencies at the request of another member or the Fund. By this procedure, the membership can increase the circulation of existing reserve currencies, which may be important for a country or countries facing a liquidity shortage. One important limitation that was placed on the use of SDRs is that they cannot be exchanged in private financial market activity, which has limited their role as an international financial asset beyond their use in official transactions.

In 1969, when the SDR was created, it was expected that it would provide an alternative reserve asset for countries to accumulate instead of dollars or gold. However, the creation of the SDR came too late to play any role in maintaining the Bretton Woods system. An allocation of SDR 9 billion was agreed to be distributed in three installments during the period 1970–1972, but during this period the United States closed the gold window and effectively ended the system as it had been designed.

The Post-Bretton Woods System

With the closure of the US gold window, the international monetary system essentially changed to a de facto, fiat dollar standard. Attempts were made in the remainder of 1971 and 1972 within the G10 to re-establish a network of fixed exchange rates similar to the par value system of the Fund, but these were unsuccessful because of the role of currency speculation. As a result, in March 1973, a period of generalized floating of currency values began among the major shareholders of the Fund, similar to the experiences following the breakdown of the gold standard after WW1 and again after the onset of the Great Depression in the 1930s. What ensued was a period of debate on international monetary reform (1972–1974) that was managed by the so-called Committee of 20 (C20) within the Fund, representing the twenty constituencies of members at the time in the Fund. These discussions were the last occasion in which formal debate on international monetary reform was taken up in a multilateral setting.[12] Even though they were not successful, it is useful to touch briefly on some of the major issues raised in these discussions as they relate to the role of the dollar in the international monetary system.

The C20 debates focused on establishing a workable system of adjustable, fixed exchange rates similar to the Bretton Woods par value system, but with more prompt adjustment action by both deficit and surplus countries in order to avoid the "dynamic instability" problem of the earlier system. Under one proposal designed to trigger policy action to eliminate payments imbalances, the IMF would administer a system of reserve indicators for countries to observe and respond to. In this respect, the proposal was somewhat similar to the basic idea behind Keynes' Plan for an International Clearing Union. The European representatives were particularly interested in this idea in order to avoid the unlimited accumulation of dollar liabilities that plagued the Bretton Woods system. The United States was sympathetic to the use of reserve indicators as a means of triggering upward exchange rate adjustments by the European countries, if warranted, in order to maintain the competitiveness of the dollar. In the end, however, there was no agreement on this issue, in part because the United States was reluctant to invest the Fund with the increased authority it would need to administer the system of reserve indicators.

Much discussion also focused on the important role that SDRs could play in the international monetary system as the principal reserve asset of the system, instead of gold or the US dollar. SDRs were seen as superior to gold, because their growth would be set by the members of the Fund in line with the perceived need for global liquidity that would avoid the vagaries and uncertainty of new monetary gold becoming available. They were also seen as preferable to the foreign liabilities of a single country (i.e., the United States) and the risks this dependence would create for the stability of the system, if these liabilities were allowed to grow without check. In view of the large overhang of dollar liabilities held by European countries as reserves, there was some discussion of the possibility of setting up a Substitution Account in the Fund from which countries could draw SDRs in exchange for their dollar holdings. One issue that remained unresolved was how any losses that the Fund might incur on its holdings of dollars vis-à-vis the SDR would be covered, whether by the United States alone or by the advanced countries in proportion to the weight of their currencies that determined the value of the SDR. A Substitution Account continues to attract interest in debates on international monetary reform, as discussed in Chapter 8.

In view of the failure to agree in the C20 on a revision of the par value system of Bretton Woods of adjustable, fixed exchange rates, work proceeded on a revision of the Fund Agreement to guide countries on their exchange rate policy. In the second amendment of the Agreement in 1978 (the first amendment of 1969 introduced the SDR), it was decided that Fund members would be free to choose any kind of exchange rate system they deemed appropriate (fixed or flexible or somewhere in between), which could vary depending on the country's stage of development. Under this arrangement, the role of the IMF was changed from one of administering the rules for a universal fixed exchange rate system to that of exercising surveillance over the specific exchange rate arrangement that each country selected (and communicated to the Fund) to ensure that it was being managed in a way that was consistent with internal and external balance. The Fund was also charged with overseeing the international monetary system to ensure its sound operation, which is to "provide a framework that facilitates the exchange of goods, services, and capital among countries, and that sustains sound economic growth" (Article IV). These references to the international monetary system, the role of capital, and the bilateral and multilateral surveillance responsibilities of the Fund were important changes made to the Fund Agreement that have guided the work of the Fund up until the present day. The objective of current account liberalization remained unchanged.

In a formal sense, the "non-system" for exchange rate arrangements, as it has been called, that was reflected in the revised Agreement embodied an implicit contract that more flexibility in exchange rate management would allow countries to implement a sound and stable macroeconomic policy framework, with the expectation that such a contract would bring about stability for the international monetary system as a whole. However, as before, the stability of the system has still depended to a large extent upon the sound macroeconomic policy management of the United States, as the leading economic and financial power in the system. This fact has become clear with the great expansion in economic and financial globalization that has taken place in the post-Bretton Woods era and the continuing dominance of the US dollar. One indicator that captures this fact is the share of dollars over time in the official reserves of IMF members. After reaching a peak of 70% in 1966, there was some decline during the late 1960s and early 1970s with the breakdown of the Bretton Woods system, but since then the dollar's share has remained within a range of 60–65% through 2020, far above the share of any other currency.[13] The other dimensions of the global currency power of the US dollar in an age of globalization are examined in Chapter 3.

Notes

1. The comparison of the work between the League and its Financial Committee and the IMF is discussed in Pauly (1996).
2. The reference to the share of dollar-based bond issuance is taken from Cooper (1987, p. 176).
3. The share of dollars in foreign exchange holdings of countries participating in the gold exchange standard is taken from Eichengreen and Flandreau (2008, p. 12).
4. Data on the gold holdings of gold standard countries can be found in Eichengreen (1996, p. 65) (Table 3.1).
5. A more elaborate discussion of the Bretton Woods system can be found in Elson (2011).
6. As one example of this literature, see Alessandrini and Fratianni (2009).
7. In September 2019, Kristalina Georgieva, a national of Bulgaria, was chosen as Managing Director of the Fund, with the strong endorsement of the members of the European Union, to which Bulgaria belongs. Ms. Georgieva represents the first non-Western European national to occupy that position.
8. Robert Triffin, a Belgian-born economist, explained this dilemma in Triffin (1960).

9. The term "exorbitant privilege" is attributed to the French Minister of Finance Valery Giscard d'Estaing in 1965, although it is difficult to document this fact. When foreign officials expressed concern about the external payments deficit of the United States, they were referring to a"basic" or "official settlements" payments deficit that included current account transactions, as well as long-term capital flows (such as foreign direct investment). During the period 1954–1971, the external current account of the United States was in surplus or in balance, which was offset or exceeded by long-term capital outflows, thus giving rise to a basic payments deficit. By contrast, in the period leading up to the Global Financial Crisis (2008–2009) there was much concern in official circles about "global imbalances", or the large current account deficit of the United States and the large current account surpluses of East Asian countries (esp. China) and oil producers.
10. An analysis of the operations of the gold pool can be found in Eichengreen (2007).
11. A recent discussion of the swap network of the 1960s, from which the figure cited in the text is drawn, can be found in McCauley and Schenk (2020).
12. The Report of the Committee of Reform on the International Monetary System and Related Issues (Committee of 20) was issued on June 14, 1974 (IMF: Washington, DC).
13. These estimates are drawn from Fig. 7.1 (p. 119) of Eichengreen et al. (2018).

References

Alessandrini, Pietro and Michele Fratianni (2009) "Resurrecting Keynes to Stabilize the International Monetary System" *Open Economic Review*, vol. 20, pp. 339–358.

Cooper, Richard (1987) *The International Monetary System: Essays on the World Economy* (Cambridge, MA: MIT Press).

Eichengreen, Barry (1996) *Globalizing Capital: A History of the International Monetary System* (Princeton, NJ: Princeton University Press).

Eichengreen, Barry (2007) *Global Imbalances and the Lessons of Bretton Woods* (Cambridge, MA: MIT Press).

Eichengreen, Barry and Marc Flandreau (2008) "The Rise and Fall of the Dollar, or When Did the Dollar Replace Sterling as the Leading International Currency?" NBER Working Paper #14154 (July).

Eichengreen, Barry et al (2018) *How Currencies Work* (Princeton, NJ: Princeton University Press).

Elson, Anthony (2011)*Governing Global Finance: The Evolution and Reform of the International Financial Architecture* (New York, NY: Palgrave Macmillan).

McCauley, Robert and Catherine Schenk (2020) "Central Banks Swaps Then and Now: Swaps and Dollar Liquidity in the 1960s" BIS Working Paper #851 (April).

Pauly, Louis (1996) "The League of Nations and the Foreshadowing of the IMF" Princeton Essays in International Finance #201.

Triffin, Triffin (1960) *Gold and the Dollar Crisis: The Future of Convertibility* (New Haven, CT: Yale University Press).

CHAPTER 3

The Growth in the Role of the Dollar as a Global Currency Power

With the end of the Bretton Woods era in 1973, the dollar entered a new period as a global currency power. The revised Bretton Woods Agreement of 1978 did not formally endow the US dollar with a central place in the international monetary system as an institutional requirement, as it had under the gold exchange system of the Bretton Woods era. Nevertheless, the dollar continued to function as the key reserve currency in the system, notwithstanding the emergence of new reserve currencies such as the Deutsch mark, the yen and the euro. In some respects, the key role of the dollar as a global currency power has expanded beyond what it had been, in particular as the globalization of trade and finance has intensified in recent decades following the reduction in trade barriers and the elimination of capital controls among the advanced countries.

While there are clear reasons why the dollar has continued to play this central role, as explained in this chapter, it is of historic interest to note that the signatories of the revised Bretton Woods Agreement (including the United States) agreed to "collaborate with the Fund and with other participants (i.e., members) ...with the objective of making the Special Drawing Right (SDR) the principal reserve asset in the international monetary system (Article XXII)". The failure of this objective to have been achieved reflects to a large extent the lack of interest on the part of the United States, as an enhancement of the SDR would have threatened or reduced the global currency power of the dollar.

A. Elson, *The Global Currency Power of the US Dollar*,
https://doi.org/10.1007/978-3-030-83519-4_3

The remainder of this chapter focuses on the highlights of the globalization era in which the dollar has maintained its role as the dominant currency with a discussion of the key metrics that illustrate that role in quantitative terms and the main factors that account for it. This discussion leads to an explanation of the special role that the United States and the dollar play as a global financial intermediary, which gives rise to a modern version of "exorbitant privilege". The benefits and costs of the dollar-dominated international monetary and financial system are discussed in subsequent chapters.

The Contours of Globalization Under the Dollar Standard for Trade

The period of the dollar standard following the Bretton Woods era was one of rapid growth in trade and financial globalization. In the area of trade, a sharp recovery in trade occurred in the immediate aftermath of WW2, but then international trade reached a plateau in the 1960s where the ratio of trade to global GDP averaged around 18%. Thereafter, it expanded more rapidly with the ratio more than doubling to reach 44% by 2017. This result was the combined effect of a number of factors working together. One was the rapid economic growth of the countries of the North Atlantic region following the post-war recovery effort in Europe, together with the liberalization of exchange and trade restrictions promoted by the IMF and the General Agreement on Tariffs and Trade (GATT). The United States was a key force, not only in the promotion of mutual growth as the largest and most robust economy in the global system, but also in leading the multinational liberalization of trade and payments. In the case of the GATT, for example, as a result of its eight rounds of multilateral trade negotiations and various other regional and bilateral trade deals, the United States reduced its average import tariff on dutiable merchandise imports from 33% in 1944 to 1–2% today (prior to those introduced by the Trump administration), which set the pace for other advanced economies.

Towards the close of the second half-century, these sustained factors were buttressed by the impact of certain technological changes that reduced transport and communication costs and changed the nature of trade. One of these changes was the development of containerships that facilitated and expanded ocean trade through greatly reduced shipping and transport costs. Advances in information and communication technology (ICT) in the late 1980s and early 1990s also contributed to lower trade costs and the development of global value or supply chains that fundamentally altered the basis of trade. Whereas in the first technological revolution of trade involving steam and telegraph in the nineteenth century, it became possible to connect the point of export manufacturing production to the point of consumption more quickly and cheaply, towards the end of the twentieth century it became possible to separate the process of production into various components along a geographic supply chain where certain elements of the manufacturing process could be completed overseas more cheaply, and then assembled and distributed across a global network of consumers more efficiently. Since the early 1990s, sharply rising international trade data have reflected this intensified process of trade with an expansion not only in the value of final goods trade, but also in the trade of intermediate goods (or those used in the process of production), as they passed from one point of processing to another along the value chain. Multinational corporations participating in global value chains (GVCs) were able to increase their export production with the advantage of lower costs of production abroad, while increasing their participation in the early and later stages of the manufacturing process related to R&D, design, engineering and marketing, along with the high tech-intensive components of the manufacturing process.

Throughout the post-WW2 era, the United States has been the dominant trading nation in the global economy for both export and import merchandise trade, although in recent years, it has ceded that position to China in the case of exports. In 1950, according to data from the World Trade Organization (WTO), the United States accounted for nearly 16% of total world trade, with similar ratios for both exports and imports. At the end of the century, this total ratio was virtually unchanged, but with a lower ratio for exports and a higher one for imports. After 2000, with the explosive growth in China's trade, following its accession to the WTO, the ratios for the United States declined, while those for China sharply increased. By 2015, the import ratio for the United States was still higher than China's, but the one for US exports was significantly lower.

What is remarkable about the trading position of the United States is that the share of global trade that has been invoiced and settled in dollars has been far greater than the ratios noted in the previous paragraph. Recent studies have shown that the share of global import trade that is denominated in dollars has been around 60%, or 4.7 times the

US share of such trade. By comparison, this ratio is only 1.2 in the case of the euro, the next currency most frequently used in the invoicing of third-party trade.[1] For most other countries, the share of their trade that is denominated in their own currency is well below one, and in many cases, it is close to zero. This dominance of the dollar in the invoicing of trade has expanded with the development of GVCs, which account for around 50% of global trade and where the presence of US multinational corporations is very large. The invoicing in dollars of the components of traded goods in the process of production within GVCs managed by US companies has been simply a matter of convenience. As a result of this phenomenon, the dollar has also assumed a major role in the valuation of bank credit for trade operations, where its share has been estimated to be around 80%.[2]

The Contours of Globalization under the Dollar Standard for Finance

The developments in the globalization of finance tell a similar story to that of trade, with the United States and the dollar in persistently dominant positions. In the mid-1970s, with the end of the Bretton Woods era and the beginning of the dollar standard, the United States had become the first country to remove all restrictions on international financial transactions of resident individuals and bank and non-bank institutions, recognizing the erosion of capital controls that had occurred with the rapid growth of the euro-dollar market during the 1960s. Over the course of the next couple of decades, there was a rapid decline in capital account restrictions for the advanced countries as a group. In the 1970s, roughly half of these countries had liberalized their capital account restrictions, as measured on a de jure basis, and by the year 2000, around 90% of these countries were in that position. Progress among the emerging and developing economies was much slower, with less than 50% without capital controls in recent years.[3]

A similar picture of financial liberalization and the expansion of financial globalization is captured by the IMF's data on countries' international investment position (IIP) that provides a de facto measure of financial openness as reflected in the increase in the sum of a country's foreign financial assets and liabilities as a ratio to its GDP. In the case of the United States, this measure was equivalent to 30% of its GDP in 1970 and by 2008, at the peak of the global financial crisis, it had reached around

300%, following a very rapid rise after the turn of the new century. Since that time, there has been relatively little growth in this ratio, as financial institutions have cut back their international investment activities. The United States has by far the largest IIP of any country. At the end of 2019, the total foreign assets and liabilities of the United States amounted to nearly US$70 trillion, which was around 2 ½ times larger than the stocks of the next two countries in size (the United Kingdom and Luxembourg), even though they are both major international financial centers.[4] These indicators provide strong evidence of the dominant size and position of US financial markets in the international financial system, which can also be judged by the fact that the value of stock market capitalization in the United States represents around one-half the corresponding value of global stock markets.

The United States and the dollar are the major players in the global financial system for the mobilization and allocation of investible funds, given the size and scope of the country's financial markets and the role of the dollar as the dominant currency in the system. As in the case of trade, the dollar is the prime currency used for the valuation of international financial transactions, in particular with respect to international banking operations and international bond placements. In the case of international banking, at the end of 2019 total cross-border claims of all banks on a global basis amounted to US$31 trillion, of which roughly one-half was denominated in US dollars (or US$15 trillion).[5] In the case of international debt securities (i.e., securities issued in markets outside the issuer country by governments and financial and non-financial institutions), a similar share (47%) of those debt placements issued by countries other than the United States was also denominated in dollars (US$11.7).[6] Thus, at the end of 2019, around one-half of all the cross-border bank loans and international debt securities (amounting to US$26.7 trillion) were denominated in US dollars.

In the case of global cross-border bank loans in dollars, the US banking system is the largest single source vis-a-vis non-residents at around US$3 trillion, as one might expect, while it is also the largest recipient country of cross-border US dollar lending (US$6 trillion) based on end-2019 data. These facts imply that most of the dollar-denominated credit identified in the previous paragraph (as well as its funding) reflected non-US bank operations between non-US banks and non-US counterparties, mainly among countries in Western Europe, Canada and Japan, and more recently China. These operations are the legacy of the Eurodollar off-shore banking activity of the late 1950s and 1960s that led to the breakdown of the Bretton Woods fixed exchange rate system, as discussed in Chapter 2. This activity has steadily increased over time with the expansion of trade denominated in dollars and the desire of corporate borrowers to have access to finance for trade, investment and other business operations, which is itself mostly denominated in dollars.

The United States continues to be the single largest source of funding for the current level of international banking, but the share of that funding raised in the United States has been declining since the global financial crisis, as banks have been relying more on sources within their home jurisdictions (more than 50% as of mid-2018). While European countries had been predominant in this respect prior to the global financial crisis, Canada, Japan, Australia and China (in that order) have played a more important role since then.[7]

The amounts of dollar-based bank claims (US$15 trillion) discussed above does not cover the full extent of dollars raised by non-US bank as they are widely known to use off-balance sheet derivatives (such as swaps and forwards) as an additional, marginal source of dollar funding for their operations. However, the available data do not provide a direct estimate of this funding source. Nevertheless, the total dollar-denominated, cross-border claims and liabilities of non-US banks amounted to around US$29 trillion at the end of 2019.

In order to get a broader picture of the size of dollar-based activity in the global financial system, one can add to the amount of balance sheet data of non-US banks just mentioned, the amount of US treasury securities held by non-residents and the share of US currency used by non-residents. Of the total US government debt circulating publicly at the end of 2019 (US$17 trillion), around 40% or US$6.8 trillion was held by non-residents. In the case of US dollar notes (US$1.7 trillion), around 60% was estimated to be held by non-residents, or US$1 trillion. Finally, one can add to these figures the amount of dollar-denominated debt securities issued by foreign countries, noted earlier, amounting to US$11.7 trillion. With these additions, the stock of dollar-denominated financial assets and liabilities circulating in the global financial system amounted to US$48.5 trillion at end-2019 (US$29t + US$6.8t + US$1t + US$11.7t). This figure is almost certainly an under-estimate, as it excludes any estimate for non-resident holdings of US corporate bonds and equity shares. Even so, it is a very large number, especially when one compares it to the equivalent values for resident holdings in the United

States. For example, the assets and liabilities of the US (domestically chartered) commercial banking system at end-2019 amounted to US$29 trillion, which rises to US$40 trillion when one adds in the amount of dollar notes (UD$0.7 trillion) and treasury debt (US$10.5 trillion) in local circulation. Adding to this figure the amount of domestic debt issued by US resident entities other than the US treasury (US$21.6 trillion), one derives a base of domestic loans and securities of nearly US$62 trillion at end-2019 (US$29t + US$0.7t + US$10.5t + US$21.6t). By these calculations, the value of the dollar-based international assets and liabilities held by non-US residents is equivalent to close to 80% of the value of comparable holdings by domestic residents.

What is remarkable about the dollar-based international financial system is the variety of entities, sectors, jurisdictions and instruments involved in the lending and funding operations that one can detect in the available databases. The fact that non-US banks do not have access to the kind of stable consumer deposit base in dollars that US domestic banks have means that they need to rely on a variety of wholesale sources of funding linked to the issue of short-term instruments such as repurchase agreements, commercial paper, foreign exchange swaps and forwards, and certificates of deposit, as well as bonds of different maturities. This funding arrangement exposes them to various kinds of risk related to interest rate and exchange rate fluctuations, as well as the uncertainty of rolling over short-term funding sources during times of market stress. To some extent, these risks can be mitigated through the use of hedging instruments such as swaps and forwards or by matching an entity's asset structure in the currency and maturity of its funding (so-called "natural hedges").

Many of the transactions in the dollar-based international financial system involve cross-currency risks to some degree. For example, a non-bank financial institution in Japan will lend or sell dollars to a pension fund in Japan to invest in dollar-denominated US securities in the United States, when that fund has pension obligations in yen. Alternatively, a non-US bank with a balance sheet of largely local currency items may issue commercial paper to a US-based money market fund through a subsidiary or foreign branch to raise dollars that it lends to another non-US bank for investing in US dollar assets.[8] These two examples involve a variety of balance sheet, currency and timing mismatches that can pose great risks for those involved in times of market stress. The global financial crisis of 2008 and the beginning of the Covid-19 in March 2020, discussed in Chapter 1, were two such events where these risks erupted in severe market turmoil and the Federal Reserve and other advanced country central banks had to get involved through bilateral swaps and other emergency funding operations to provide dollar-based liquidity and maintain functioning markets for major financial instruments.

The size of foreign exchange operations monitored by the Bank for International Settlements (BIS) gives another image of the dollar's dominant role in the global financial system. According to its latest triennial survey for 2019, average daily foreign exchange transactions amounted to US$7 trillion, for which the US dollar was on one side or the other for nearly 90% of the trades.[9] Some of these transactions were related to the settlement of trade transactions, but most of them were related to transactions in the dollar-based global financial system, either for the funding or allocation of investments or for the hedging of currency risk involved in those transactions through spot and forward trades, as well as swaps and cross-currency swaps. (Spot foreign exchange transactions are outright purchases or sales of foreign exchange, whereas forwards represent a commitment to buy or sell foreign exchange at some future date, typically less than 6 months from the start of the contract. A foreign exchange swap is a contract to exchange currency (e.g., dollars for euros) for a specified period of time (less than 6 months), at the end of which the exchange is reversed. A cross-currency swap is similar to a swap, but has a longer maturity (of more than 1 year) with the exchange of floating interest rate payments during the lifetime of the contract.)

A number of factors motivate the participation of resident and non-resident entities in the exchange of dollar-based financial assets and liabilities. US-based entities may be interested in lending dollars to non-residents as they may be more willing to pay higher rates of interest than domestic borrowers and as a means of diversifying their portfolio of assets. Foreign entities may want to buy US dollar assets in order to earn higher yields than may be available from asset investments in their home country and for the purpose of portfolio diversification. In this regard, US dollar-based assets, such as US treasuries and investment-grade corporate debt, are known for their "safe haven" characteristics of increased value and liquidity during times of market stress, as noted in Chapter 1. These assets may have less risk from the impact of inflation and exchange rate depreciation than comparable investments in the home country of the investor. Foreign entities may want to borrow dollars because of the access this action brings to a broader and deeper investor base with lower costs than they may face in their home country. Access to these lending sources may also diversify their funding sources.

It is also important to understand the source of dollars that foreign entities may have available to invest in dollar-based assets. One important source is the official reserves that foreign central banks hold in dollars. At the end of 2019, these official reserves amounted to the equivalent of US$6.8 trillion, which to a large extent are invested in US treasury securities of various maturities and represent the largest share of the foreign holdings of these bonds noted earlier. In addition, international trading firms may hold dollars overseas for managing the settlement of trade transactions that they may want to hold in temporary dollar investments. Similarly, foreign banks or non-bank financial intermediaries may hold dollars from their financial transactions or dealings with multinational corporations that they may want to invest in US dollar assets to match the currency exposure of their liabilities to those firms. In essence, these various motivations suggest strongly that the dollar-based international financial system is one of convenience, reliability and diversity that can satisfy a variety of needs and provide a number of benefits to the private entities involved.

Long-term Indicators of the Global Currency Power of the Dollar

In order to develop a longer time perspective on the dominant currency status of the dollar, it is interesting to examine two broad indicators, for which data are available on an annual basis since the end of the Bretton Woods era in the early 1970s. The dollar's status with respect to these indicators reflects its importance across a variety of functions including not only the invoicing and settlement of trade and the valuation of financial assets, but also more broadly as a reference rate for the management of a country's exchange rate and monetary policies. One of these indicators is the currency composition of official foreign reserves and the other is the extent to which the dollar is used as a peg, anchor or reference rate for the management of a country's exchange rate. Some countries such as the United States allow their currency to float freely in response to changes in the demand and supply of that currency in foreign exchange markets, but most countries tie the value of their currency to one of the currencies of the advanced countries by means of a peg or an adjustable peg in the case of a fixed exchange rate system; in the case of a flexible exchange rate system, the currency of an advanced country is often used as a reference rate for the conduct of a country's monetary and fiscal policies according to which it allows the value of its currency to fluctuate within a certain fixed or moving band. According to both of these indicators, the dollar has been the dominant currency throughout the post-Bretton Woods era up until the present day as discussed further below.

In the case of official foreign reserves, the dollar has clearly dominated the currency composition of reported foreign reserves, with its share well over 50% since the early 1970s, as noted in Chapter 2. Initially during the early post-WW2 era, the dollar's share was in the range of 70–80%, given its role as the principal reserve currency under the Bretton Woods system. This percentage share dropped to the low 50s by 1990, as other currencies such as the German mark and Japanese yen attracted some attention as reserve currencies. Thereafter, the dollar's share increased to the mid-60s even as the euro gained some status as a competitive reserve currency to the dollar, while the yen and pound continued to play residual roles.[10] A country that allocates a high share of its official foreign reserves to dollar-denominated investments is also likely to be one in which a large share of its trade is invoiced and paid for in dollars and foreign borrowing is largely denominated in dollars. These features of private sector activity dictate that the central bank maintain a significant share of its official reserves in dollars in order to be able to resolve temporary interruptions in the flow of these dollar-denominated transactions.

The evolution of the dollar's role as a peg, anchor or reference rate for other currencies tells a similar story to the one just discussed. Over time, there has been a steady increase in the number of countries that use the dollar as their reference currency in some manner, as more countries have become independent since 1970, first with the collapse of the European colonial empires and more recently with the break-up of the Soviet Union. When one weights those countries that are tied to the dollar by their share of global GDP, one can define an effective dollar zone for the global economy that is quite large. In the early 1970s, it represented around 70% of global GDP, but then this share dropped to around 50% in the late 1980s and early 1990s, with the competitive role played by other reserve currencies such as the mark, yen and, more recently, the euro, as noted earlier. However, since then, the size of this dollar zone has increased to around 65% of global GDP, involving more than half of the 195 countries in the global system with separate currencies.[11] The euro zone, the next largest currency zone, is less than half as large as the dollar zone, even though its share of global GDP is roughly the same as that of the United States (on a purchasing power parity basisi). The dollar currency zone can be understood as one in which the dollar and the United States predominate in the pricing and flow of trade, foreign borrowing and investment, and in which the policies of the Federal Reserve have significant spillover effects on monetary policies in the countries of the zone.

Factors Leading to Global Currency Power

There are a number of factors than can account for the global currency power of the dollar that has endured from the time of the Bretton Woods Agreement up until the present day. At a global level, the primary status of the United States as the largest economic, financial and military power within the international system must be recognized. These attributes have been reinforced by the long-standing commitment of the United States to the defense and maintenance of a liberal international economic order and its institutional infrastructure that has promoted sustained growth of the global economy over the long term.

Even though the share of the United States in global GDP has fallen steadily since the end of WW2 with the growth and expansion of other advanced countries and, more recently, the emerging market economies in East Asia, the United States is still the largest country within the global economy with a share of around 24% (measured at current exchange rates). As such, it has been the largest trading nation until very recently with the emergence of China as an export powerhouse. Most countries of the world count the United States among its major trading partners. The United States moved to a status of virtual free trade before any other country after WW2 and has been the leader in promoting the removal of trade barriers through the GATT, the WTO, and a variety of regional and bilateral trade pacts.

The dominant status of the United States as a trading nation has encouraged the use of the dollar as a unit of account (for invoicing) and medium of exchange (for the settlement of trade transactions) over time. As noted earlier, this trend has been intensified in recent decades by the development of GVCs, in which the United States' manufacturing and services sectors have played a major role, as part of the process of growing trade integration within the global economy. The expanding use of the dollar in conducting international trade has also been encouraged and reinforced by its prominent role as a peg, anchor or reference rate for the currencies of the largest share of the membership of the IMF since its founding compared with other reserve currencies.

As a financial superpower, the United States has been recognized for the size and scope of its financial markets, which are unparalleled for their breadth, depth and liquidity. As noted in Chapter 2, the growing sophistication of US financial markets was one of the main factors that led to the beginning of the transfer process from the pound to the dollar of its role as a global currency power during the 1920s. What has also been critical to the primary role of the dollar in financial transactions is the full convertibility of the dollar and the free and open access of non-resident individuals and enterprises to US financial markets for legitimate transactions. One sign of the special role that the United States plays as an international financial marketplace is the dominance of the dollar in global foreign exchange transactions, noted earlier. Some of these transactions relate to basic trading operations and financial flows, but most of them relate to a variety of derivative transactions involving swaps and forwards for managing risks in those basic trades or for the short-term management of funds related to them.

The long-term macroeconomic policy management and strong rule of law that exist in the United States have also solidified its position as a global currency power. In its rule of law, the United States is recognized for its strong protection of property rights and independent judicial system that are available to residents and non-residents alike for the safeguard of their trading contracts and financial transactions. These legal attributes give the United States a pre-eminent role in the international economic system.

The long-term macroeconomic policy management of the United States is another factor that has sustained the pre-eminence of the dollar vis-à-vis other currencies. While the United States has experienced certain periods of higher than normal inflation and weak economic growth, by and large over the long term it has sustained a solid pace of growth in its real GDP of close to 2½%, on an average annual basis for 1991–2020, close to its potential, with average inflation at a stable rate of around 2%. This performance has provided in effect an anchor for the global economy as a stable trading power with positive spillover effects on other countries. Since the conquest of high inflation in the early 1980s, the Federal Reserve has gained a strong reputation for its non-partisan, sound technocratic administration of monetary policy that has helped to sustain the long-term growth and inflation performance noted above. This policy has been accompanied by a long-term commitment of the US government to the implementation of sound fiscal and budgetary policies that have inspired confidence within the global economy of its commitment to debt sustainability and the protection of the "safe haven" status of US government securities.

The global financial crisis which originated in the United States in 2008 raised questions about the reliability of the government's regulatory and supervisory frameworks vis-à-vis the large commercial banks and the growing, virtually unregulated non-bank financial sector (so-called "shadow banks"), as well as the role of monetary policy in contributing to the development of a large property price bubble that preceded the crisis. These developments raised questions for the first time in recent history about the inherent instability of the global financial system linked to the United States and the central role of the dollar. These questions and doubts have been raised again in relation to more recent developments in US government policy that are examined in Chapters 5 and 6.

One other factor of a non-economic nature that has played a role in the determination of the dollar as a global currency power is the national security relationships of the United States with certain countries, such as Germany and South Korea. Countries that have security or military alliances with the United States may find it convenient to see the United States not only as a source of their security guarantees, but also as the financial center through which they can manage their borrowing and investment needs. Such an arrangement has been shown to increase the share of the country's official reserves that are denominated in dollars. According to recent empirical studies, such a relationship is estimated to account for a 30% higher share of official reserves in dollars for countries such as Germany, Japan, Saudi Arabia, South Korea and Taiwan with strong security links to the United States compared with other countries with similar trading links to the United States.[12]

In addition to the fundamental forces discussed above that can account for the global currency power of the dollar, one needs to consider the network and reinforcing effects and externalities associated with the use of the dollar as a global currency that have bolstered its widespread international use as a unit of account, medium of exchange and store of value. The fact that the dollar is only one of 195 national currencies suggests that there are forces of a natural monopoly that impel the international economy to the selection by market forces and government policy of one or a few currencies as global reserve currencies. The fundamental forces outlined above suggest why it is the dollar that has been chosen as the global currency power. In addition, there are natural links between the choice of the dollar by a country for the invoicing and settlement of its trade with the United States that can easily spread to other countries of a regional trading bloc and then, more generally, among countries with strong trading ties with that country because of the lower transaction costs involved. The use of the same currency (i.e., the dollar) for trading relations has also been convenient from the point of view of comparing prices and transport costs. The selection of the dollar for the pricing of primary commodities, first in the case of petroleum and then, more generally, for other products, has also reinforced the tendency to use the dollar for invoicing and settling foreign trade. These network effects operating at the trade level can then have repercussions for the development of dollar-based international financial transactions. At first, it may be the actions by national and/or foreign banks in arranging loans for businesses involved in foreign trade that develop into other forms of dollar-based foreign finance, for example, for the management of short-term dollar funds of these businesses and the expansion of their trading operations more generally, on possibly better terms than available in the local currency.[13]

These developments at the levels of trade and finance lead to a third level in the hierarchy of reinforcing relationships, which is linked to the choice of dollar-based investments by a country's central bank for the management of its official reserves, as noted earlier. In a country where the dollar plays an important role as a unit of account and medium of exchange for its trade and financial relationships with other countries, it is natural for the central bank in that country to hold dollar-based investments as a store of value for its official reserves. For temporary needs or to facilitate trade and financial flows, the central bank can then lend dollars to domestic businesses or purchase and sell the dollars they use in international transactions, while maintaining close working relationships with counterpart central banks in other important trading partners or source countries for dollar finance.

The Special Role of the United States as a Global Financial Intermediary

As noted earlier, the United States has the largest international investment position of any country in the global economy. As such, it has played an indispensable role as an international financial intermediary that has been closely related to the role that many of its financial assets, in particular US government securities, have played as "safe haven" or "safe" assets for foreign entities. This role of the US economy and its dollar-based assets has been a key feature of the global financial system since the time of the Bretton Woods Agreement and has expanded significantly during the post-Bretton Woods era. The prominence given by foreign entities to US government securities as safe assets is another factor that has solidified the position of the dollar as a global currency power. US treasury securities have historically been considered risk-free and near-cash, as they retain their value and can be easily sold in what is the largest bond market in the world, in both normal times and at times of market stress. They also provide a benchmark for the pricing of other debt of similar maturities and thus have an impact on the interest rates that private and public agents pay on loans in many countries with open capital accounts.

Safe assets have appeal to both domestic and international investors for their characteristics of ease of transfer (i.e., liquidity), sustainability (i.e., high credit rating of issuing entity) and maintenance or increase in value during times of stress (reliability). As such, investors are willing to pay a premium or receive a lower yield than that of other financial assets of similar duration. In addition to US government securities, which have received wide recognition as a safe asset, highly rated debt of other US government agencies, such as the Government National Mortgage Association (Ginnie Mae), municipal debt, commercial paper and highly rated corporate bonds have been given safe asset status. Prior to the global financial crisis, mortgage-backed securities (MBS) and collateralized debt obligations (CDOs) that had been used extensively during the housing boom in the United States that preceded the crisis were also given safe asset status by domestic and foreign investors because of their AAA ratings. These derivative instruments had been created by investment banks as a means of converting conventional housing loans into tradable securities composed of mortgage financial instruments of varying quality from sub-prime to highest quality and sold publicly as medium-to long-term bonds to domestic and foreign investors. Unfortunately, the rating agencies that evaluated these securities in many cases did not conduct a careful analysis of their underlying quality and often conferred AAA ratings on them under pressure from the investment banks that created them. This lack of independence and due diligence on the part of the rating agencies in many cases was due to the fact that they had close working relationships with the investment banks for a variety of business functions.

When it became widely understood by market participants that many of the highly rated MBS/CDOs were in fact of dubious quality, this change became the trigger for panic selling and a breakdown in the short-term financial arrangements that were used by investors to acquire them. This sudden change in the financial markets was particularly problematic for European banks that had been major investors in MBS/CDOs on the mistaken assumption that they had "safe haven" status. These banks had in many cases issued commercial paper or repurchase agreements (REPOs) on an overnight basis to money market funds in the United States, often through a branch or subsidiary located there, to acquire dollars for the purchase of these securities. (A REPO is a financial transaction in which cash is provided by a non-bank financial intermediary, such as a money market fund, to another financial entity, often on an overnight basis, against the collateral provided by the security purchased by the REPO seller.)

The case just described is another example of the cross-currency, resident-non-resident financial transactions discussed earlier that pose significant risks as a result of balance-sheet mismatches of currency and maturity for the investors involved, where foreign exchange swaps and forwards would be involved. Nevertheless, when the global financial crisis erupted in late 2008, the European banks found it very difficult to arrange overnight financing or swaps to sustain their acquisition of MBS/CDOs because of their significant loss in value and the unwillingness of money market funds to roll-over the REPOs that they had acquired from the banks. In these circumstances, the European banks were unable in many cases to raise the dollars needed to cancel the REPOs and, ultimately, they had to rely on the European Central Bank for temporary assistance through dollar funding that it arranged through a bilateral swap with the Federal Reserve.

The major losses suffered during the global financial crisis by investors in MBS/CDOs resulted in a substantial reduction in the size and scope of dollar-based safe assets, given the widespread popularity of these securities, and increased sharply the demand for US Treasury securities in the period thereafter. Throughout the post-Bretton Woods era, the global demand for these securities has been the source for significant inflows of capital to the United States in its external accounts. During the early part of the post-Bretton Woods era, these inflows were offset by capital outflows in the form of foreign direct investment and portfolio investment abroad by domestic US investors with the result that the United States had a balanced financial account in its external balance of payments equal to a balanced current account comprising its exports and imports of goods, services and income. These results gave rise to the image of the United States as a global financial intermediary, given the size of these capital inflows and outflows and their different characteristics. The capital inflows or sales of mainly US Treasury securities abroad were viewed as analogous to liquid short-term deposits captured by domestic banks. These liabilities would be offset by business loans or investment by the banks on the asset side of their balance sheet that could be seen as roughly equivalent to the long-term capital outflows of the United States in the form of its foreign direct investment and portfolio investment abroad noted earlier. The transformation by a bank of short-term deposits on the liability side of its balance sheet to longer-term loans or investment on the asset side of its balance sheet is inherent to the process of financial intermediation. So too, in the external accounts of the United States, one can see an analogous process at work within the global financial system. Thus, the United States came to be known as "global banker to the world".

What is also unique to the role of the United States as "global banker" is that the United States has earned a significant net interest gain on the difference between the interest it paid on its liabilities or capital inflows and the yield it has earned on its foreign investments or capital outflows. To a large extent, this difference arises from the fact that foreign entities have been willing to pay a significant premium or accept a lower interest payment for the safety and security of US Treasuries as global safe assets than they have been for other types of investments, as noted earlier. According to one prominent study, the difference between the income earned by the United States on its foreign assets and the interest paid on its liabilities amounted to around 3.5% per year during the post-Bretton Woods era (1973–2015), compared with 1.3% during the Bretton Woods era (1952–1972).[14]

The authors of the study just cited argue that these two figures (3.5 and 1.3%) are a true measure of the "exorbitant privilege" that has accrued to the United States during the Bretton Woods era and since. Others have argued that the "exorbitant privilege" for the United States arises simply from the fact that it has been able to run current account deficits in its external balance of payments for sustained periods of time without any external pressure to make policy adjustments in the same way other countries are required to do in order to reduce or eliminate such deficits. The increase in the positive interest rate differential earned by the United States for its global borrowing and lending operations during the post-Bretton Woods era also reflects a growing spread in that differential over time as resident US investors have shifted to increasingly more risky foreign investments with correspondingly higher yields with the increase in financial integration and financial globalization. Because of this shift, some analysts have suggested that the role of the United States as a global financial intermediary has changed over time from that of "global banker" to that of global "venture capitalist".[15]

When viewing the large interest rate differential in favor of the United States as a reflection of its "exorbitant privilege" in the global financial system, economists have also argued that the premium paid by foreign investors for US Treasury securities is a form of insurance payment for their safe asset status, as they maintain or increase their value during times of financial market stress. These securities increase in value not only because of increased demand, but also because of an appreciation of the US dollar that increases the value of dollar-based portfolios vis-à-vis those denominated in other currencies. By the same token, the appreciation of the dollar represents a loss for the United States, as its foreign claims are denominated mainly in other currencies that decrease in value. The combined effect of a decline in the dollar value of US foreign assets and little or no change in the dollar value of its foreign liabilities at a time of financial stress or crisis represents a substantial transfer of wealth from the United States to the rest of the world that economists have characterized as an "exorbitant duty" offsetting the "exorbitant privilege" that the United States enjoys in more normal times. During the global financial crisis of 2008–2009, the impact of fulfilling this "exorbitant duty" by the United States as a global financial intermediary was estimated to amount to 19% of US GDP.[16] The "privilege" and "duty" just described are unique to the role of the United States as the hegemonic power within the global financial system and the global currency power of the dollar.

This positive interest rate differential for the United States in its external accounts also means that it can run a deficit in the balance of its trade in goods and services equivalent to the net interest income associated with this differential without incurring an overall current account deficit. This result is a benefit or privilege enjoyed by few other countries. In balance of payments accounting, the current account of a country's balance of payments includes receipts and payments between residents and non-residents (i.e., inflows and outflows) for goods, services and income. Interest received on foreign assets (or loans) and that paid on foreign liabilities (or debt) is included within the income component of the current account just mentioned. The current account is matched by the capital and financial account, which means that a current account deficit is offset by a capital and financial account surplus or net capital inflows, whereas a current account surplus is matched by a capital and financial account deficit or net capital outflows, as the overall result of the balance of payments must sum to zero. In the discussion that follows, the capital and financial account is referred to as simply the financial account for convenience, since capital account transactions for the United States are relatively minor in comparison with those of its financial account.

Beginning in the mid-1980s, the capital inflows of the United States began to exceed its outflows such that it was generating a financial account surplus that offset a deficit in its current account. (Over time, this result has steadily expanded, giving rise to a large, cumulative negative imbalance in its net international investment position that was discussed earlier.) At one level, this is a necessary result of balance of payments accounting as explained above, without any implications for causality. At another level, in order to explain this growing current account deficit of the United States and its financial account surplus, one must look to domestic developments and the difference between aggregate domestic savings and investment. A current account deficit implies that domestic expenditure for consumption and investment is greater than the value of domestic production, or that saving (i.e., production minus consumption) is less than investment, with the imbalance covered by an excess of imports over exports. In the case of the United States, one can see that its savings–investment imbalance has been reflected primarily in a steady erosion of domestic savings, as investment fluctuated within a relatively narrow range of 20–25% of GDP until 2009 when it fell below 20% of GDP for the first time. The erosion in savings, however, can be linked to both a steady increase in personal consumption as a share of GDP and an erosion in government savings reflecting an increase in fiscal imbalances over time. The fiscal position of the US government shifted from overall balance during the 1950–1970 period to a deficit of around 5% of GDP in the mid-1980s and to one of 7% during the period 2008–2012. This expansion in the size of the overall government imbalance has accounted for most of the increase in the savings–investment gap and external current account deficit noted earlier.

If allowed to grow unchecked, this pattern of growing fiscal imbalances will raise questions in the minds of domestic and foreign investors about the stability of US government finances and the sustainability of the government's debt position. These concerns have taken on greater importance in light of the adverse economic effects of the Covid-19 crisis and its major fiscal impact, both in terms of lost revenue and the massive increases in spending incurred to offset those effects. Up until now, the safe asset status of US government debt has been reflected in a steady decline in government bond yields, as domestic and foreign demand for these assets has tended to exceed their supply. However, there is no guarantee that this situation will continue indefinitely, which is an issue taken up in Chapters 5 and 6.

Notes

1. These ratios for the dollar and euro are drawn from Gopinath (2015).
2. This estimate has been taken from Bruno et al. (2018).
3. The de jure measure of capital controls cited in this paragraph is the Chinn-Ito index of capital controls, which is available athttps://web.pdx.edu/~ito/Chinn-Ito_website.htm..
4. These estimates of the international investment position of Luxembourg, the United Kingdom and the United States are drawn from the Balance of Payments and International Investment Position database of the IMF which is available at data.imf.org.
5. The data reported in this paragraph come from the locational bank statistics database of the BIS (available at stats.bis.org), which is estimated to cover around 95% of global banking operations, based on reports from 48 countries and off-shore financial centers, with the largest international banking operations involving counterparties in 200 countries.
6. The share of dollar-denominated debt securities is based on the BIS international debt securities database, which is available at stats.bis.org.
7. The source of dollar funding for non-US international banks at the global level has been examined by Aldasoro and Ehlers (2018). An additional source of information can be found in Annex 5 of IMF (2019).

8. The content of this paragraph is examined more fully in BIS Committee on the Global Financial System (2020).
9. The BIS Triennial Report on "Foreign Exchange Turnover in April 2019" (September 16, 2019) has further details on these transactions.
10. The currency composition of official foreign reserves cited in this paragraph is drawn from the estimates produced by Eichengreen et al. (2018) that are presented in Fig. 7.1.
11. The estimates for the size of the dollar zone in the global economy are drawn from Ilzetzkiet al. (2019).
12. This relationship is examined in Eichengreen et al. (2017).
13. The externalities and network effects of the use of the dollar in trade and finance are examined at a conceptual level in Gopinath and Stein (2018).
14. These calculations are laid out in Gourinchas, Rey and Govillot (2010).
15. This shift in the role of the United States was first proposed in Gourinchas and Rey (2007).
16. This estimate is drawn from the paper of Gourinchasetal. (2010).

References

Aldasoro, Inaki and Torsten Ehlers (2018) in "The Geography of Dollar Funding of non-US Banks" *BIS Quarterly Review* (December), pp. 15–26.

BIS Committee on the Global Financial System (2020) "US Dollar Funding: An International Perspective" CGFS Paper #65 (June).

Bruno, Valentina et al (2018) "Exchange Rates and the Working Capital Channel of Trade Fluctuations" BIS Working Paper #694 (January).

Eichengreen, Barry et al (2017) "Mars or Mercury? The Geopolitics of International Currency Choice" NBER Working Paper # 24145 (December).

Eichengreen, Barry, Arnaud Mehl and Livia Chitu (2018) *How Currencies Work: Past, Present, and Future* (Princeton, NJ: Princeton University Press).

Gopinath, Gita (2015) "The International Price System" NBER Working Paper #21646 (November).

Gopinath, Gita and Jeremy Stein (2018) "Banking, Trade, and the Making of a Dominant Currency" (March 28), Harvard Working Paper, which is available at http://scholar.harvard.edu.

Gourinchas, Pierre-Olivier and Helene Rey (2007) "From World Banker to World Venture Capitalist: US External Adjustment and Exorbitant Privilege" in Richard Clarida (ed.) *G7 Current Account Imbalances: Sustainability and Adjustment* (Chicago, IL: Univ. of Chicago Press).

Gourinchas, Pierre-Olivier, Helene Rey and Nicholas Govillot (2010) "Exorbitant Privilege and Exorbitant Duty" Bank of Japan Institute for Monetary and Economic Studies Discussion Paper #2010-E-20 (August).

Ilzetzki, Ethan, Carmen Reinhart and Ken Rogoff (2019) "Exchange Arrangements Entering the Twenty-first Century: Which Anchor will Hold?" *Quarterly Journal of Economics* (May), vol. 34 (2), pp. 599–646.
IMF (2019) *Global Financial Stability Report* (October).

CHAPTER 4

The Benefits of the Dollar System to the United States and the Rest of the World

The dollar-based international monetary and financial system, which has been in existence since the end of World War II and has intensified during the last couple of decades, has provided a number of benefits to the United States. Some of these have been suggested in previous chapters, along with certain benefits for the rest of the global economy. The purpose of this chapter is to bring these ideas together and examine them in more detail. Chapters 5 and 6 will then look at the problems and defects associated with this dollar-based system that pose a threat to global financial stability over the medium term. Chapters 7–9 examines various reforms and institutional changes to deal with these problems.

The benefits that have accrued to the United States from the global currency power of the dollar can be broken down into those that pertain most directly to private traders and investors and those that apply mainly to the US government for the conduct of its foreign economic and national security policies. In reality, these two sets of benefits cannot be separated, as the first have been a derivative of the second. However, the first have largely been the result of spontaneous market forces, whereas the second relate to conscious policy decisions. The chapter closes with a discussion of the positive externalities of the dollar-based international monetary system for the rest of the global economy.

A. Elson, *The Global Currency Power of the US Dollar*,
https://doi.org/10.1007/978-3-030-83519-4_4

The Benefits of the Dollar System for Private Traders and Investors

As was noted earlier, there is a natural tendency for one or a few national currencies to emerge as the dominant currency for the invoicing and settlement of trade within a region or among close trading partners. Within Europe, for example, the establishment of a dominant currency was achieved by common agreement among the members of the European Union to replace a number of separate national currencies with a new currency, the euro, in 1999. This decision has been the foundation stone for a strong process of trade and economic integration in the period since. Key to this process has been the elimination of administrative and transactional expenses related to the exchange of separate currencies among trading partners and the comparison of price data needed for trade. In the case of the US dollar, the process of becoming a dominant currency for trading purposes has been a naturally evolving one. Given the major role that the United States has played as a trading partner for many countries, it became convenient for certain countries to price their exports and imports in dollar terms given the relative stability of dollar trading prices and the absence of exchange risk in such a practice. The international practice of setting the export prices for primary commodities in dollars that started with petroleum in the 1970s would have reinforced a country's decision to price its trade in dollars. This tendency would have been greater for a country with strategic complementarities in trade with the United States, the more open it was to trade, and the greater its reliance on dollar imports as inputs for domestic production. The decision of a country to invoice its exports in dollars instead of its local currency also would have avoided the cost and inconvenience of swapping a future payout in local currency for dollars using some hedging device. Once certain trading partners of the United States had established dollar pricing for their trade, the favorable effect of network externalities would have encouraged this practice among other trading partners of the United States, especially if various trading partners of the United States had among themselves important trading relations.[1]

Once established as a dominant currency for the invoicing and settlement of trade, it is easy to see how this practice could lead to the demand for dollars as a safe asset for financial transactions. Importers with dollar funds would have more predictability in terms of their import cost requirements, especially if their domestic expenditures are very dependent on imported goods, while exporters with dollar receipts may find future projects easier to finance with dollar loans from foreign banks (using exports as collateral) that are likely to carry a lower interest rate than borrowing from banks in their home country. With the dollar as a dominant currency for international bond issues, borrowers in foreign countries issuing dollar-denominated bonds would find it easier for international investors to compare the yields on their bond offerings, while facilitating the issue of debt of new borrowers in international financial markets.

For traders and investors in the United States, the convenience of using the dollar as a dominant currency brings a number of benefits. The invoicing and settlement of trade in dollars eliminates the cost and inconvenience of foreign exchange transactions and the associated problem of exchange risk. The search for trading partners on the export or import side is easier to the extent that a wide range of countries use dollars in the pricing of their trade. This process is enhanced by the large presence of major US banks in foreign markets which can help to establish trading links and manage the financing of trade once it is established. This advantage for US-based traders has been particularly important in the development of global value chains that account for a major share of US trading activity. In financial transactions, US-based investors have a rich variety of dollar-denominated bond offerings from foreign borrowers to consider for their portfolio choices. At the same time, corporate borrowers in the United States have a potentially large market for their bond placements given the strong global demand for dollar-denominated financial assets. The large scope of dollar-based banking outside the United States also has facilitated the financing of foreign direct investment projects by American businesses in many countries. The benefits from the global currency power of the dollar for the trade and financial transactions noted above extend quite widely given the large size of the dollar currency zone that covers around two-thirds of global GDP.

The Benefits of the Dollar System for the US Government

There are two broad sets of benefits that the US government has enjoyed from the global currency power of the dollar. One is best captured under the term "exorbitant privilege" and the other relates to its use in meeting certain foreign policy objectives. Both of these sets of benefits are quite distinct.

The term "exorbitant privilege" as applied to the United States has come to have two separate meanings or interpretations. The first, as noted in the previous chapter, originated during the latter part of the Bretton Woods era, and was formulated by the French government as a criticism of the dollar-centric international monetary system, which allowed the United States to run persistent current account deficits financed by the issue of US Treasury debt that other countries needed for their reserve holdings. This privilege was not without limit, however, as the viability of the Bretton Woods Agreement depended upon the commitment of the United States to keep its outstanding dollar liabilities to other countries below the value of the stock of its gold holdings. Because of excessively expansionary monetary and fiscal policies, the United States was unable to keep this commitment and thus the Bretton Woods era came to an end. Nevertheless, even though the United States suspended its obligation under the Bretton Woods Agreement to convert outstanding dollar liabilities into gold, under the de facto dollar-based system that has been in place since the mid-1970s, the United States has continued to run persistent current account deficits. From the mid-1970s to the mid-1980s, the United States maintained either a small surplus or approximate balance in its current account transactions, but since then, the current account balance has turned negative and has continued to increase up until the present day. Once again, the causal factor for these deficits has been an expansionary fiscal policy. At the same time, these deficits have been financed by the sale of US Treasury debt to foreign investors and institutions, which have viewed it as the pre-eminent "safe" financial asset of the global financial system.

This capability to run "deficits without tears" has served the United States' foreign policy interests very well given the global reach, for example, of its military outlays and the deployment of military personnel and equipment in more than 70 foreign countries. The global currency power of the US dollar is perfectly suited for this essential activity of the United States as a global hegemonic power in its role as the protector of the liberal international economic order and an international political system without major war for the last 75 years.

The absence of a significant external constraint on the United States and the continued, strong foreign demand for its Treasury debt as a global safe asset have given it great autonomy in the conduct of macroeconomic policies and the unique power to delay the implementation of any policy adjustments to deal with its current account imbalance. This autonomy, however, is not without limit and depends upon the positive assessment of foreign investors and creditors that the United States will be able to maintain a sustainable fiscal and debt position in the future. Prior to the Covid-19 crisis, serious concerns with regard to this issue had not been raised, but in the period since they have been, given the magnitude of the problems caused by the pandemic and the major fiscal response. These issues are explored in more detail in Chapter 6.

In principal, the provision of safe assets by the United States in the form of Treasury debt does not require it to run a current account deficit, as the liabilities issued by the United States by way of Treasury debt could be offset in its external financial account by the accumulation of foreign assets in the form of foreign direct investment and an increase in equity stakes abroad by private investors and businesses. This historic pattern in the United States' external financial account transactions is what has led analysts to describe as typical of a global financial intermediary which issues short to medium term, "safe" financial notes and bonds on the liability side of its external balance sheet that is matched by investments in long-term risky assets abroad on the asset side of its balance sheet. None of these transactions are the result of conscious policy decisions or deliberate actions on the part of the US government, but rather they represent the result of countless market-based decisions of different entities at home and abroad that reflect the comparative advantage of the United States in providing financial services to the rest of the world. The fact that this process has occurred in the context of a growing current account deficit on the part of the United States can only be explained by domestic economic forces that have created a growing fiscal imbalance and a relatively high level of private consumption.

The persistence of the US current account deficit has been a major factor in the emergence and persistence of the problem of global imbalances. These imbalances represent the aggregate sum of current account deficits and surpluses of major countries or geographic regions of the global economy. Conceptually, the sum of the deficits should match the sum of the surpluses, with capital outflows from countries or regions in the latter group providing the financing required by countries or regions in the former group (with some allowance for statistical discrepancies and mismeasurement). The size of these imbalances tended to be in the range of 2–3% of global GDP from the mid-1970s to the mid-1990s, but after the latter time period, they expanded sharply and reached a value equivalent to 6% of global GDP just prior to the global financial crisis of 2008. The United States has been the main source of the deficit side of these global imbalances, and during the period preceding the global financial crisis was absorbing around two-thirds of the global current account surplus or net savings of the rest of the world. The surplus side of the global imbalances was more diversified in its geographic origins and reflected the net aggregate savings generated by major oil exporters, China and other emerging export economies of East Asia. In the period since the crisis, the size of the global imbalances has been reduced, although the United States has continued to be the dominant factor on the deficit side.

The other more recent meaning of "exorbitant privilege" as applied to the United States relates to the significant risk premium that it has earned on the asset structure of its external financial account in relation to the cost of its liability structure. As noted in the previous chapter, this risk premium has been estimated at around 3.5% a year for the period 1972–2015, which implies that the United States has generated a significant difference between what it earns on its foreign assets and what it pays on its foreign liabilities, even though its net international investment position (NIIP) has become increasingly negative since the mid-1990s. In 2019, the NIIP of the United States amounted to minus US$11 trillion, according to estimates of the IMF, compared with minus US$1.9 trillion in 2005.[2] Despite this significant negative trend, during the same time period, the net primary income of the United States (related to its earnings of interest and dividends) in its external current account increased from US$54 billion in 2005 to US$257 billion in 2019. This net flow of income from abroad has been an important offset to a growing trade deficit on the part of the United States amounting to US$866 billion in 2019; without this net income from abroad, the current account deficit and external financing requirement of the United States would have been correspondingly larger.

Another less important aspect of the "exorbitant privilege" enjoyed by the United States is the "seigniorage" that it earns on the use of its currency abroad. Seigniorage represents the implied savings that a country accrues in terms of goods and services from the issue and public use of its notes and coins as interest free debt, compared with the issue of normal government debt. Of the total notes and coins issued by the United States, it is generally assumed that roughly 60%, or around US$1 trillion is held overseas; on the assumption that alternative financing for the government of this amount would cost 1%, then seigniorage for the United States would amount to US$10 billion, or less than 5% of the net primary income earned by the United States in 2019.[3]

Apart from the benefits associated with its "exorbitant privilege", the United States has gained significant advantages in the conduct of its national security and foreign policy from the global currency power of the dollar. These can be understood in terms of the use of the dollar as both a "carrot" and "stick" device, with the former taking the form of special aid packages and the latter taking the form of economic sanctions. Each of these is elaborated in the paragraphs below.

As the dominant reserve currency in the international monetary system, access to dollars, especially for emerging and developing economies, is a valued resource. Throughout the post-WW2 era, the United States has maintained an active program of foreign assistance since the early 1960s, administered mainly by the US Agency for International Development (UDSAID). Initially, this assistance was primarily in the form of concessional loans linked to bilateral or multilateral programs in support of economic development, but over time it has shifted mainly to grants for a wider range of purposes (see below). By and large, this assistance has been offered to countries with which the United States had good diplomatic relations as an inducement for them to maintain strong economic ties to the United States as distinct from Communist China or the Soviet Union. Currently the US government has more than 150 countries as aid recipients, but some of this aid may only take the form of small grants to selected non-governmental or humanitarian institutions in certain countries. In many cases, foreign assistance has been viewed as a "carrot" to induce behavioral changes on the part of a recipient government through a manipulation of the benefits and costs they face. This definition suggests that once established, the threat or act of withdrawing foreign assistance can also be used to bring about a change in a recipient's policy or actions, thus acting as a "stick" or sanction.

Probably the most successful aid operation of the United States was launched in the immediate aftermath of WW2 with the Marshall Plan (1948–1952) that was focused on the economic recovery of Western Europe with assistance amounting to US$13 billion for 16 countries. This operation has been the largest program of foreign assistance carried out by the United States, and in current dollars it represented 2–3 times the entire current budget for foreign aid of nearly US$50 billion. During the 1960s, the focus of US aid operations shifted to a variety of goals including (a) multiple aspects of economic development, (b) humanitarian assistance and health improvement and (c) military defense and security assistance, with each of the three components just listed accounting for roughly one-third of the foreign assistance budget in recent years. Significant amounts have been channeled through the United Nations in support of its varied programs. Since 9/11, measures to promote counterterrorism have become an important focus of US foreign assistance within its operations for military defense and security assistance.

With these wide-ranging objectives, it is no surprise that US aid operations are funded and administered by at least 20 different government agencies and departments. The United States is the world's largest donor country in the current value of its aid, even though its foreign assistance as a share of GDP is one of the lowest among the advanced countries. Currently, five countries account for the largest share of US bilateral assistance, namely Afghanistan, Israel, Egypt, Jordan and Iraq with each country receiving annually at least US$1 billion (Iraq) up to a maximum of US$6 billion (Afghanistan). Each of these programs has been sustained on a long-term basis, involving a heavy political commitment of the US government (involving both the executive and congressional branches) to the sustained existence of the country in question and its resistance to subversive forces.[4]

One example of a more limited and broadly successful program of long-term aid by the United States is the case of Colombia and its efforts to resist and finally defeat the FARC guerrilla movement as reflected in a negotiated peace treaty in 2016. The aid program for Colombia ("Plan Colombia") involved a range of government agencies covering economic development, counternarcotics, governance reform and military assistance. In each of these areas, the focus was on strengthening the Colombian government's capabilities in the achievement of economic, political and military objectives. In the military sphere, the goal of a limited group of US military personnel was solely for the purpose of training and strengthening Colombian forces in their battles with the FARC. Over a period of 16 years (2000–2016), a total amount of US$10 billion was disbursed in loans and grants in support of Plan Colombia, as well as for military equipment and training.[5] While the aid program has yielded very mixed results in the reduction of narcotics production and trafficking, the negotiated peace settlement has triggered a sustained period of economic growth, structural reform and improvements in macroeconomic policy implementation, building on the economic and social gains fostered by Plan Colombia. In this respect, the US aid program has been widely recognized as having saved Colombia from disintegrating into a narco-state. One clear recognition of this achievement has been the decision of the IMF to grant Colombia access to its Flexible Credit Line (FCL) in 2016, with renewals in 2018 and 2020.[6] This line of assistance is granted on a contingency basis to countries to be used in the event of unexpected external shocks and requires ex ante conditionality in terms of very strong macroeconomic fundamentals and strong records of policy implementation. Chile, Mexico, Peru and Poland are the only other countries that have been granted access to the FCL. In April 2020, Colombia became only the third Latin American country to be granted membership in the OECD, along with Chile and Mexico, a further sign of its developmental gains.

Foreign assistance has been provided for a number of different objectives that have not always been clearly identified and prioritized, with the result that it has been difficult to measure its success. For example, agricultural assistance has been provided to Uzbekistan, mainly for purposes of securing overflight privileges for US military aircraft bringing troops and supplies to Afghanistan, without careful attention given to its links to other development objectives of the Uzbek government. In other cases, agricultural assistance was provided on the condition that food aid would be shipped from US farm sources and shipped in US flagged vessels, regardless of the higher cost involved for the aid recipient compared with other sources.[7] In fact, the "tying" of foreign aid to the procurement of US goods and services is a fairly common practice and is a feature of around 40% of the bilateral development assistance component of US foreign aid. Generally, studies have concluded that US foreign assistance has not been as well integrated with the government's overall foreign policy objectives as it should be and that it needs tighter coordination and evaluation.

One of the less widely understood programs of US bilateral assistance takes the form of dollar loans that are administered by the US Treasury Department through its Exchange Stabilization Fund (ESF), which are not counted as part of the US government's foreign assistance budget. Unlike other programs of economic assistance that require annual funding authorizations from the US Congress, the ESF has existed for many years as a separate source of financial assistance under the control of the Secretary of the Treasury. Originally, it was created by Congress in the Gold

Reserve Act of 1934 as a fund to be used by the Treasury Department to support the value of the dollar in foreign exchange markets following the government's decision to abandon the gold standard in the wake of the Great Depression. More recently, it has been used by the government to provide short-term stabilization loans to countries that are trying to restore exchange rate stability following a period of sudden capital outflows or to implement a macroeconomic adjustment program in response to a currency or debt crisis. A number of these loans have been authorized in connection with multilateral assistance from the IMF. Argentina, Brazil and Mexico have been recipients of this assistance on several occasions in the context of financial crises, while Indonesia and South Korea received ESF loans during the Asian financial crisis of 1997–1998. Lending programs of the ESF are initiated solely on the authority of the Secretary of the Treasury, with the approval of the President. The US Treasury Department considers the ESF to be an important instrument of financial assistance to contain the spread of financial crises among emerging market economies.

As of end-September 2019 (the most recent date of published financial data), the ESF held US$95 billion in assets comprising foreign currencies (mainly euros and yen), SDRs and foreign government securities. During the five-year period ending September 2019, the only ESF country assistance operation was the annual renewal of a short-term swap line of credit with the Bank of Mexico as called for under the NAFTA/USMCA Agreement (initially set at US$3 billion and raised to US$9 billion in November 2018), under which no drawings have been made.

The ESF has taken on a new, special role in the context of the US government's response to the Covid-19 crisis, which is completely different from its previous operations in that it is implementing loan programs to domestic recipients (businesses and local governments) and providing support for emergency lending activities of the Federal Reserve. This exceptional financing role has been made possible with funding provided by the US Congress amounting to US$500 billion under the Covid-19 Aid, Relief and Economic Security (CARES) Act of March 27, 2020.

The other instrumentality the dollar has provided the US government has come through the use of economic sanctions. The United States has been an active user of economic sanctions, which have been broad-ranging from comprehensive, i.e., covering all commercial activity as in the case of Cuba and North Korea, to more selective (e.g., asset freezes or restrictions on financial transactions) in the case of foreign individuals and organizations suspected of criminal or terrorist behavior. Some of these have been imposed in concert with other members of the United Nations, but many have been implemented on a solo basis. In the latter category, the United States has been more active than any other advanced country and currently has comprehensive economic sanctions in effect against 20 countries. As in the case of foreign assistance, many government departments within the US government can be involved in the implementation of economic sanctions, with the President's National Security Council acting as the main coordinating unit.[8]

In the financial sphere, the imposition of sanctions by the United States can be quite restrictive. If foreign individuals or companies are restricted from having commercial or financial relations with American banks or businesses, this limitation will represent a near comprehensive global ban, as most global payments are cleared and settled in dollars either through the CHIPS (Clearing House International Payments System) financial network, a private clearinghouse operated by the largest US banks, or FEDwire, a clearinghouse operated by the Federal Reserve system. This dollar-based payment system is nearly fully reliant on the SWIFT messaging service that is used by virtually all of the international correspondent banks involved in cross-border payments and transfers. The use of financial sanctions by the US government, which are managed by the Office of Foreign Asset Control in the US Treasury Department, has increased sharply in recent years. The current list of targeted individuals and entities (or "Specially Designated Nationals") filled a report of 1530 pages as of the end of 2020 with more than 6000 names. Most of these names originate from Iran, Syria, Ukraine, North Korea, Russia, Venezuela and China.[9]

The increased use of financial sanctions has raised numerous complaints about the US government's excessive actions in "weaponizing the US dollar". Apart from the financial burden on US banks in ensuring their compliance with the SDN list through self-monitoring, some of the sanctions have been applied to non-US entities (banks, insurers and transport companies) which have done business with firms or individuals on the list, even though they operate in countries friendly to the United States. These countries have complained about the extra-territorial reach of the US sanctions. This concern has led to the establishment of an alternative messaging system (INSTEX—the Instrument in Support of Trade Exchanges) by a number of European countries in early 2019 to facilitate non-dollar trade with Iran under the JCPOA agreement (see below). In this connection, it is interesting to note that China had made a similar move of instituting its own messaging service for processing international trade and payments in renminbi in October 2015 (CIPS—the Cross-border Interbank Payments System). Both of these initiatives represent a challenge to the long-standing use and dominance of the dollar for the conduct of cross-border payments.

Perhaps one of the more successful uses of financial sanctions was launched by the United States against Iran during the period leading up to active negotiations of a nuclear arms agreement (the Joint Comprehensive Plan of Action—JCPOA) by the United States and other members of the UN Security Council (the so-called P5 + 1, the five permanent members of the Security Council and Germany). The United States has a long history of sanctions against Iran dating back to 1979 and the Iran hostage crisis. Beginning in 2005, it introduced successive rounds of economic sanctions against Iran in response to actions it was taking to enhance its capacity for nuclear weapons development that led to an intensified period of negotiations after 2010 with the P5 + 1. The sanctions introduced by the United States were accompanied by sanctions authorized by the UN and EU. These sanctions in the context of an intensified diplomatic effort to contain Iran's nuclear development program can be viewed as a successful use of economic sanctions given the results achieved by the JCPOA and represented an effective alternative to the use of military force. In the period leading up to the final rounds of negotiations in 2013–2015, the economic sanctions were clearly having a severe economic impact on Iran in terms of their effect on oil production, exports, domestic manufacturing production and foreign direct investment.[10] In July 2015, the JCPOA was agreed and in January 2016, the United States lifted a wide range of its sanctions, including the phased release of US$100 billion in frozen financial assets related to past oil exports. Notwithstanding this action, a number of other US sanctions remained in place related to Iran's support of terrorist action and militant Islamic groups such as Hezbollah. Unfortunately, the success of these sanctions was short-lived as the United States decided to pull out of the JCPOA in 2018 on the basis of a flawed analysis and re-assessment of its potential impact. However, under the administration of President Biden that took office in January 2021, an attempt is being made to re-establish US participation in the JCPOA agreement.

The Benefits of the Dollar System for the Rest of the World

The dominance of the dollar within the global financial system reflects certain unique strengths of the US economy which have had both positive and negative spillover effects on the rest of the global economy. The benefits associated with the positive effects of the dollar system are examined in the rest of this chapter, while the defects are examined in the next chapter.

A number of the benefits that can be associated with the dominance of the global dollar system have already been identified in previous chapters and cover a range of issues. At a very general level, the dominance of the dollar has reflected the major role that the United States has played through its global military presence and active leadership in a number of multilateral institutions or groups (such as the IMF, the World Bank, the OECD and the G7) in promoting a liberal international economic order supportive of a sustained growth in real per capita income, a reduction in income inequality, and economic and financial integration. The overall prosperity and endurance of this post-WW2 era of growth and development (1945–2020) contrasts quite sharply with the previous 75 years of the global economy in which a shorter period of economic globalization was followed by the tumult and economic destruction of two world wars and the Great Depression. While the hegemonic role the United States has played in the pst-WW2 era as described above has clearly served its interests, it has also provided certain benefits to the rest of the global economy as well.

Under the current system, the United States has generally maintained a record of sustained economic growth and low inflation that has provided a relatively stable anchor for the rest of the world, as reflected in the expansion and size of the dollar currency zone and the widespread use of the dollar in trade invoicing, the denomination of international bank and debt flows, and the currency composition of official foreign reserves. Consistent with its dominant position in international trade and finance, the dollar has maintained a relatively stable, trade-weighted value in real terms vis-à-vis other currencies during the post-Bretton Woods era, with some cycles of appreciation and depreciation around that value. These results of the US macroeconomic performance have helped to maintain the stability of the global economy to the benefit of most of its participants.

The central position of the dollar within the global financial system is consistent with the free access that the rest of the world has to the US financial markets which are unparalleled in terms of their breadth, depth and liquidity. One manifestation of the dominant position of US financial markets in the global financial system is the special role that the dollar plays as a funding currency for a large network of diverse borrowers and lenders that is geographically dispersed and that interact among themselves and with the United States through a range of intermediaries and financial instruments. The extensive use of the dollar as the dominant funding currency for global financial flows brings certain benefits to the rest of the global economy arising from the positive network effects associated with lower costs and risk in the transfer of capital.

In keeping with its dominant role in the global financial system, the dollar has provided access to a range of "safe haven" or safe financial assets for the rest of the global economy, the main one of which has been US Treasury debt. Other government agency debt and highly rated corporate bonds have also played this role. The exceptional role of US government debt securities has been reflected in the fact that nearly half of its existing debt stock has been held by non-residents of the United States, who have been prepared to pay a significant premium or convenience yield for their acquisition. The attraction of these safe assets is that they are highly liquid and tend to appreciate in value during times of financial stress, thus acting as a hedge for investors against market turmoil. The wide circulation of the dollar and the high marketability of these safe assets make them an ideal financial instrument for a variety of short and medium-term uses. The provision of these safe assets represents a key benefit of the dollar-based system for the rest of the world economy.

A central underlying principle of the appeal of US Treasury bonds as an international safe asset is that the US government will not take any action to jeopardize the service of this debt and that over time it will maintain a sound fiscal situation consistent will full debt sustainability, as it has in the past. This is an essential commitment for the United States to be able to maintain its hegemonic role within the global financial system and the global currency power of the dollar. Prior to the global financial crisis, this issue was not a concern given the relatively low level of government debt to GDP and the likely path of "debt dynamics" as determined by the size of the primary government balance (i.e., revenue less non-interest expenditure) and the relationship between the interest rate on government debt and the growth rate of nominal GDP. If the primary government balance is greater than zero and the difference between the interest rate and the growth rate of GDP is less than zero, then the "debt dynamics" are positive and the debt to GDP ratio will tend to decline.

With the global financial crisis, however, there was a marked increase in the ratio of government debt to GDP and the outlook for debt dynamics became more adverse, but this outlook was countered by a reduction in the primary deficit in the following years and a rise in the rate of GDP growth above the rate of interest. However, this improvement was reversed by fiscal developments in 2017–2018 and the impact of the Covid-19 crisis that have created major challenges for fiscal management and debt sustainability once the pandemic is brought under control and economic recovery is fully in place. The implications of these issues for the viability of the dollar system are examined in more detail in Chapter 6.

A final benefit of the dollar-based system for the rest of the global economy relates to the role of the Federal Reserve (the Fed) in the conduct of monetary policy and as an unofficial international lender of last resort. Both of these features of its behavior have been critical to the global currency power of the dollar and the stability of the dollar-based global financial system. In the conduct of its monetary policy, the Fed has played an indispensable role in the maintenance of relatively low inflation since the conquest of US inflation in 1982 and in keeping the US economy close to its potential rate of growth since that time. These attributes of its policy were most clearly in evidence during what has been called the "Great Moderation", a time period running from the mid-1980s up to the onset of the global financial crisis in 2007.[11] The global financial crisis was obviously a severe aberration from that record of good macroeconomic performance, reflecting in part a weakening in government financial regulation and supervision; nevertheless, the Fed played an essential role in resolving the crisis, both at home and abroad, and in promoting a sustained economic recovery thereafter through the use of innovative approaches to monetary policy. The period 2009–2019 was one of the longest periods of sustained economic growth and employment gains for the global economy in the post-Bretton Woods era.

The Fed's roles as an unofficial international lender of last resort (ILOLR) was most clearly on display during the global financial crisis of 2008–2009 and the Covid-19 crisis of 2020, as noted in the previous chapter. Both of these crises had severe international ramifications that triggered bold and decisive action on the part of the Fed, without which a major upheaval and disruption of the dollar-based global financial system would have occurred. In both cases, the Fed established a network of bilateral swaps with 14 other central banks including the major central banks of the advanced countries (the European Central Bank, Bank of England, Bank of Japan, Swiss National Bank and Bank of Canada) and the central banks of a mixed group of 9 other advanced and emerging market economies (Australia, New Zealand, Denmark, Norway, Sweden, Brazil, Mexico, South Korea and Singapore).

A central bank swap is an exchange of currencies between two central banks in which one central bank offers its currency in exchange, for example, for dollars it wishes to receive from the Fed at a market-determined rate of interest for a set period of time. One can think of the operation as the equivalent of an exchange of loans by each central bank, with each loan denominated in the national currency of each central bank. After a pre-determined set of time, the loans are reversed. Since it is usually the foreign central bank that is interested in acquiring dollars, one can also think of the swap as a kind of REPO facility in which the foreign central bank borrows dollars from the Fed against the collateral of an equivalent amount of its own currency.

During the global financial crisis, the Fed initiated its central banks swaps in December 2007 and reached a peak disbursement of around US$580 billion with ten of the swap network participants in December 2008 (four central banks did not use their swap lines); these credits were fully paid by mid-February 2010. During the Covid-19 crisis, a period of intensive use of the Fed's swap lines ran from late March to late May 2020, with a peak disbursement of around US$450 billion, most of which was repaid by late September 2020. One innovation the Fed introduced in April 2020 shortly after the financial turmoil created by the Covid-19 crisis was to establish the Foreign and International Monetary Authorities repo facility (FIMA) for foreign central banks which were not granted access to its swap network. Under this facility, foreign central banks could borrow US dollars for a short period of time and at a set rate of interest in exchange for the temporary surrender of US treasury securities that they held. This facility not only increased the amount of dollar liquidity globally on a temporary basis, but it also reduced the potential need for sales of US Treasury securities, thus mitigating pressure in the market for those securities. Initially this facility was established for a period of six months, but it was later extended through September 2021. Through the end of 2020, the stock of net drawings under FIMA amounted to US$1 billion.

Early on in both crises, the Fed activated these swaps, along with a number of other emergency lending facilities, some of which were available to non-resident banks with branches/subsidiaries in the United States, in order to deal with major shortfalls in liquidity in the dollar-based international credit system described in Chapter 3. This system involves cross-border banking operations with significant balance sheet mismatches involving dollar funding with short-term REPOs, commercial paper and foreign exchange swaps and long-term investments and loans. When panic about the implications of the crises erupted in the financial markets, the short-term funding operations dwindled or disappeared, thus confirming the high roll-over risk they entailed. All at once, the affected banks faced large liquidity needs or the prospect of severe losses in their loan portfolio. In these conditions, the dollar swap lines established by the Fed were essential to the financial stability of the system. During the outbreak of the Covid-19 crisis, the dollar swap lines were also important in providing funding to foreign bank branches in the United States from their home offices abroad in order to meet increased demand for credit from US corporations under existing lines of credit with these branches that they could not fund from other sources.[12]

During the Covid-19 crisis, the Fed conducted an additional operation as an unofficial international lender of last resort that was critical to the safe haven status of the US treasury securities. Unlike the global financial crisis, in March 2020, many investors in these securities decided to sell them in large quantities at a moment of turmoil in order to accumulate positions in cash (e.g., through shares in money market funds) to manage what they expected to be major payment requirements at a time when the economy would be operating well below capacity and personal and business income would be sharply curtailed. In these conditions, the Fed intervened strongly in the market for government securities by buying them without limit in order to reverse a temporary drop in price and jump in yield that had taken place. Such action was essential for maintaining the attributes of these safe assets that domestic and foreign investors had come to expect over many years. No other public financial institution could have acted so quickly and decisively to the benefit of the global economy. In this respect, the Fed was acting as a "market-maker of last resort" in addition to providing emergency lines of credit to financial institutions as a "lender of last resort".

Without the ILOLR operations of the Fed, as described above, the global currency power of the dollar would have been seriously damaged.

Even so, the global financial crisis and the central role that the United States played in its origins and evolution triggered widespread debate on the defects, both real and potential, of the dollar-based global financial system, which are discussed in the next chapter.

Notes

1. Gita Gopinath of Harvard University has done much work in quantifying the extent of dollar-denominated trade in the global economy and in conceptualizing the benefits for traders and investors that are reflected in the opening paragraphs of this chapter; see, for example, Gopinath (2015) and Gopinath and Stein (2018).
2. A recent analysis of the US NIIP can be found in Milesi-Ferretti (2021).
3. A broader discussion of the recent trend of cash holdings in the United States and calculations of its seigniorage revenue can be found in Rogoff and Scazzero (2021).
4. A good overview of US foreign assistance can be found in Lawson and Morgenstern (2020).
5. For a review of US-Colombia relations during Plan Colombia, see Beittel (2019). This case has also been analyzed in a recent book by Robert Gates (2020), a former US Secretary of Defense, as an example of a successful US program of multifaceted and inter-agency foreign assistance.
6. Colombia has been granted access to the Flexible Credit Line of the IMF on a continuous basis since 2009, when the FCL was established, thus being the only Fund member country in that position.
7. These two examples were cited in Lawson (2016).
8. For a recent discussion of the role of the US Commerce, State and Treasury Departments in implementing and assessing the effectiveness of sanctions, see US Government Accountability Office (2019).
9. For a good discussion of the US Treasury Department's program of financial sanctions, see Schott (2021).
10. These economic effects are analyzed in World Bank (2015).
11. The "Great Moderation" is discussed in various places in Elson (2017).
12. This example of the indirect benefit of the Fed's central bank swap lines for credit conditions in the United States is examined in Cetorelli, Nicola et al. (2020).

References

Beittel, June (2019) "Colombia: Background and US Relations" Congressional Research Service Report #43813 (November 29).

Cetorelli, Nicola et al (2020) "How Fed Swap Lines Supported the US Corporate Credit Market amid COVID-19 Strains" Federal Reserve Bank of New York Liberty Street Economics (June 12).

Elson, Anthony (2017) *The Global Financial Crisis in Retrospect: Evolution, Resolution and Lessons for Prevention* (New York, NY: Palgrave Macmillan).

Gates, Robert (2020) *Exercise of Power: American Failures, Successes and New Path Forward in the Post-Cold War World* (New York, NY: Knopf).

Gopinath, Gita (2015) "The International Price System" in the *Jackson Hole Symposium* of the Federal Reserve Bank of Kansas City, vol. 27.

Gopinath, Gita and Jeremy Stein (2018) "Banking, Trade and the Making of a Dominant Currency" Harvard Working Paper (March 28), which is available at http://www.scholar.harvard.edu.

Lawson, Marian (2016) "Does Foreign Assistance Work? Efforts to Evaluate Foreign Assistance" Congressional Reference Service Report #42827 (July 22).

Lawson, Marian and Emily Morgenstern (2020) "Foreign Assistance: An Introduction to US Programs and Policy" Congressional Research Service Report #40213 (April 30).

Milesi-Ferretti, Gian Maria (2021) "The United States Is an Increasingly Debtor Nation: Should We Worry?" Brookings Institution Hutchins Center on Fiscal and Monetary Policy Commentary (April 14), which can be found at www.brookings.org.

Rogoff, Kenneth and Jessica Scazzero (2021) "COVID Cash" Working Paper #002 (February 11), CATO Center for Monetary and Financial Alternatives.

Schott, Jeffrey (2021) "Raising a Caution Flag on US Financial Sanctions Against China" Peterson Institute for International Economics Policy Brief #21–1 (January).

US Government Accountability Office (2019) "Economic Sanctions" Report # GAO-20–145 (October).

World Bank (2015) "Economic Implications of Lifting Sanctions on Iran" MENA Quarterly Economic Brief (Issue #5) July.

CHAPTER 5

The Defects of the Dollar-Centered Global Financial System

The United States has the largest and most sophisticated financial markets in the global financial system, and as a source and destination for international financial flows, it is larger than for any other country. Dollar-denominated assets and liabilities also circulate more widely within the global financial system than those of any other currency. In these respects, the dollar is the center-piece of the international financial system. This chapter will consider the actual or potential defects of these arrangements and their implications for global financial stability. These defects can be considered under three broad topical areas: (1) the nature of capital flows and their volatility; (2) the provision of safe assets; and (3) the balance of payments adjustment process. Each of these topics is taken up in turn.

The Nature of Capital Flows

Cross-border capital flows are usually identified as bringing a number of benefits for countries that are both sources of capital flows and their recipients. At a basic level, short-term capital flows are a necessary accompaniment of foreign trade in terms of the financing of trade and the disposition of proceeds from the settlement of trade transactions. International capital flows can also allow for the diversification of investments and greater investment opportunities for the residents of

A. Elson, *The Global Currency Power of the US Dollar*, https://doi.org/10.1007/978-3-030-83519-4_5

one country, while for another they can be a source of consumption-smoothing during periods of income variability and provide the funding of important business or development projects.

The trouble with this benign image of capital flows is that it ignores the fact that they are highly volatile. They are certainly more volatile than trade or output. On the inflow side, they can be subject to "surges" and "sudden stops", whereas on the outflow side they can take the form of "flight" and "retrenchment", as they are often characterized by analysts. With the spread of financial globalization since the mid-1980s, there has been a sharp increase in the magnitude of international financial flows, as reflected in the international investment positions of both advanced countries and leading emerging market economies. International capital flows have displayed significant variation around that rising trend.

As one major example, in the period leading up to the global financial crisis of 2008–2009 and the immediate aftermath, international capital flows, both inflows and outflows, were subject to dramatic change. In the years preceding the crisis, capital inflows to advanced economies had been on a sharply rising trend or "surge", increasing from an amount equivalent to around 16% of their group GDP in 2005 to around 26% of GDP in mid-2007. Then with the collapse of Lehman Brothers in September 2008, there was a "sudden stop", as these inflows suddenly slowed and fell to a negative amount equivalent to nearly 4% of GDP by the end of 2009.[1] They subsequently recovered to an amount equivalent to 12% of GDP by 2011, but then fell to around 6% of GDP during 2013–2014 before rising again to 12% of GDP by the end of 2015. Emerging market economies also experienced a "surge" and "sudden stop" in capital inflows at the time of the global financial crisis, with inflows more than doubling in the two-year period preceding the crisis to nearly 11% of their group GDP, and then falling to around 2% of GDP by early 2009.

In the case of the advanced countries, outflows initiated by domestic investors are as volatile as capital inflows, with the result that net inflows are much less volatile than inflows and outflows. However, this is not the case for emerging market economies, where domestic investors are not as important as their counterparts in the advanced countries as sources for capital flows to other countries, since the latter tend to have larger foreign asset positions. Accordingly, net inflows are dominated by the pattern of inflows and thus, are more volatile for emerging market economies and potentially more disruptive of macroeconomic behavior. In the case of the global financial crisis, one can see a shift in net capital inflows from a positive 6% of GDP in 2007 to a negative 5½% in late 2008.[2]

In considering the volatility of capital flows, one needs to distinguish among the main components of these flows, i.e., foreign direct investment (FDI), portfolio flows (debt and equity securities), and bank and non-bank financial flows. FDI is far more stable than either of the other two components, with financial flows the most volatile. Excluding FDI, private flows are more volatile than public flows, as are bank flows compared with non-bank flows.

Many studies have tried to determine whether "push", "pull" or "pipe" factors have been more important in determining the pattern of capital flows and their variability.[3] "Pull" factors have been identified with the investment and growth prospects of recipient countries and their macroeconomic performance based on the assessment of market investors. "Push" factors have been associated with global economic and financial conditions that affect the availability of funds and international investors' risk appetite, such as movements in the real rate of interest, the growth outlook and measures of risk aversion in major advanced countries of the global financial system, in particular the United States. A relaxation of monetary policy by the Federal Reserve, as measured by changes in the federal funds rate, typically has operated as a "push" factor and an inducement to capital outflows from the United States.

"Push" factors have proven to be more important than "pull" factors in explaining changes in capital flows and have been linked to changes in US monetary policy and the behavior of the so-called VIX indicator. This latter indicator is a measure of uncertainty and risk aversion in the financial markets of the United States as reflected in the expected volatility of the S&P 500 stock market index (see below). The "pipes" of international capital flows refer to the institutional infrastructure through which capital flows move (i.e., the "plumbing" of the international financial system, so to speak). Since the global financial crisis, the shift from bank-based to non-bank financed sources of capital flows and the diversification of funding sources have represented important changes in the "pipes" of capital flows. The "push" and "pull" factors tend to determine the volume of capital flows, whereas the "pipe" factors have been important in determining the volatility of capital flows.

The VIX is an index sold on the Chicago Board Options Exchange (CBOE) that is based on the prices of options to buy and sell contracts related to the future value of the S&P 500 index, which has been shown to be a good forward-looking measure of market risk and investors' sentiments. The VIX indicator tends to move inversely with the expected movement of the S&P 500 index. When it is relatively low in value, say 12 or below, it correlates with buoyancy in the stock market and low risk version. When it is high in value, say 30 or above, it correlates with expectations of turmoil and uncertainty in the financial markets and is considered a "fear" gauge.[4] For example, higher levels of global risk, as reflected in increases in the VIX indicator, are positively associated with "stops" and "retrenchments" and negatively associated with "surges" and "flights". The importance of the two indicators described above as "push" factors, one for the stance of monetary policy in the United States and the other for a measure of buoyancy or turmoil in the stock market of the United States, suggests the heavy weight of US financial conditions in the determinants of international capital flows. This relationship also points to the dominant role of the dollar as a funding currency for international financial intermediaries and for the denomination of international portfolios.

The major evidence for the weight of US financial conditions can be found in the existence of what economists have identified as a "global financial cycle" in capital flows that is closely related to changes in the monetary policy stance of the Federal Reserve, as reflected in its federal funds rate (and other policy rates) and the behavior of the VIX indicator. The global financial cycle can be observed in the behavior of bank credit, house prices, equity prices and long-term interest rates.[5] More specifically, a shift of the Federal Reserve to a stance of monetary tightening through an increase in its federal funds rate will lead to deleveraging on the part of financial intermediaries, a cutback in international credit flows and a tightening of foreign financial conditions, and a decline in domestic credit expansion globally.[6]

One example of the cycle can be seen in the behavior of bank credit and housing prices in the period leading up to the global financial crisis 2008–2009. While the United States was at the center of the crisis as reflected in a pre-crisis surge in capital inflows, a sharp rise in financial credit and a housing price bubble, these phenomena were also in evidence in many countries of the European Union, in particular, the UK, Ireland, Spain, Portugal and Greece. When the housing price bubble burst as a result of an increase in central bank policy rates, there was a sharp retrenchment in capital inflows, a "sudden stop" in financial credit and a collapse of confidence in non-bank financial institutions, as investors sought the safety of US government securities.

An important factor in the propagation of the global financial cycle is the behavior of global banks, both resident to the United States and non-resident, that deal in dollar-denominated credit transactions throughout the dollar-based international financial system, as described in Chapter 3. Changes in the tide of capital flows may or may not be convenient for the conditions of individual countries, especially among emerging market economies. In a number of cases, surges in capital inflows have been associated with a rapid growth in domestic bank credit, speculative high-risk activities, bank insolvencies and even a banking crisis, with resulting damage to output and employment.

It is clear that in a growing age of dollar dominance and capital flow volatility the incidence of financial crises has increased. During the period 1980–2007 prior to the global financial crisis, for example, there were 150 banking crises in 110 countries throughout the global economy compared with only 10 during the preceding years of the post-WW2 era, when capital controls and tight regulation of domestic banks were common throughout the membership of the IMF. Not all of the crises in the more recent period were associated with capital flow volatility, but most of them did occur in countries of high capital mobility.[7]

The obvious question and problem for countries in the dollar-dominated global financial system is what kind of policy measures can they introduce to deal with the external financial pressures. The existence and growing strength of the global financial cycle has created a fundamental challenge to one of the basic tenets of international financial policy as reflected in the so-called Mundellian Trilemma or "impossible trinity", that is identified with the teachings of Robert Mundell, a Nobel Laureate in economics. The trilemma postulates that a country wishing to maintain an independent monetary policy must choose between capital mobility and a flexible exchange rate system or a fixed exchange rate system and capital controls. It cannot conduct an independent monetary policy with a fixed exchange rate and capital mobility, which is identified as the "impossible trinity". This trilemma has governed thinking about international monetary policy for decades prior to the age of full financial globalization and dollar dominance. For many years, it was the basis of a view that as long as countries followed the principles of the "impossible trinity" in order to pursue a sound domestic macroeconomic policy program, such an arrangement would be consistent with global financial stability and sustained growth of the global economy. The trilemma was also developed for an international economy that existed without dollar dominance and the global financial cycle.

In the light of the global financial cycle and capital flow volatility, many economists have more recently adopted the view that there is an "irreconcilable duo" between free capital mobility and an independent monetary policy, regardless of the exchange system that a country maintains. According to this view, countries must introduce capital controls (or capital flow management tools) and /or macroprudential policies, as complements to monetary and exchange rate policies in order to limit the impact of surges and retrenchments in capital flows associated with the global financial cycle. Macroprudential policy is associated with the financial regulatory framework of a country that deals with the behavior of the banking or non-banking sector as a group, as distinct from the performance of individual banks which is covered under microprudential regulatory policy. Macroprudential policy measures cover the use of instruments, such as countercyclical capital charges or loan to value ratios for mortgage financing, that are aimed at controlling the pace of credit creation regardless of whether the funding for such credit has an external source or not. This broader array of policy options than suggested by the "impossible trinity" for countries to consider in dealing with the problems of capital flow volatility has been labeled the "Integrated Policy Framework" by the IMF, which has incorporated it into its analysis and policy recommendations.[8]

In line with this new policy approach, it is significant that the IMF has introduced since the time of the global financial crisis the new dimension of capital flow management policies to its country surveillance work in the case of advanced countries and emerging market economies, precisely to take account of the possible problems associated with the "irreconcilable duo". Under this rubric, the Fund staff and country authorities consider measures by way of capital controls and/or macroprudential policy to address issues related to the management of capital flows and their spillover effects on domestic policy management. Part of the significance of this change in the Fund's surveillance work is that it only has very limited authority under its Articles of Agreement to recommend changes in a country's capital controls, as distinct from the case of changes in exchange restrictions, controls or other aspects of the exchange rate system that affect a country's current account transactions for goods, services, income and transfers. This issue is examined again in the context of IMF reforms in Chapter 8.

The Provision of Safe Assets

Intimately related to the dollar dominance of the global financial system is the provision of safe assets by the United States, mainly in the form of government securities. These assets provide unique attributes of safety and liquidity that are valued by domestic and foreign investors. For these services, they are prepared to pay a premium vis-à-vis the securities of other governments and accept a yield that is less than what they can earn on those other securities. This difference in yields has been designated as a "convenience yield". In this respect, the US government earns seigniorage from the issue of its securities, as it does for the wide use of its currency as a medium of exchange in international transactions. During the 1990–2017 period, it has been estimated that the convenience yield for US government securities generally varied within an estimated range of zero to 300 basis points, and averaged around 100 basis points.[9]

Given these attributes of dollar-denominated safe assets, foreign corporations and other borrowers have an incentive to issue bonds or seek credit denominated in dollars in international financial markets, a tendency that is confirmed in the data. As of December 2020 (data for December 2019 in parentheses), 72% (75%) of the share of foreign currency-denominated credit (i.e., bank loans and debt security issues) by non-bank borrowers outside the United States was denominated in dollars, compared with only 25% (23%) by non-resident borrowers outside the eurozone in euros and 3% (2%) in yen for borrowers outside Japan; the ratio for the dollar was 63% in 2000, signaling an increase in the dominance of the dollar during this time period.[10] These aspects of dollar funding in international financial markets have been self-reinforcing with the dominance of the dollar in trade invoicing discussed earlier.

The dominance of US government securities as global safe assets has created a number of anomalies, distortions and significant risks for the global financial system. One anomaly is that a number of emerging market economies, in particular in East Asia, have increased substantially their holdings of US government securities as part of an effort to bolster their official foreign reserves, thus creating a net flow of capital to the major advanced country of the global system. This trend, which was particularly pronounced during the period 1998–2014, has been reflected in the pattern of global imbalances, with the emerging market economies showing a surplus in their current account balances and the United States a deficit. The anomaly and distortion in this pattern of capital flows is that it reverses the normal flow that one would expect from a development perspective. Given the differences in per capita income between the United States and the emerging market and developing economies (EMDEs), one would expect capital to flow from the advanced countries to the EMDEs, reflecting the large investment opportunities to exist there and the higher returns to be expected.

From the perspective of the EMDEs, the demand for safe assets and higher levels of official reserves are related to their concern about the volatility of capital flows and the high incidence of financial crisis that has come with the age of financial globalization. A high level of official reserves is now seen as the best defense against sudden withdrawals of capital or fears of a collapse of the currency by foreign investors in response to unexpected developments in the global financial system. During the period of the Bretton Woods system, it was generally recommended that EMDEs maintain a level of official reserves equivalent to around three months of import payments, as this item was a key component of their consumption and investment requirements. Today, this metric has changed substantially and is commonly expressed in terms of covering the stock of a country's short-term external debt, the size its current account deficit (if one exists) or the stock of broad money, or some combination of these three indicators, depending upon the specific circumstances of the country.[11] Each of these three indicators focuses on a different aspect of a country's financial accounts, rather than the level of its imports as used to be the case, and leads to a much higher level of recommended official reserves than in the past.

As a result of this expanded demand for official foreign reserves, there has been a major expansion in the stock of these reserves since the beginning of the new century. In 2000, the aggregate level of gross official reserves amounted to around US$2 trillion (5.9% of global GDP), which then increased to around US$11.5 trillion by 2010 (17% of global GDP) and to an estimated US$13.5 trillion at the end of 2020 (16% of global GDP); most of this increase was accounted for by the EMDEs, which held around two-thirds of the amount registered in 2020. China held the largest share of these reserves at around US$3 trillion.[12]

This accumulation of official reserves by the EMDEs has come at a significant economic cost for these countries. In most cases, the counterpart of an increase in official reserves would have been a surplus in the current account of these countries, which implies that domestic demand and economic growth were being suppressed below what they would have been otherwise in order to generate the desired amount of foreign reserve accumulation. In addition, the large holdings of official reserves would be earning much less of an economic return, given the significant convenience yield on US government securities (the main component of the reserves) compared with alternative investments, domestic or foreign, that would have been available to these countries. This opportunity cost will translate into lower economic growth in the future. If the country wished to sterilize the counterpart of its acquisition of foreign exchange by domestic borrowing of the same amount, it is very likely that the interest it would pay on its domestic borrowing would be significantly higher than the interest earned on its foreign exchange holdings abroad, thus giving rise to a significant quasi-fiscal cost to its self-insurance goal.

One obvious problem in the international monetary system that these conditions reveal is the inadequacy of the global financial safety net (GFSN). Ideally, countries would not be accumulating large stocks of official reserves as a self-defense mechanism, if there was an easily accessible international lender of last resort they could turn to for emergency financial assistance in the event of a sudden stop in capital inflows or major pressure on its exchange rate because of capital flight. The Federal Reserve has taken on some of this role through its network of swaps with the central banks of other major currency countries, but these swaps have only been made available to a small, select group of emerging market economies. The IMF is the obvious candidate to play the role of international lender of last resort for the rest of the global system; however, its financial resources are relatively limited in relation to the potential demand and are mostly available on a conditional basis. It has experimented with the creation of quick-disbursing financial arrangements, but these have only been available to countries with very strong macroeconomic fundamentals. As a result, official foreign reserves of individual countries comprise by far the largest component of the GFSN, with the IMF, central bank swaps, and regional financial arrangements accounting for the remainder. Since 2000, there has been a major expansion in each of these four components of the GFSN in response to the risks associate with financial globalization, but in a fairly haphazard, uncoordinated fashion, with the result that official reserves have outweighed the other three components by a factor of 3–4 in the period through 2020. The excessive reliance on self-insurance by the EMDEs is the clearest symptom of the inadequacy of the formal institutional bases of the GFSN. The reform of this feature of the international financial architecture is taken up in Chapter 8.

Up until now, there has been an increasing demand for safe assets within a growing global economy, especially on the part of countries whose share of that economy has been growing (e.g., China and other large emerging market economies). This tendency is reflected not only in the growing share of US treasury securities that are held by non-residents (e.g., foreign central banks), but also in the long-term decline in the medium and long-term interest rates on US treasury debt. During the last 20 years, the yield on 10-year US government bonds has declined from 6½% to just under 1%. Similar declines can be seen in the comparable bond yields of other advanced countries given the dominant influence of the US treasury market. Other factors have also been identified as playing a role in this declining trend, such as an increase in savings associated with an ageing of the US population and a decline in productivity growth, but the safe asset demand appears to be dominant.[13]

There are certain problems that can be associated with these developments. One is that the equity risk premium has risen sharply since the global financial crisis with the strong demand for safe assets, creating an inducement to high-risk lending and financial investment. The risk premium is the difference between the yield on relatively risky assets, such as equity in an investment, and that on a risk-free asset such as US government securities. Since the global financial crisis, the former has declined by around 200 basis points from around 12 to 10% on an annualized basis, while the risk-free rate has declined from around 5% to close to zero at present. With the decline in the risk-free rate has come a sharp decline in bank lending rates, which may further lead to an increase in the financing of risky projects in search of the higher returns. Such conditions may also be conducive to the development of bubble phenomena, e.g., in housing and financial markets, with risks to financial stability. Another concern arises from the fact that as the yield on US government debt approaches zero, a further increase in demand cannot be satisfied by a decline in this yield, and downward pressure on economic activity becomes the only way to contain this demand, thus putting a brake on the growth of actual output.[14]

Another difficulty for the global financial system with the dominance of the dollar as a safe asset provider is the sustainability of this arrangement. This issue has been captured by references to what has been called the "new Triffin Dilemma". The original "Triffin Dilemma", as discussed in

Chapter 2, related to a fundamental inconsistency in the Bretton Woods system between the role of the United States as the main provider of official reserves for IMF member countries through the issue of US treasury securities to finance its balance of payments deficits and its commitment under the system to accept those liabilities in exchange for gold from its reserve stock. At some point, Professor Triffin argued, if the United States continued to maintain balance of payments deficits because of its lax fiscal and monetary policies, its foreign liabilities would rise to a level where they would exceed the value of its gold stock and countries would want to convert those liabilities into gold, and the system would break down. As we know from Chapter 2, that point came in 1971.

The "new Triffin Dilemma" refers to a somewhat similar problem arising from the United States' provision of safe assets in the form of treasury securities associated with its persistent current account deficits and the sustainability of this arrangement within a growing global economy. The inconsistency in this arrangement is that the relative share of the United States economy has been shrinking (from 19% of GDP on a PPP basis in 2005 to 16% in 2020) and the demand for safe assets by countries with a growing share of the global economy is increasing. Accordingly, with a continuation of this trend, there will come a point in time when the United States will be unable to continue to satisfy a growing demand for safe assets without other countries becoming concerned about the debt sustainability of the United States. When that point is reached, the United States will lose its convenience yield, a crisis of confidence will erupt, and it will be faced with a very sudden fiscal adjustment. How and when such a point is reached is hard to predict, but it will be possible to make some judgement from the medium-term path of fiscal adjustment that the US government lays out, once the Covid-19 pandemic is brought under control and the economic recovery is firmly in place. This issue is examined in Chapter 6.

The existence of the "new Triffin Dilemma", the growing demand for safe assets, and the dependence of global financial stability on the Federal Reserve as an international lender of last resort raise basic questions as to whether the dollar dominance of the global financial system is a stable system when the share of the United States in the global economy is shrinking over time. At present, there are no rules on how the Federal Reserve will act in response to threats to global financial stability as an unofficial international lender of last resort, nor ex post-explanations for the decisions that it takes. For example, the swap network that the Fed created during the global financial crisis and the Covid-19 crisis was an ad hoc construct in the sense that 5 central banks (the Bank of Canada, European Central Bank, Bank of England, Bank of Japan and Swiss National Bank) were given permanent status, whereas the other nine central banks that participated were chosen according to its own non-public, internal procedures and excluded other countries that asked to be included, but were not. At the same time, the extraordinary influence that monetary and fiscal policy decisions of the United States have on the rest of the global economy implies that the global financial system does not have a fully secure anchor for monetary and financial stability, given the primary focus of those decisions on domestic conditions in the US economy and the accountability of the Fed's Board of Governors exclusively to US domestic political authorities. These questions are taken up further in Chapter 7.

The Balance of Payments Adjustment Process

A third area of concern with the dollar-centered global financial system is the defective process for adjusting balance of payments imbalances among countries with significant current account surpluses and deficits. In particular, these imbalances expanded sharply in the period leading up to the global financial crisis and became the channel through which excess savings in a number of East Asian countries flowed to the United States in search of safe assets for their official reserves. These flows financed persistent current account deficits of the United States related to a credit bubble supporting speculative activity in the housing sector.

In the case of the United States, there has not been an effective constraint on its current account deficits that have persisted on a virtually uninterrupted basis since the early 1980s because of the "exorbitant privilege" it has been given by other countries seeking to obtain safe assets in the form of US treasury securities. This tendency on the part of the United States creates an expectation that the dollar will depreciate over the medium to long-term time frame, which reinforces the "new Triffin Dilemma" discussed earlier and the inherent instability of the dollar-dominated global financial system. For other countries, the adjustment process operates in an asymmetric manner with pressures on deficit countries (other than the United States) to adjust arising from the demands of international creditors, but no similar pressure exists for surplus countries. As a result, this condition creates a deflationary bias in international monetary relations. This bias can also be seen, for example, within the European Monetary Union and the constraint on regional economic growth associated with the large surplus position of Germany and its reluctance to expand demand for the benefit of its EMU partners.

This deflationary bias is augmented by certain implications of the dominance of the dollar in trade invoicing for those countries that are members of the dollar currency zone. For example, when a country's currency depreciates because of pressures arising from a current account deficit, there is no benefit for its exports as these are priced in dollars and are thus unaffected by the exchange rate adjustment. However, the price of imports in domestic currency does increase, so that all of the adjustment takes effect through the higher domestic cost of imports, which imparts a deflationary bias to the trade adjustment for this country. This tendency is reinforced by the increased cost of dollar financing with currency depreciation, if as is likely for countries with dollar invoicing for trade, they also rely on dollar-based loans for their financing. Also, since the exchange rate depreciation only operates through imports and not exports (at least in the short run), a larger exchange rate adjustment may result than would be the case if exports were affected as well, in order to bring about a sufficient import reduction to correct the current account imbalance. More generally, when the dollar appreciates against other currencies, this movement leads to a reduction in imports among those countries that invoice their imports in dollars. This is the case because these countries will confront a higher price for their imports, which will result in lower demand for imports and correspondingly lower trade with other countries.[15]

What is missing in these conditions is a central coordinating mechanism that can bring about an effective adjustment process among all countries, both surplus and deficit. In the era of the gold standard prior to WW2, this process of adjustment was in principle automatic and operated on a decentralized basis. This system broke down under the pressures of the Great Depression and two world wars. Then, with the rules for adjustable fixed exchange rates under the Bretton Woods system, countries were required to adjust their exchange rates if they moved beyond certain fixed limits in response to a "fundamental disequilibrium" in their balance of payments. This system became untenable, however, because the United States failed to play its essential role under the system, while the expansion of capital movements made it necessary to have more exchange rate flexibility.

By contrast, the current system is completely ad hoc, as countries are free to adopt any exchange rate arrangement that suits their particular circumstances, as long as they accept the obligations of Article VIII of the Fund Agreement to refrain from any restrictions on their current account transactions. In this connection, it is interesting to note that the Fund's Annual Report on Exchange Arrangements and Exchange Restrictions (AREAER) lists ten different types of exchange rate arrangements currently being implemented by Fund member countries, ranging from fixed exchange rates to freely floating exchange rates.[16] Under this system, countries have continued to face problems of currency or balance of payments crises and difficulties in maintaining internal and external balance for their economies, in part because there are no clear "rules of the road" for most of the intermediate exchange rate regimes that exist.

Within this current system, the IMF has attempted to facilitate and promote effective balance of payments adjustment through its bilateral and multilateral surveillance activities. Each year, member countries of the IMF are required to consult with the Fund on its macroeconomic and external payments situation and discuss possible policy changes to deal with emerging problems or difficulties they are facing. Excessive current account imbalances would certainly be focused on in these discussions. The result of these discussions and the outlook for the medium term are then presented in a report that is discussed by the Fund's Executive Board representing the full membership. A summary assessment of the country's policy framework and outlook is then conveyed to the country authorities with any recommendations for further policy action. These recommendations can then be reviewed in a subsequent surveillance exercise. In this way, the Fund brings to bear both its own technical expertise, as well as the "peer pressure" of its global membership, to promote appropriate policy changes to deal with defects in a member country's current economic situation. It needs to be recognized, however, that the Fund has no power to force countries to introduce policy changes, except if a country wishes to borrow its financial resources to deal with an external payments problem. In that situation, it would have to agree with the Fund on certain conditions in the form of policy adjustments in order to qualify for the loan and make periodic disbursements once the loan is approved. In this respect, the IMF is playing the role of an international creditor in the asymmetric adjustment process discussed earlier.

The IMF also makes an important contribution to the elimination of global imbalances through its various multilateral surveillance exercises, in particular its annual External Sector Report. This exercise is focused on the conditions of the major advanced countries and emerging market economies that account for most of the global imbalances. The centerpiece of the exercise is an effort by the Fund to identify for each of these countries a sustainable current account position consistent with maximum employment, low inflation and external debt sustainability. These positions are then compared with the actual current account position of each country to determine the extent of adjustment that would be appropriate and the range of policy measures that could be adopted to eliminate any difference between the actual and desirable current account positions. The possibilities for policy coordination among certain countries are also discussed. The conclusions of these discussions can then be followed up in the Fund's bilateral surveillance exercise with each of these countries. Again, it must be noted that the Fund has no power in these discussions to compel policy changes on the part of those countries involved in its External Sector exercise, and it is therefore up to each country to cooperate with the Fund in trying to bring about a suitable degree of adjustment to the problem of global imbalances. This basic fact and the limits on what the IMF can do in its multilateral surveillance exercises was highlighted in the 2018 exercise by the then Economic Counsellor of the Fund (Maurice Obstfeld):

> Our objective is to alert the membership to the potential risks from these imbalances and to highlight countries' shared responsibility to address them in an appropriate manner.... Surplus and deficit countries must work together to reduce excess global imbalances in a manner supportive of global growth and stability.[17]

The Main Defects: A Summing up

In light of the broad-ranging discussion above, it may be useful to highlight and summarize the main defects of the dollar-centered global financial system that were identified and the difficulties and problems they pose for global financial stability. These issues are then addressed in the reform proposals that are taken up in Chapters 7–9. The following points should be made:

1. The dollar-centered global financial system is marked by substantial capital flow volatility that can create significant problems in

macroeconomic policy management for EMDEs when capital flows take the form, for example, of "surges" and "sudden stops".

2. Capital flows can also take the form of a global financial cycle operating over a number of years where there is synchrony in capital flows, asset prices, bank leverage and credit growth. On the upswing of these cycles, bank-led capital flows to EMDEs can induce rapid growth in domestic bank credit that can lead to financial crises. The problem for these countries is that the conventional view that a flexible exchange rate system can provide an effective insulating device from these flows no longer seems to apply.
3. Dollar-based international bank credit can be a major force in the transmission of the global financial cycle and shows a strong link to changes in US monetary policy and market perceptions of uncertainty and risk aversion as reflected in the VIX financial market indicator. The relatively large size of the dollar-denominated international bank credit system and the dollar currency zone imply that the spillover effects from these developments in US financial markets can be very significant. The existence of these cycles implies that the global financial system is lacking an anchor for the expansion in global liquidity and international credit growth, which increases the likelihood of financial crises. Another implication is that there is a lack of clear institutional oversight for the global financial system, as there is for the international monetary system (the IMF) and the global trade system (the WTO).
4. Within the dollar-centered global financial system, it is also quite evident that there has been a significant "up-hill" flow of capital from the EMDEs to the advanced countries, in particular the United States, related to the acquisition of its safe assets in the form of US treasury securities. This flow reverses the normal expectation of capital flows and foreign savings from the advanced countries to the EMDEs that are needed to supplement domestic savings in order to cover their investment requirements for economic growth and development.
5. The acquisition of safe assets by EMDEs for their official reserves has been a response to the volatility of international capital flows and to what they perceive to be the lack of an effective, international lender of last resort that they can rely on in periods of sudden changes in capital flows. This accumulation of official reserves has come at a significant economic cost in terms of the compression of

domestic demand needed for the generation of a current account surplus as a counterpart of those reserves, the foregone investment associated with those reserves, and their relatively low yield.

6. The global demand for dollar-based safe assets represents the existence of an "exorbitant privilege" that the United States has enjoyed in different ways since the beginning of the post-Bretton Woods era. However, it represents a threat to global financial stability in that it cannot be maintained indefinitely without creating a problem of debt sustainability and the likelihood of a debt crisis for the United States. This problem arises because in a global economy where the share of the United States is declining and the demand for safe assets by countries with a growing share of the global economy is increasing, the United States will not be able to satisfy that demand without threats arising to its debt sustainability (the "new Triffin Dilemma").
7. The growing demand for safe assets provided by the United States has led to a significant reduction in the long-term yields on US treasury bonds in recent years. At the end of 2020, those rates were close to zero. In such circumstances, the risk premium has increased and borrowers are facing rates for their loans from banks and investors that do not adequately reflect the risk of the projects they are undertaking. These conditions represent a further threat to global financial stability. They may also represent a threat to global economic activity, if yields on safe assets cannot decline in response to the continuing growth in their demand, in which case market equilibrium can only be maintained by a compression in actual and potential output and a corresponding cutback in the demand for safe assets.
8. While there is an excessive reliance on the provision of safe assets by the United States in the light of the defects raised above, there is also an excessive reliance on the Federal Reserve to act as an informal international lender of last resort for the global dollar-centered financial system. Up to now, as reflected by its actions in response to the global financial crisis and the Covid-19 crisis, the Fed has implemented that role very effectively, but there is no guarantee that it will continue to do so in the future. Its bilateral swap network is largely ad hoc and has only covered a select group of 14 countries. The rest of the global system obviously has no role

in the Fed's decision-making, outside of certain selective consultative mechanisms that its Board of Governors has with other central banks. By law, the Fed is fully accountable only to US domestic political authorities.

9. The Fed's role as an informal international lender of last resort points to clear deficiencies in the global financial safety net (GFSN). The GFSN comprises the lending facilities of the IMF, central banks swap networks, regional financing arrangements and official foreign reserves of individual countries. During the past 20 years, official reserves have expanded to become by far the largest component of the GFSN, mainly because of perceived deficiencies in the other three components, which are too limited in the size of their financial resources or in the range of countries that have access to their lending facilities.
10. The dollar-centered international monetary system lacks a symmetric balance of payments adjustment mechanism to deal with global imbalances. Because of its "exorbitant privilege", the United States, which has maintained a chronic current account deficit, has not been subject to any pressure to adjust, unlike other deficit countries that need to satisfy their international creditors. By contrast, those countries that maintain a current account surplus enjoy the freedom to determine if and when they will adjust. If global imbalances expand, as they did prior to the global financial crisis, they can be the source of distorted capital flow movements that lead to excessive credit creation in deficit countries, the development of asset price bubbles and possible financial crises.
11. The gold standard of fixed exchange rates and the Bretton Woods system of adjustable fixed rates were based on rules that allowed, in principle, for symmetric current account adjustment. The current system, by contrast, is defined by an ad hoc system of exchange rate arrangements where each country pursues its own rules for maintaining internal and external balance, subject only to the general rule of refraining from any restrictions on current account transactions. The IMF has oversight responsibility for this system and through its bilateral and multilateral surveillance activities attempt to promote an appropriate level of global imbalances. However, it has no power to enforce its policy recommendations in support of

this goal, except in cases where a member country wishes to have access to its financial resources.

12. At the country level, there is a separate problem of balance of payments adjustment for those countries that are subject to dollar invoicing for their trade transactions. In the event of a depreciation of their currency against the US dollar, these countries will not benefit from a decline in the foreign currency value of their exports, since these are priced in dollars. However, the local currency price of their imports will increase, so that any reduction in the size of their trade deficit will only occur as a result of a decline in imports. The asymmetry in this adjustment process may require a larger exchange rate depreciation than would be the case if the foreign price of exports was reduced, with the result that there may be a larger than desired compression of domestic demand in order to bring about a suitable adjustment in the trade balance. This bias towards import compression is reinforced by dominant dollar financing if, as is likely, importers rely on dollar-denominated credit for their import payments.

Notes

1. The data on capital inflows cited here were drawn from the European Central Bank IRC Task Force Report (2015) Chart 1. Capital inflows can be positive or negative, as they involve both buying and selling transactions by foreigners or non-residents.
2. The data reported here can be found in Pagliari and Hannan (2017).
3. A recent study that examines the "push", "pull" and "pipe" factors in international capital flows can be found in the report of the BIS Committee on the Global Financial System (2021).
4. The role of the VIX in the global financial cycle is discussed in Kalemni-Ozcan and Kwak (2020).
5. The existence of a global financial cycle is most closely associated with the research of Helene Rey of the London School of Economics; see, for example, Rey (2013). Potjagailo and Wolters (2020) provide a long historical study of the existence of global financial cycles. Some skepticism about the strength of the global financial cycle in recent times can be found in Cerutti et al. (2017).
6. The relationship between US monetary policy and the global financial cycle is explored in Miranda-Agrippino and Rey (2020).
7. The information for this paragraph is drawn from Reinhart and Rogoff (2009), Appendices A.3 and A.4.

8. For a recent IMF presentation of the Integrated Policy Framework, see IMF (2020).
9. These statistics are drawn from Krishnamurthy and Lustig (2019), Fig. 9, p. 28.
10. These data are drawn from the Global Liquidity indicators published on a quarterly basis by the BIS, which can be accessed at https://stats.bis.org.
11. The IMF's *Guidance Note on the Assessment of Reserve Adequacy and Other Considerations* (June 2, 2016) provides one discussion on the notion of reserve adequacy, which can be accessed at www.imf.org.
12. These data on official reserves are drawn from Martin et al. (2020).
13. For one summary of the factors leading to the long-term decline in the real rate of interest, see Stephen Cecchetti and Kermit Schoenholtz "What's in Store for r*?" Money, Banking and Financial Markets blog (www.moneyandbanking.com), November 24, 2020. A more extensive study can be found in Ferreira and Shousha (2021).
14. This argument and the data on the equity risk premium were presented by Caballero et al (2017).
15. These features of the adjustment process associated with the dollar as a dominant currency for trade invoicing were first analyzed by Gita Gopinath. For a recent statement, see Gopinath et al. (2020).
16. This information is provided in the IMF's *Annual Report on Exchange Arrangements and Exchange Restrictions* 2019 (August 10, 2020), p. 9, which can be accessed at www.imf.org. In a detailed academic study of existing exchange rate arrangements, Ilzetzkiet al. (2019) define 15 different exchange rate arrangements currently in effect based on a more detailed differentiation of intermediate, flexible exchange rate systems according to the degree of their variation with respect to their anchor currency.
17. Maurice Obstfeld "Addressing Global Imbalances Requires Cooperation" IMF blog (September 24, 2018).

References

BIS Committee on the Global Financial System (2021) "Changing Patterns of Capital Flows" CGFS Papers #66 (May).

Caballero, Ricardo et al (2017) "The Safe Assets Shortage Conundrum" *Journal of Economic Perspectives*, vol. 31(3), Summer, pp. 29–46.

Cerutti, Eugenio et al (2017) "How Important Is the Global Financial Cycle? Evidence from Capital Flows" IMF Working Paper #17/193 (September).

European Central Bank IRC Task Force Report (2015) "Dealing with Large and Volatile Capital Flows and the Role of the IMF" Occasional Paper #180 (September).

Ferreira, Thiago and Samer Shousha (2021) "Supply of Sovereign Safe Assets and Global Interest Rates" Federal Reserve Board International Finance Discussion Papers #1315 (April).

Gopinath, Gita et al (2020) "Dominant Currencies and External Adjustment" IMF Staff Discussion Note (SDN/20/05), July.

Ilzetzki, Ethan, Carmen Reinhart and Ken Rogoff (2019) "Exchange Arrangements Entering the Twenty-First Century: Which Anchor Will Hold?" *Quarterly Journal of Economics*, vol. 134(2), pp. 599–646

IMF "Toward an Integrated Policy Framework" IMF Policy Paper (October 2020).

Kalemni-Ozcan, S. and J.H. Kwak (2020) "Capital Flows and Leverage" *The Annual Review of Economics*, vol. 12, pp. 833–846.

Krishnamurthy, Arvind, and Hanno Lustig (2019) "Mind the Gap in Sovereign Debt Markets: The US Treasury Basis and the Dollar Risk Factor" Proceedings of the 2019 Economic Policy Symposium (Jackson Hole), Federal Reserve Bank of Kansas City.

Martin, Fernando Eguren et al (2020) "Capital Flows During the Pandemic: Lessons for a More Resilient International Financial Architecture" Bank of England Financial Stability Paper #45 (December).

Miranda-Agrippino, Silvia and Helene Rey (2020) "US Monetary Policy and the Global Financial Cycle" *Review of Economic Studies*, vol. 87(6) (November).

Pagliari, M.S. and S. A. Hannan (2017) "The Volatility of Capital Flows in Emerging Markets: Measures and Determinants" IMF Working Paper #17/41 (February).

Potjagailo, Galina and Mark Wolters (2020) "Global Financial Cycles Since 1880" Bank of England Staff Working Paper #867 (May).

Reinhart, Carmen and Kenneth Rogoff (2009) *This Time Is Different: Eight Centuries of Financial Folly* (Princeton NJ: Princeton University Press).

Rey, Helene (2013) "Dilemma Not Trilemma: The Global Financial Cycle and Monetary Policy Independence" Proceedings of the 2013 Economic Policy Symposium (Jackson Hole), Federal Reserve Bank of Kansas City, pp. 285–333.

CHAPTER 6

Prospects for the Dollar

The problems associated with the global currency power of the dollar that were discussed in Chapter 5 need to be balanced against the risks it faces over the near to medium term in order to determine when a trigger point for its decline as the dominant currency of the global economic and financial system could occur. These risks are associated with a weakening in the US government's commitment to its hegemonic role in the global system and the economic effects of its response to the Covid-19 crisis during the 2017–2020 period. These two developments are examined in this chapter, and their implications for the evolution and reform of the international monetary system are taken up in Chapters 7, 8 and 9.

The United States and Its Support for the Liberal International Economic Order

Throughout the post-WW2 era from the time of the Bretton Woods Conference up until recently, the United States has demonstrated a strong commitment to, and leadership of, the liberal international economic order that has promoted economic and financial globalization and a record of sustained growth and poverty reduction for the global economy. This hegemonic role has been reflected in a vigorous pace of trade and capital account liberalization, strong support for an international institutional framework to promote inter-governmental cooperation in

A. Elson, *The Global Currency Power of the US Dollar*,
https://doi.org/10.1007/978-3-030-83519-4_6

managing the global economy, and the exercise of extraordinary monetary and fiscal actions to stabilize the global economy in times of financial stress.

In recent years, however, the United States has adopted a more anti-globalist stance in its foreign policy that has been reflected in a variety of actions and statements. One of its first actions in the economic sphere was to withdraw from the Trans-Pacific Partnership in January 2017, soon after the inauguration of a new presidential administration, with virtually no explanation provided. This regional trade agreement had been negotiated and agreed among 12 countries in the Pacific region by a previous administration and would have, among other things, promoted US exports to that region and strengthened its intellectual property protections. It also would have represented an effective pressure point against China, which had wanted to participate, but was not included because it did not meet certain minimum trade policy standards required by the agreement. The existence of this agreement would have represented a more effective tool for the United States in its trade policy negotiations with China than the use of bilateral tariffs that it introduced in mid-2018. In the absence of the TPP, the other 11 signatory countries finalized the agreement without the participation of the United States in March 2018 and then concluded a separate, but less ambitious, Regional Comprehensive Economic Partnership with China, also without the United States. As a result, the United States has weakened its economic ties with the Asia Pacific region, while focusing more exclusively on a bilateral confrontation with China over its trade and economic practices.

Initially, the change in the US government's stance towards China was motivated by its concern with the size of its bilateral trade deficit with that country and complaints about unfair trade practices on the part of China that were promoting that deficit. This complaint was then expanded to include China's practice of imposing rules for technology transfer through joint ventures on any company seeking access to China's domestic market. While there is merit to these complaints, it needs to be recognized that the US government's concern about trade imbalances with China are misguided on two grounds. One is that the deficit with China is exaggerated in the sense that it reflects the peculiar nature of the supply chain trade that the United States has with that country. China's exports to the United States include a large component of intermediate goods that it has imported from other countries for processing in the assembly of final goods that it ships to the United States. As a result, the value added of export trade from China to the United States is significantly much lower than the gross export value. This difference exaggerates the true imbalance of US trade with China and cannot be attributed to unfair trade practices on its part. The difference between gross exports and net exports (i.e., excluding the import value of intermediate goods for processing exports) is particularly evident in the case of Apple's iPhones, which it imports from China after final assembly there following processing of many components in other countries in Asia. The value for final assembly and testing of the iPhone in China represents only around 2% of its total imported value recorded in US bilateral trade with that country. The other reason the US government's focus on its bilateral trade deficit with China has been misguided is that it is the overall trade balance, and not a bilateral balance with one particular country, which should be the focus of policy concern.

Notwithstanding these considerations, the United States does have legitimate grounds for raising concerns about China's trade and business practices that are shared by other advanced countries. In that case, it would have been more effective if the US government had worked jointly with those countries, either through the World Trade Organization or on a separate track, to bring pressure on China to modify its policies. Instead, it introduced a number of unilateral trade actions, mainly in the form of tariff increases against China and some of its other trading partners in the case of other disputes, that violated WTO rules and threatened the multilateral trading system developed since the early post-WW2 years.

The retreat from a regional or multilateral approach to foreign economic policy was expounded in December 2017 with the publication of the US Government's "America First National Security Strategy".[1] This is a remarkable document in that it reflects an almost exclusive focus on bilateral trade relationships as a key concern of foreign economic policy: "trade imbalances" and "fair and reciprocal trade practices" are mentioned throughout the report, more it seems than any other concept. The focus on trade imbalances in the report ignores completely any link to the domestic macroeconomic imbalances that give rise to them and reflects a mercantilist approach to foreign trade that ignores the benefit of imports and only promotes exports. One can also read the document and not find any appreciation of the global currency power of the US dollar, the advantages the United States has gained from this power, and the hegemonic role that the United States has played in defending the liberal international economic order. Any reference to multilateralism is absent from the document, and the United Nations, IMF, World Bank and WTO are mentioned once each in isolated references of no particular importance. Everything is reduced to bilateral economic relationships with no emphasis on regional alliances.

Consistent with the spirit of the 2017 strategy paper, the US government took a number of actions to curtail its affiliation or commitment to multilateral arrangements. In addition to the withdrawal from the TPP, the government cancelled its membership in UNESCO, the UNWRA and, in the midst of the Covid-19 crisis, the WHO. It also removed itself at an early stage in the negotiations of the Global Compact on Migration that were managed by the International Organization of Migration and approved in December 2018. The United States also refused to agree to the replacement of four judges of the trade Dispute Settlement Body of the WTO, thus bringing the important work of this international forum to a halt. From the end of August 2020 until March 2021, the WTO was without a Director-General following the resignation of its last leader, as the United States and China were unable to agree on a suitable replacement. (Following the inauguration of a new US President in January 2021, a new Director-General was selected in mid-February 2021.) Consistent with the spirit of the National Security Strategy, there was some question as to whether the United States would withdraw from the WTO, as it has made a series of threats since 2017 about such a move.

In addition to these actions, the United States signaled its intention to withdraw from the International Climate Accord that was finalized in 2015 and cancelled its adherence to the Joint Comprehensive Plan of Action (JCPOA) with Iran, which a previous administration had taken the lead in negotiating. The United States also expressed dissatisfaction with NATO, again threatening withdrawal from what has been a major foundation of US–European relations since the end of WW2. Finally, the United States weakened its leadership within the G7 and G20, which has limited the effectiveness of these groups in fostering a multilateral approach to the solution of international economic and political problems, while using more aggressively than in the past its own bilateral trade and financial sanctions to handle its international disputes.

The change in the traditional leadership role of the United States in international relations described above has been particularly apparent in the case of the Covid 19 crisis. When the Covid-19 epidemic became widespread in early 2020, the United States downplayed its significance and was slow in adopting domestic measures to deal with it. When its global crisis dimensions became apparent, it soon became an additional source of conflict on the part of the United States with China because of that country's failure to contain its international transmission, and then with the WHO, because of the latter's alleged bias and favoritism towards China. The US concern over the nature of the WHO's relationship with China led to its decision in August 2020, at the height of the Covid-19 crisis, to announce its withdrawal from the organization. No other action could have given a greater signal on the part of the United States of its disdain for a multilateral approach to the solution of global problems and lack of interest in assuming a leadership role in their solution, as it has done so often in the past.

This change in posture on the part of the United States has been made more pronounced by the failure of its efforts to contain the spread of the epidemic within its own borders. Instead of seeing the United States assume a leadership role in the management of the epidemic, other countries witnessed its inability to come to grips with a health crisis because of a weak governmental response at the national level, with major adverse economic effects as a result. Rates of infection and death from the coronavirus have ranked the United States among the highest of any country and have led to extraordinary fiscal measures to mitigate their broader economic and social effects that far exceed those of any other country, both in absolute terms and in relation to GDP.

The description of the United States reflected in the paragraphs above represents a radical change from the past and a major departure from the hegemonic role that it has played in the international system since the end of WW2. It is important to understand why this shift has taken place, because if it continues, it will mark the beginning of a change in the international monetary system and the global currency power of the dollar. A change like this could not take place without some grounding in the domestic politics of the United States. Even though the president of the United States who was responsible for the changes described above did not remain in office with the results of the presidential election of November 2020, it is still important to try to assess whether or not the political forces that supported him will continue to be a factor in American political life. If so, and the United States does not resume its traditional leadership role in the international system, that development will weaken the confidence that other countries have had in US hegemony of the global economic and financial system, thereby exacerbating the negative features of that system discussed in Chapter 5.[2] These considerations, together with an assessment of how the United States will manage the economic effects of the Covid-19 crisis, which are discussed in the second part of this chapter, will determine when and how the global currency power of the dollar will begin to change.

Domestic Factors Behind the Change in the US Hegemonic Role

President Trump, who was responsible for the changes in the US hegemonic role described above, is a populist leader whose basic support sprang from non-college-educated workers in industrial and farm states of the mid-west and south of the United States that had not fared well since the beginning of the current century under the impact of globalization. Many of these had been adversely affected, in particular, by the effects of the increased trade with China following its accession to the WTO in 2001. It was these workers and their experience that President Trump had in mind when he complained about the unfair trade practices of China and its large trade surplus with the United States. Negotiations with China to reduce that surplus were a major priority of his administration throughout his term in office, even though the actions it adopted in trade policy did nothing to reduce that surplus.

As a result of a major export drive by China and its accession to the WTO, that country did raise its share of global export trade substantially after 2000, from 3.9% in 2000 to 13.8% in 2015. Much of that increase was reflected in bilateral trade with the United States, to a significant extent because of the supply chain trade that was noted earlier. Accordingly, China's share of total US imports of manufactured goods rose from 10.9% in 2001 to 23.1% in 2011. The global status of the dollar played a role in this bilateral relationship as the pricing of goods in the supply chain trade and assembled in Special Export Zones in China was all managed in dollars. It is this trade that has given rise to the critics of globalization who claim that many jobs in the US manufacturing sector were transferred to China during the first decade of the new century to take advantage of lower wages for similar work in that country, as well as other countries in the Asian region that were supplying intermediate goods for the final assembly of manufactured goods in China for the US consumer market.

Initially, it was thought that increased US trade with China (and other developing economies) would bring about a commonly expected effect of expanding international trade between a developed and a less developed country as regards the distribution of gains from this trade. Within this standard analytical framework, the developed country exporting capital intensive goods would experience an increase in the relative share of income of capital and of skilled workers, whereas the same effect would apply to the other country exporting labor-intensive goods for the relative share of income accruing to labor and unskilled workers in that country. At the same time, there would be a tendency for income of unskilled workers in the developed country to decline and for the wages of unskilled workers in the less developed country to increase until they were roughly the same. In this process of convergence, it was expected that the income gains to workers in the expanding share of production in each country would be greater than the income losses to workers in the declining share. Finally, it was believed that those workers in the import-competing sector adversely affected by trade could readily find work due to flexible labor markets in other regions of the country, with the benefit of governmental re-training and relocation allowances, if needed. The effects of foreign trade just described reflected a consensus among economists prior to the massive increase in US trade with China beginning in the late 1990s.

As a result of the research by David Autor, a labor economist at MIT and his colleagues, it was shown that this consensus was flawed, especially as regards the labor adjustment effects of international trade.[3] Instead of a shift of labor from sectors or regions experiencing import competition from China, many of the affected communities witnessed an increase in unemployment or a decline in labor force participation over a period of a decade after the initial impact of increased trade. This result varied according to wage levels, with those at the higher end of the wage scale demonstrating mobility, but those at the middle and lower levels very little. One of the reasons for this result was the inadequacy of the government's response to the change in labor conditions in those communities most exposed to increased trade with China, in particular its program of Trade Adjustment Assistance (TAA). Even counting the response of all of the government's social assistance programs, including TAA, medical payments, disability benefits and unemployment insurance, these programs covered only around 10% of the income loss of those workers most affected by the rising trade with China.

What is of particular significance for the topic of this section of the chapter is that the researchers cited above were able to show that the trade effects described above had a significant impact on the Republican Party vote shares in the Presidential election of 2016. In those states that were critically important for Mr. Trump's Electoral College victory (i.e., Michigan, Pennsylvania and Wisconsin), Autor and his colleagues were able to demonstrate statistically that these states would have voted for the Democratic candidate, as they had in previous elections, if the growth in import competition from China had been 50% less than it actually was during the 2000–2016 period.[4] These authors saw this result as consistent with a broader conclusion in the political economy literature, which has shown that adverse economic effects in certain sections of the country in recent years have led to ideological shifts in voter sentiment that have contributed to changes in economic policy of the kind that were described in the previous section of this chapter.[5]

In the national political debate, the adverse economic effects of recent years are associated not only with increased trade with China, but also to the impact of globalization more generally. Professor Larry Summers recently captured the sentiment very well in an interview he gave to *The American Interest* magazine. On globalization, he said, "Someone put it to me this way: First, we said you are going to lose your job, but it was okay because when you got your new one, you were going to have higher wages thanks to lower prices because of international trade. Then we said your company was going to move your job overseas, but it was really necessary because if we didn't do that, then your company was going to be less competitive. Now we're saying that we have to cut taxes on those companies and cut the calculus class from your kid's high school, because otherwise, we won't be able to attract companies to the United States, and you have to pay higher taxes and live with fewer services. At a certain point, people say 'This whole thing doesn't work for me', and they have a point".[6]

Within the impact of globalization, one must also add the concern that many workers have over the sharp increase in inequality that has occurred in the United States in recent decades. In the first few decades after the end of WW2, income and wealth inequality were on a declining trend, but then beginning in the late 1970s this trend was reversed and the measures of inequality intensified after the late 1990s. Following the Great Depression, for example, the Gini coefficient of income inequality had been on a declining trend, reaching a ratio in the range of 0.36–0.39 in the years immediately following WW2, where it stayed until the early 1980s, but then it rose to 0.45 in the years just prior to the global financial crisis, and more recently to 0.47 in 2018, close to where it was in the late 1920s. (The Gini coefficient ranges from zero, or perfect equality, to 1, or perfect inequality.) By these measures, the United States has at present the highest level of inequality among all the OECD countries, except for Chile and Mexico.

Other measures show a similar trend, as reflected in the declining share of labor income in national income and the divergence between real wages (or hourly compensation for workers adjusted for inflation) and the growth in labor productivity (or the rise in production per hour of work). In the case of real wages, there was a strong similarity in its growth path and that of productivity during the period 1948–1979, with real hourly wages rising by 93%, as one would expect for an economy operating at close to full employment with competitive labor markets. However, since then, there has been a sharp divergence in the growth rates of these two indicators, with productivity rising by 69.6% through 2018 and real wages by only 11.6%.[7]

The degree to which globalization can account for the decline in manufacturing jobs (as reflected in trade with China) and the increase in income inequality has been a subject of extensive debate, but undoubtedly it has played some role. In the first case, it needs to be recognized that employment in manufacturing has been on a declining trend since 1950 because of productivity improvements, the effects of automation and a structural shift in the US economy towards one based on services. This downward trend accelerated after the turn of the new century with employment in manufacturing falling from 17 million in 2000 to 11.4 million in 2011, a fall of one-third precisely during the period of intensified trade with China. Studies have shown that roughly one-third of that decline, or 2 million workers, can be attributed to increased trade with China, of which roughly one-half was related to the direct effect of imports of manufactured goods from China and the other half to the indirect effect of the loss of manufacturing on the activity of its suppliers of intermediate goods in its domestic supply chain.[8]

However, when one considers import trade with China within a broader context of US exports and imports of goods and services, it turns out that the net employment effect of the growth in total trade was positive.[9] To a great extent, the gains in employment offsetting the loss in manufacturing jobs associated with increased trade with China were reflected among skilled workers in high-tech manufacturing and services, as one could predict on the basis of the trade theory summarized earlier. Nevertheless, this outcome does not diminish the burden of the adjustment problem for the many workers adversely affected by the increased trade with China, who happened to be concentrated in parts of the mid-West and Southeast regions of the United States that voted in favor of the populist Presidential candidate Trump in 2016.

Questions have also been raised about the impact of globalization on the increase of income inequality. In the example just described at the end of previous paragraph, one can see how the increase in trade can exacerbate income inequality, as it favors the income of workers in the dominant skill-intensive sectors of the economy and weakens the income of labor in import-competing or less-skilled intensive sectors of the economy (e.g., basic manufacturing). However, studies have shown that only around 10–15% of the wage differential between skilled and non-skilled workers can be attributed to international trade, whereas most of it is due to the so-called "college premium", or the widening dispersion of wages between those workers with a college education or higher and those with a high school education or lower.[10] It turns out that those who have not benefitted from the "college premium" overlap to a significant extent those workers negatively affected by the growth in US trade with China and supported the anti-globalist stance of the populist Presidential candidate in 2016. These workers have also been an important source of the "politics of humiliation" that Mr. Trump exploited in the 2016 election. A college degree has been the gateway to a remunerative career and social esteem, and those without one have come to feel that they are seen as less worthy, or "a basket of deplorables", as Hilary Clinton expressed the idea in the 2016 Presidential campaign. This sense of humiliation has created resentment on the part of those without a college degree and has further strengthened the forces supporting an anti-globalist agenda in American politics.[11]

Financial globalization may have also contributed to some degree to the problem of rising income inequality. In the period leading up to the global financial crisis of 2008–2009, the US financial industry was involved in a great deal of rent-seeking behavior and speculative activity that contributed to the onset of the crisis. This conclusion is consistent with the fact that the financial sector increased sharply its income as a share of total GDP in the period prior to the crisis to a level that has been shown historically to be a negative factor for gains in productivity and real income.[12] The financial crisis also was a factor in the exacerbation of income inequality because of the sharp contraction in income and employment it produced, as well as the slow recovery of income of lower and middle income groups compared with those of the top 10 and 1% of the income scale in the period after.

Apart from any negative effects of globalization, it must be recognized that a major factor that has contributed to the appeal of populist leaders and their anti-globalist stance in foreign economic policy is the weakening of the social safety net that had been established in the United States during the Bretton Woods era. During the early post-WW2 decades, there was an implicit contract among business, labor and government to support a strong manufacturing-based economy through government policies promoting full employment and the commitment of labor to a stable, loyal workforce for industry in exchange for sound wages, health and pension benefits from business. High marginal income tax rates, together with government transfers for education, social security and unemployment insurance, maintained income inequality at relatively low levels. Labor unions were an active force in representing the interests of workers in dealings with business and government.

With the decline in manufacturing and the shift to a more service-oriented economy, many of these institutional safeguards began to erode. This trend has been intensified with the opening of supply chain trade and the off-shoring of many unskilled labor functions to foreign countries. This development has dampened wage increases for basic workers, while the share of income accruing to business owners and shareholders has increased, aided in particular by a sharp decline in tax rates at the highest income tax brackets. There has also been a rise in contingent labor contracts where workers were being given contracts for part-time, temporary work with no benefits. With the relative decline of the manufacturing sector in the US economy, union density and strength has declined. Whereas in the mid-1950s, around 35% of private sector workers were members of a labor union, that share dropped to 6% by 2019.

One particular area where the United States has weakened its social safety net is in regard to active labor market policies (ALMP), as distinct from passive labor market policies that cover social security and unemployment insurance and respond automatically to changes in the business cycle. The former cover policies that promote re-employment of workers in conditions of structural change where labor positions or companies have been eliminated. Such policies are particularly relevant in an age of globalization where pockets of unemployment have developed, as noted earlier, because of technological change, off-shoring and supply chain trade or import competition. These policies include employment services, re-training programs and relocation assistance. In the case of the United States, these programs are highly fragmented across the federal government, with as many as 40 programs spread across 14 agencies; the TAA cited earlier is one of these agencies dedicated to trade-related adjustment problems for workers. Nevertheless, the total amount of government funding for these programs amounts to only 0.1% of GDP. By this measure, the United States again ranks as the lowest of any OECD country, except Mexico. Germany spends around 0.6% of GDP for ALMP, while France and Sweden allocate more than 1% of GDP to these programs.[13] Notably, the current allocation of the US government for ALMP is less than what it was in 1985 (i.e., 0.25% of GDP), but still very low in comparison with European countries.

The previous discussion makes clear that there are many structural and institutional factors that are affecting the welfare of unskilled or low and middle-income workers. These are not likely to be changed quickly and will continue to be an influence in domestic American politics. They also will require a sustained effort on the part of the US government to overcome with important fiscal implications. How this effort will be managed in a way that does not weaken the debt sustainability of the US government is a topic that is discussed in the next section of this chapter.

In a discussion of the social and economic impact of globalization on US workers, one must also take note of the impact of immigration. While most studies have concluded that immigration has not had an adverse effect on the economic welfare of American workers, it is nonetheless true that immigration has aroused feelings of "white supremacy" among certain domestic groups that were evident in the failed insurrectionist attempt of January 6, 2021. While it is certainly the case that extremist and domestic terrorist groups, such as "the Proud Boys" or "Oath Keepers", were active participants in the attack on the Capitol on that day, they represented only around 12% of the mob. By contrast, it has been shown that a significant number of the first 377 individuals convicted for criminal behavior on that day were middle-class white men who came from counties throughout the United States that had been experiencing a rapidly rising proportion of Hispanic or other minority groups.[14] These individuals are very likely to have characterized themselves as the victims of the "Great Replacement", which is based on the notion that rising immigrant groups and non-white minorities are rapidly replacing the white population in the United States because of mass immigration policies and high birth rates. Accordingly, these individuals were motivated to participate in the violent attacks of January 6 because of their white supremacist views and a fear of social and economic loss associated with the rapid increase in the share of immigrant groups in the United States in recent decades. They also believed that President Trump shared their fear and distaste for the "Great Replacement".

As in the case of workers adversely impacted by globalization, workers motivated by feelings of "white supremacy" will continue to have an impact on domestic politics in future years. Notwithstanding the marked change in the foreign outlook and orientation of the new US presidential administration that took office in January 2021, the anti-globalist and weakly hegemonic stance of its predecessor government still has a strong political base that may resist and frustrate attempts of the current government to reestablish the United States' traditional role in the international economic system.

The Outlook for US Debt Sustainability

In addition to the domestic political forces discussed above that have been supporting a weakening in the hegemonic role of the United States in the global economy, one must consider the prospects for US government debt remaining a global safe asset in order to assess the future of the global currency power of the dollar. With the onset of the global financial crisis, the US government entered a new phase of debt accumulation. At the beginning of the global financial crisis in 2008, following a period in which US government debt in the hands of the public as a ratio to GDP had been stable or declining, it then doubled from less than 40% of GDP to close to 80% within a period of six years as a result of the programs it put in place to deal with the crisis. This experience will be repeated, if not exceeded, as a result of the Covid-19 crisis (see discussion below).

In the light of these developments, analysts have been debating whether the United States will be the center of a "new Triffin Dilemma" in which foreign governments and investors will begin to question the ability of the US government to maintain debt sustainability and lose confidence in the "safe haven" status of Treasury securities. As noted in Chapter 5, this new "Dilemma" differs from the original "Triffin Dilemma" of the Bretton Woods era that was discussed in Chapter 2, as that "dilemma" predicted that the expansion of Treasury securities during the 1960s would inevitably exceed the US government's gold stock, with the result that it would not be able to maintain its commitment under the Bretton Woods system to redeem those securities for gold, and the system would collapse. The "new Triffin dilemma" predicts that government debt and its ratio to GDP will continue to expand and that at some point foreign creditors and investors will lose confidence in the ability of the US government to repay its debt and manage its debt burden, and a debt crisis will then ensue.[15] This dilemma is given more potency by virtue of the fact that the share of the United States in global GDP has been on a declining trend, as emerging market economies (especially China) have experienced higher rates of growth than the United States. This fact magnifies the burden on the United States to maintain large fiscal and external current account deficits in order to satisfy the growing demand for safe assets on the part of these economies.

The issue of debt sustainability is usually considered within the framework of "debt dynamics" that was cited in Chapter 4. This framework posits that changes in the government's debt to GDP ratio can be explained in terms of two variables: one is the primary fiscal balance, or the difference between government revenue and non-interest government expenditure, which determines the net impact of non-interest government spending on the size of the government's debt ratio; and the other is the difference between the nominal rate of interest on government debt and the growth rate of nominal GDP, which determines the impact of macroeconomic factors (the interest rate on government debt, the growth in real growth and the rate of inflation) on the numerator and denominator of the debt ratio. For example, if interest rates go up, this will increase the size of government debt and the debt to GDP ratio, if not offset by other factors; and if the rate of inflation or real GDP increase, then the debt ratio will decline. In algebraic terms, the "debt dynamics" can be expressed in the following simple formulation: $d/y\ (\mathrm{t}) = -\ ps/y\ (\mathrm{t}) + (r - g)\ x\ d/y\ (t - 1)$, where d is the stock of government debt for the end of the current year (t), y is nominal GDP for the current year, ps is the current year's primary government surplus, and $(r - g)$ is the difference between the nominal rate of interest on government debt and the growth rate of nominal GDP in the current year, and $(d/y\ (t - 1)$ is the debt ratio at the end of the previous year.

According to this formulation, the government debt ratio will decline (increase) in the current year if the government runs a primary surplus (deficit) in its fiscal operations measured in relation to GDP, but the debt ratio will increase (decline) if the difference between the rate of interest and the growth of GDP multiplied by the debt ratio at the end of the previous year is positive (negative). These two factors can obviously work in the same direction. If the government maintains a primary fiscal deficit, and the $(r - g)$ factor is positive, then the debt ratio can rise quite rapidly and quickly become unsustainable. At the same time, if the debt ratio is very high and the $(r - g)$ factor is positive, then the government will need to maintain a primary budget surplus in order for the debt ratio not to rise or actually decline. As an example, if the debt ratio is 100%, and the $(r - g)$ factor is 2%, then the government will need to maintain a primary surplus of 2% of GDP in order for the debt ratio not to rise. If the debt ratio were 150%, then the primary surplus would need to be 3%, but if the ratio were 50%, then the primary surplus would need to be only 1%.

In the consideration of the future debt prospects for the United States, it is useful to examine the experience of the government in managing its debt the last time it exceeded 100% of GDP. This situation arose as a result of the extraordinary outlays for WW2 when government debt (in the hands of the public) reached a peak level equivalent to 106% of GDP at the end of 1946. During the next 24 years, this debt ratio was reduced to 27% by the end of 1970, a decline of nearly 80 percentage points of GDP, which was an unprecedented outcome in American fiscal history. Notably, in that experience, the primary surplus of the government and the $(r - g)$ actor were generally working in the same direction to bring about such a dramatic decline. During the first half of this time period from the end of 1946 to the end of 1958, the government maintained an average primary surplus of 1.8% of GDP, while the $(r - g)$ actor registered a minus 3.9%. For the second half of the period under consideration, these factors were somewhat weaker, while still both contributing to a decline in the debt ratio. The primary surplus amounted to 2% of GDP, on average, during the 1959–1970 time period, and the $(r - g)$ factor was 0.4%. For the two periods as a whole, the $(r - g)$ factor contributed nearly two-thirds of the reduction in the debt ratio, with the remainder accounted for by the primary surplus.[16]

The fact that the rate of average growth in nominal GDP (6.2%) was so significantly larger than the rate of interest (2.3%) during the 1947–1958 time period suggests that there may have been some special factors contributing to this result, and indeed this is the case. The early post-WW2 years were ones of relatively high inflation, in particular 1947, 1948 and 1951. At the same time, this time period was one of financial repression, in the sense that there were government controls on interest rates, both for government bonds and for commercial bank deposits. In the case of government debt, there was an understanding during the war years and afterward between the Federal Reserve and the US Treasury Department to impose limits on the interest rates for government debt for the explicit purpose of reducing debt service outlays for the government. In 1951, an "Accord" was agreed between the two institutions to remove those limits, but the Fed continued to take measures to limit the increase in government yields.

As a result of this policy, the average annual yield on 10-year government bonds amounted to 2.5% during the 1947–1958 time period, while the average annual rate of inflation was 3.4%. This pattern was reversed in the next 12-year time period, with average yields on government bonds at 4.5% and the average rate of inflation at 2.5%, thus implying a more normal (positive) level for the real interest rate. The high rates of inflation recorded in 1947, 1948 and 1951 (averaging 10% per annum) had two important effects. One is that it reduced the debt/GDP ratio by a substantial amount on account of the rapid growth in nominal GDP resulting from high rates of inflation, which was significantly larger than the increase in debt associated with interest payments on the existing stock of debt.

The second effect of high inflation is that the average interest rate on government bonds in real terms in the three years noted above amounted to minus 8.2%. A negative interest rate of this magnitude implied a significant, implicit transfer of income from creditors to the government, which could be considered equivalent to a tax. Such a tax would have been easier to impose by the government through a temporary period of high inflation than it would have been directly through an increase in existing taxes. The amount of this implicit transfer or tax, which could be called a "financial repression tax", was quite large when measured as the negative interest rate multiplied by the existing stock of government debt.[17] On average, the financial repression tax for the three years in question (1947, 1948 and 1951), when measured in the way just described, amounted to 6.6% of GDP or 30% of government revenue for each of those three years. These measures are substantial by any standard, especially when one considers that they represent the savings in interest payments that the government obtained from high inflation or the improvement in the primary government surplus that would have been required if real interest rates had not been negative. They could also be considered a hidden "liquidation effect" associated with high inflation in reducing the debt/GDP ratio.[18] At 6.6% of GDP for each of the three years in question, the total effect was nearly 20% of GDP, or around one-quarter of the reduction in the debt-GDP ratio that was achieved during the 1947–1970 time period discussed earlier.

It is difficult to think that high inflation could be used now as a method for reducing the government's debt/GDP ratio in the period ahead once the economic recovery from the Covid-19 crisis is solidly in place. Given the Congressional mandate under which the Federal Reserve operates, it would feel compelled to resist any accumulation of inflationary pressures once the rate of inflation exceeded its annual medium-term target rate of 2%.[19] Also, a new "accord" between the Treasury Department and the Federal Reserve would be resisted by the latter, as any new agreement by the two government agencies on keeping the yields on government debt negative in real terms would damage the independence of the Fed in carrying out its operational and policy decisions, which has been built up so carefully over the last three to four decades.

What is the outlook for the government debt/GDP ratio over the next 5–10 years? This is an important question in light of the demands on the US government in trying to deal with the Covid-19 crisis. These demands have been far larger than those associated with the global financial crisis that led to the jump of 40 percentage points in the government debt/GDP ratio noted earlier. The perceptions of financial markets and foreign investors about the ability of the US government to manage its debt burden and the prospects for achieving and maintaining a sustainable level of debt will be critical for determining whether or not the "new Triffin Dilemma" becomes a reality or not.

According to the Congressional Budget Office's (CBO), the overall government budget deficit in 2020 (or the fiscal year ending September 2020) was equivalent to 15% of GDP, which was the highest on record since the WW2 years, and higher than the deficit recorded in 2009 (9.8% of GDP) as a result of the effects of the global financial crisis and the government's response to its effects.[20] In this baseline scenario (of early March 2021), the deficit falls to 10% of GDP in 2021 and then stays at an average of around 4% of GDP through 2031, the end of the projected 10-year period. The projections assume a relatively benign outlook for interest rates, with annual rates on government debt averaging around 2.2%. With the average rate of growth in nominal GDP projected at 4.2% of GDP, the $(r - g)$ factor for debt dynamics is projected to be, on average, around minus 1.8.

This result would be a positive element for debt reduction and sustainability; however, it is offset by a sustained primary government deficit of around 2.8% of GDP, implying that the government debt/GDP ratio will increase from 100% at the end of 2020 to 107% by the end 2031. Even though that debt ratio would be the highest on record, slightly exceeding the previous peak of 106% of GDP in 1946, it would not be an alarming result for debt sustainability, as long as interest rates on government remained at the relatively low level cited above and the government had put in place a medium-term fiscal adjustment plan before the end of the current decade that would reduce the primary deficit to a balanced position or a small surplus. If not, the CBO long-term budget outlook (of early March 2021) points to a sustained deterioration in the fiscal imbalances over the next two decades and a near-doubling of the debt to GDP ratio to 202% in 2051.[21]

The problem with these projections, however, is that we know the CBO's baseline scenario described above is almost certainly an underestimate of the government's budget outlook and that its cumulative deficits and debt accumulation for the coming decade will be much higher. For one thing, the CBO forecast described above excludes the special Covid relief package (i.e., the American Rescue Plan) of the Biden administration (amounting to $1.9 trillion) that was approved by Congress on March 10, 2021, after the release of the CBO's long-term budget outlook. In its commentary on the CBO projections, the non-partisan Committee for a Responsible Federal Budget prepared an alternative scenario in which the special relief package was included. In this alternative scenario, the overall budget deficit rises to the equivalent of 15.6% of GDP in 2021, thus exceeding the ratio registered in 2020. It will also further erode the outlook for the primary balance over the coming decade, as a result of which the primary deficit averages 3.1% of GDP, compared with 2.8% in the baseline scenario, and the government debt ratio rises to around 113% of GDP by the end of 2031 and to 259% of GDP by 2051.[22]

It is important to note that these projections assume that actions are taken to deal with the pending insolvencies of three key government trust funds that support mandatory spending in the government budget: the

Highway Trust Fund in 2022, the Medicare Hospital Insurance Trust Fund in 2026, and the Social Security Old Age, Survivors and Disability Insurance Trust Fund in 2032. If corrective tax measures to strengthen the income of these trust funds are not adopted, then significant expenditure cuts in benefits and outlays funded by these trust funds would need to be imposed.

The presentation of the Biden Budget proposal for FY2022 by the Office of Management and Budget (CBO) in May 2021 provides a basis for making a further refinement of the medium-term fiscal outlook and debt sustainability, as it incorporates the impact of the administration's major new policy initiatives as stated in the American Jobs Plan and the American Family Plan in a 10-year scenario for 2022–2031.[23] This budget proposal will increase further the overall and primary budget deficits over that time period along with the government debt ratio. Total spending is projected to rise by US$5 trillion, which will be partially offset by major new taxes and selective spending cuts of UDS$3.8 trillion, with respect to the previous scenario described above incorporating the effects of the Covid relief package (i.e., the American Rescue Plan). With these adjustments, the average primary deficit for the 2022–2031 period would rise to 3.3% of GDP, while the government debt ratio would increase to 117% of GDP by 2031. The further rise in the debt ratio reflects the fact that the primary deficit is only partially offset by a negative $(r - g)$ factor averaging −1.7% for the 10-year period. In this respect, it is clear that the government's budget proposal does very little to alter the perverse debt dynamics that underlay the CBO's original long-term fiscal outlook.

Notwithstanding the major increases in government spending and revenue in these two adjustments of the CBO's medium-term outlook, it is notable that the macroeconomic outlook has remained largely unchanged across the three scenarios. The annual rate of economic growth and inflation are both projected at around 2%, on average, while the yield on 10-year government bonds would average around 2.4% (and roughly zero per cent in real terms). These are very benign assumptions and could easily turn out to be optimistic. As one example, with the major increase in government expenditure, revenue and the budget deficit, there could be "crowding out" effects on private spending that could weaken the prospects for economic growth. In addition, the continued growth in the budget deficit and government debt ratio could induce a more rapid rise in the interest rate on Treasury securities than envisaged. In this connection, it is noteworthy that the current yield on 10-year government bonds (1.6% in May 2021) is higher than the rates projected for 2021 and 2022 in the OMB budget proposal. A further important risk factor is the outlook for inflation that could turn out to be higher than projected in view of the government's highly expansionary budget proposal and the very accommodative monetary policy stance announced by the Federal Reserve for the 2021–2023 time period. The sharp increase in the consumer price index of 5% for the 12-month period ending May 2021 raises important questions as to whether this was part of a temporary and transitory effect of the recovery from the Covid crisis or the beginning of a more sustained period of inflationary pressures that will require changes in the Fed's relaxed policy stance.

The realization of any of the risks identified above would make the fiscal outlook and the $(r - g)$ factor less favorable for debt dynamics and the debt sustainability challenge over the medium to long-term much greater. In this connection, it is interesting to note the presentation that Olivier Blanchard, a former President of the American Economic Association (AEA), made at the beginning of 2019. In his Presidential Address, he claimed that as long as the $(r - g)$ factor was negative, the fiscal costs of government debt associated with high distortionary taxes in the future to repay it would be zero, while its welfare costs associated with the crowding-out of private investment and lower output and consumption would be low.[24] However, the hidden assumption in these claims was that the primary balance was zero or in a small surplus position, which is certainly not the case at the present time or for the foreseeable future.

In the period ahead, it is impossible to know what might trigger the "new Triffin Dilemma" and when it might occur. However, it is very likely to occur in conditions when the primary balance is in deficit and the $(r - g)$ factor is a positive number, which could well be the case before the end of the current decade (i.e., 2030). The change in outlook and prospects for the US government's debt sustainability as perceived by creditors and investors could occur very abruptly and would be reflected in a sudden increase in the interest rates on new and existing government bonds in the financial markets associated with an increase in the perceived risk premium for these assets. Such an increase would be self-fulfilling in the sense that it would make the government's debt management problem much worse and the sustainability of its debt far more difficult. The government would then be forced to (a) declare default on its debt service obligations, (b) impose a sudden embargo on its non-interest outlays or (c) seek relief from the Federal Reserve in the purchase of its debt, all of which would be untenable. The first two would constitute a fiscal crisis and the third would trigger higher inflation. A fiscal crisis would have serious ramifications for the global financial sector given the important place of government securities in the portfolios of global private and public entities (e.g., banks, insurance companies and pension funds). It would also lead to a significant loss of value of the dollar in international financial markets.

The kind of budget outlooks described above does not give one a basis for being sanguine about the risks of making the "new Triffin Dilemma" a reality, especially given the perverse debt dynamics they imply. By the same token, it is difficult to imagine how the debt stabilization experience of the early post-WW2 era could be repeated in our own time. This challenge for the future is made more difficult by the wide appeal of an economic doctrine that goes under the label of "Modern Monetary Theory" (MMT).[25] Simply put, this theory states that in an advanced country that issues its own currency, such as the United States, the government does not need to be concerned about the size of its expenditure or debt outstanding as it can always pay for any expenditure (including for debt service) not covered by revenue by printing new money.

Part of the appeal of MMT is that in the current macroeconomic environment in the United States of low inflation and negative real interest rates, the traditional inverse relationship between inflation and unemployment (as demonstrated by the so-called "Phillips Curve") appears to have broken down. In this environment, it is alleged that the government has much more freedom to use its expenditure programs to deal with public policy objectives of larger output and employment without concern for inflation, as there is likely to be spare capacity in the economy. MMT further posits that as long as there are spare resources to be used in the economy, the government can expand its outlays for productive purposes without necessarily increasing revenues to pay for them. However, there is a risk of higher inflation if the government spends too rapidly, especially if the economy is already growing at a rapid rate and close to full employment. These considerations may have justified the major stimulus package embodied in the American Rescue Plan that was introduced in March 2021, but are much more difficult to justify as a basis for fiscal policy once the economy has been restored to its pre-pandemic growth path.

On its face, MMT seems to be an expansion of traditional Keynesian thinking about the role of government spending in expanding aggregate demand when the economy is in a recession or operating at less than full employment. However, it is more agnostic as to what the limits of government spending are on an a priori basis, as these need to be established empirically by trial and error. It also relegates monetary policy to a secondary role in macroeconomic policy-making and asserts that its main role is to keep interest rates at a low level for the benefit of the government's debt management through an expansion in liquidity. This objective can be achieved through direct or indirect (secondary market) purchases of government debt. If the rate of inflation does rise, this can be managed through governmental wage and price guidelines or increases in taxation to reduce the government deficit.

The implications of MMT regarding the relative unimportance of the size of the government budget deficit and its debt stock obviously run counter to the points of view and concerns raised earlier in this chapter. To the extent that its main tenets have been taken on board by a number of leading figures in the progressive wing of the Democratic Party of the United States, its popularity will help to create a political environment that is not receptive or sympathetic to proposals over the medium-term to reduce the size of the government's primary deficit. This will be unfortunate as MMT makes a number of assumptions that are difficult to justify. One is that the Federal Reserve would abandon its independence and coordinate its policy actions very closely with those of the Treasury, thus destroying the credibility it has established over many years for maintaining low rates of inflation and unemployment. The MMT also assumes that the government can institute a policy decision process in coordination with Congress that would allow for quick adjustments in tax policy, as needed for macroeconomic stabilization purposes. Such an assumption is inconsistent with past history showing significant lags between the government's decision to seek Congressional approval of measures of fiscal adjustment and the timing of that approval and then the date of its implementation, with possibly negative effects on the pace of economic activity. In addition, the MMT ignores the special role of US government debt as a global safe asset and the potential threat of "the new Triffin Dilemma" becoming a reality. In view of these concerns, the MMT is not a realistic or an appropriate framework for dealing with the very uncertain political and fiscal underpinnings of the dollar's central role in the global financial system.

Notes

1. The Strategy document can be accessed at www.whitehouse.gov.
2. For a European perspective on the damage created by the Trump administration on the global standing of the United States, see Marc Leonard "The Crisis of American Power" Project Syndicate (February 1, 2021). Mr. Leonard is the Co-founder and Director of the European Council on Foreign Relations.
3. Autor et al. (2016a and b).
4. Autor et al. (2017)
5. This conclusion is drawn by Autor et al. (2016a).
6. This interview appeared in *The American Interest* (May 22, 2020), and was cited in the *Journal of Economic Perspectives*, vol. 34(3) Summer 2020, p. 267, from which it has been drawn for this reference.
7. These data are presented in the "Productivity Pay Tracker" of the Economic Policy Institute (www.epi.org), based on data published by the US Bureau of Labor Statistics (www.bls.gov).
8. These results were reported by Acemoglu et al. (2016).
9. This statement is based on the work of Feenstra and Sasahara (2017).
10. These results are drawn from Krugman (2008).
11. The "politics of humiliation" has been examined in a book by Michael Sandel (2020), and was highlighted by Thomas Friedman in one of his columns for the New York Times (September 8, 2020).
12. This conclusion is based on the work of Cecchetti and Kharoubi (2015).
13. These data have been drawn from Atkinson (2018).
14. These data on the motivation of participants in the insurrection comes from Professor Robert Pape of the University of Chicago, who has identified the connection between the participants in the January 6 riot and their fear of the "Great Replacement" in his report "Understanding American Domestic Terrorism" The Chicago Project on Security and Threat (April 6, 2021), which is available at cpost.uchicago.edu.
15. A recent formulation and explanation of the "new Triffin Dilemma" can be found in Gourinchas et al. (2019).
16. For these calculations, the author used historical data for the US Federal Budget from the Congressional Budget Office and the Office of Management and Budget to calculate the primary balance. The interest rate for 10-year US government bonds was used for "r", and the time series for GDP was derived from the US Bureau of Economic Analysis.
17. The measure of the "financial repression tax" used here is based on the work of Reinhart and Sbrancia (2011).
18. The term "liquidation effect" is also based on the work of Reinhart and Sbrancia (2011).

19. In August 2020, the Federal Reserve announced a change in its inflation target from one based on a limit of 2% for a given period of time to one based on an average target of 2% over a given period of time, which would allow price increases to exceed 2% for a certain period of time in the future if they had fallen below 2% for a similar period of time in the past. This change in the targeting procedure of the Fed does not alter the main point raised in this paragraph about the efforts the Fed would make to resist a significant, sustained increase in the rate of inflation caused by fiscal policy.
20. The government budget outcome for 2020 and the CBO's baseline budget projections for 2021 and the following decade can be found in its report to the US Congress "Additional Information About the Budget Outlook: 2021 to 2031" (March 2021), which can be found at www.cbo.gov.
21. These projections are based on the CBO's *Long-term Budget Outlook* (March 2021), which was released on March 4, 2021 and can be accessed at www.cbo.gov.
22. This alternative budget scenario is based on two reports by the Committee for a Responsible Federal Budget: "Analysis of CBO's March 2021 Long-Term Budget Outlook" (March 4, 2011) and "New Budget Projections Show Record Deficits and Debt" (March 11, 2021), which can be accessed at www.crfb.org.
23. Office of Management and Budget (OMB) *Budget of the US Government: Fiscal Year 2022* (May 2021).
24. A summary of Blanchard's detailed paper presented at the AEA can be found in Blanchard (2019).
25. One of the economists closely identified with Modern Monetary Theory (MMT) is Stephanie Kelton (2020). A cogent critique of MMT can be found in Mankiw (2020).

References

Acemoglu, Daron et al (2016) "Import Competition and the Great US Employment Sag of the 2000s" *Journal of Labor Economics,* vol. 34(#s1) January, pp. 141–198.

Atkinson, Robert (2018) "How to Reform Worker Training and Adjustment Policies for an Era of Technological Innovation" A Report of the Information Technology and Innovation Foundation (February).

Autor, David, David Dorn and Gordon Hanson (2016a) in "Importing Political Polarization? The Electoral Consequences of Rising Trade Exposure" NBER Working Paper #22637 (November).

Autor, David, David Dorn and Gordon Hanson (2016b) "The China Shock: Learning from Labor-Market Adjustment to Large Changes in Trade" *Annual Review of Economics*, vol. 8, pp. 205–240.

Autor, David, David Dorn, Gordon Hanson and Kaveh Majlesi (2017) "A Note on the Effect of Rising Trade Exposure on the 2016 Presidential Election" MIT Working Paper (March 2).

Blanchard, Olivier (2019) "Public Debt: Fiscal and Welfare Costs in a Time of Low Interest Rates" PIIE Policy Brief #19–2 (February).

Cecchetti, Stephen and Anisse Kharoubi (2015) "Why Does Financial Sector Growth Crowd Out Real Economic Growth?" BIS Working Paper #490 (February).

Feenstra, Robert and Akira Sasahara (2017) "The 'China Shock', Exports and US Employment: A Global Input-Output Analysis" NBER Working Paper #24022 (November).

Gourinchas, Pierre-Olivier et al (2019) "The International Monetary and Financial System" NBER Working Paper #25752 (April).

Kelton, Stephanie (2020) *The Deficit Myth: Modern Monetary Theory and the Birth of the People's Economy* (New York, NY: Public Affairs).

Krugman, Paul (2008) "Trade and Wages, Reconsidered" *Brookings Papers on Economic Activity,* vol. 39 (Spring), pp. 103–154.

Mankiw, Gregory (2020) "A Skeptics Guide to Modern Monetary Theory" *AEA Papers and Proceedings*, vol. 110, pp. 141–144.

Reinhart, Carmen and M. Belen Sbrancia (2011) "The Liquidation of Government Debt" NBER Working Paper #16893 (March).

Sandel, Michael (2020) *The Tyranny of Merit: What's Become of the Common Good* (New York, NY: Macmillan).

CHAPTER 7

Possible Reforms of the Dollar-Centered Reserve System

In the light of the problems and prospects laid out in Chapters 5 and 6, the purpose of this and the following two chapters is to examine possible changes in the dollar-centered international monetary system that could remove many of the existing threats to international financial stability which may worsen with the uncertain fiscal prospects for the United States.

There are essentially three paths to international monetary reform. One is evolutionary in the sense that with changes in the relative economic strength of different currency blocks, both national and regional, there could be a shift from a reserve currency system dominated by the dollar to a multipolar or a multi-reserve currency system. The currency history of the dollar and UK pound touched on at the beginning of Chapter 2 suggests that during the inter-war years an evolutionary process was under way in shifting from a system in which the pound was the dominant reserve currency to one in which it shared this role with the dollar. By the end of this period and the end of WW2, however, the dollar had become the primary reserve currency of the international monetary system and this fact was recognized in the Bretton Woods Agreement.

A second process of reform is a formal, institutional one, as distinct from the informal, evolutionary example just noted, in which countries convene for the purpose of making reforms to the international monetary system in the face of growing problems of instability with a view to

A. Elson, *The Global Currency Power of the US Dollar*,
https://doi.org/10.1007/978-3-030-83519-4_7

improving its operation. Such a process could cover a range of outcomes depending upon the problems to be resolved and the political influence and motivation of the countries involved. Given the wide range of institutional mechanisms for international consultation and collaboration on international monetary issues that now exist, one can assume that the appropriate institutional and technical infrastructure is in place for this formal approach to international monetary reform to be effective, if there was sufficient political will among the major players to proceed.

The last successful example we have of such an approach is the Bretton Woods Conference of 1943–1944 that was guided by Great Britain and the United States and emerged from the spirit of the Atlantic Charter of 1941 for post-war planning. The Committee of 20 discussions within the IMF during 1973–1975, as noted in Chapter 2, were another example of this institutional approach to reform, on a more modest scale, which led to revisions of the Bretton Woods Agreement and the de facto recognition of the dollar-based international monetary system. Since that time, groups such as the G-7, the G-20, the Financial Stability Board, and the International Monetary and Financial Committee of the IMF, each of which are institutional elements within the international financial architecture that exists to foster consultation and collaboration on international monetary issues, have taken up particular issues related to international monetary reform, but without formal decision-making authority.[1] Given the current fragmented state of international relations among the major powers, it seems clear that a political climate does not exist at the current time to suggest that an institutional approach to international monetary reform could proceed very far.

A possible trigger for global currency reform could come about by necessity as a result of a global financial crisis that leads to a formal, institutional process of reform in an effort to restore global financial stability. In specific terms, this approach could be envisioned to take effect, for example, as a result of the realization of the "new Triffin Dilemma" that was discussed in Chapter 5. It was the original "Triffin Dilemma" that led to the breakdown of the Bretton Woods system and the IMF Committee of 20 reform discussions noted above. Such an outcome would occur presumably with the current arrangements of the dollar-centered reserve system still largely in place and prior to the completion of any transition to a multipolar or multi-reserve currency system. When such an outcome might occur is highly uncertain, but it clearly depends upon the degree to which the US economy is able to maintain the confidence of the rest of the global economy in its fiscal and debt sustainability.

A third avenue of possible global currency reform could be the result of financial innovation and rapid technological change in the field of digital currencies that have been triggered by the development of Bitcoin in 2008 and the proposal for the launching of Libra (now Diem) that was initiated in April 2019. These developments could result in an evolutionary process of currency reform to a multi-reserve system that might be similar to or different from the one envisaged in the first approach, but on a more rapid time schedule.

The three possible avenues to reform of the dollar-centered reserve system just described are examined in this and the next two chapters. The remaining body of this chapter deals with the evolutionary process of currency reform and is focused on two topics. One is a quick review of the defects and problems affecting the current dollar-based international financial system that need to be addressed. The second issue is the outlook for moving in an evolutionary fashion to a multi-reserve currency system centered on the dollar, euro and renminbi. Chapter 8 then deals with the major pieces of a formal, institutional approach to international monetary reform. Under the institutional approach, it is assumed that many of the problems associated with the current dollar-based system would require a strengthening of the IMF. Two aspects of its operations have particular relevance for improving the current system: one is its role as an international lender of last resort and the other is the potential role of the SDR as a global safe asset. Finally, Chapter 9 takes up the issue of digital currencies and their potential impact on both the evolution of the international monetary system and the role of the dollar as the primary reserve currency.

The Problems of the Current Dollar-Centered System

Chapters 5 and 6 identified a number of problems associated with the dominant reserve currency status of the dollar that have implications for the future stability of the international financial system. These are briefly summarized below.

One major issue is the relative scarcity of global safe assets to satisfy the liquidity needs of a growing global economy that have been dependent largely on the supply of US-based financial assets and US treasury debt, in particular. This problem has implications for a number of other defects in the system: one is the "up-hill" flow of capital from EMDEs to the advanced countries for purposes of reserve accumulation as a form of self-insurance against financial crises; another is the "exorbitant privilege" of the United States and the "new Triffin Dilemma" that deals with the supply of dollar safe assets; and a third is the decline in real yields on government debt resulting from the heavy demand for Treasury debt that can be a dampening factor on global economic growth, as well as a source of speculative investment activity and "bubble" phenomena.

The issue of self-insurance can be linked to another set of defects that pertain to the EMDEs. One is the volatility of capital flows and the negative spillovers of Federal Reserve monetary policy that have been reflected in the Global Financial Cycle. Another problem is the institutional weaknesses of the Global Financial Safety Net (apart from countries' own reserves). These two factors in the global financial system point to the extraordinary influence of the Federal Reserve in the international monetary system associated with its conduct of monetary policy and role as an informal international lender of last resort. Given the primary focus of the Fed on the performance of the US economy and the expected continuation of a declining share of the US economy in the global economy, questions can be raised about the stability and reliability of this arrangement.

Along with the defects of the GFSN, one can point to the lack of clear oversight of the international financial system. Currently, this oversight is shared in the work of a number of agencies within the international financial architecture, such as the IMF, the Financial Stability Board, the Organization of Economic Cooperation and Development, and the BIS, but on a selective or informal basis. In a world of financial globalization, it is essential that this oversight responsibility be clearly assigned on an institutional basis. The IMF comes the closest of any of the agencies listed above in carrying out such a responsibility, but without any formal authority in its Articles of Agreement.

Finally, there is the issue of global imbalances, which was an aggravating factor leading up to the global financial crisis of 2008–2009. While these imbalances were clearly monitored and examined for their causes and effects, there do not exist any clear rules for how these should be managed or reduced over time in cases where adjustments are called for.

The ten issues/problems listed above represent a major agenda of concerns about the current dollar-centered reserve currency system. A satisfactory resolution of all of them would require a collective effort on the part of the major advanced and emerging market economies over a number of years. In the discussion below an effort is made to identify how effective an evolutionary approach to currency reform could be in dealing with them.

The Shift to a Multi-Reserve Currency System

While the current system is one in which the dollar is clearly dominant, it is also true that other currencies play secondary roles as international reserve currencies, such as the euro, the pound, and the yen. The euro is clearly in the lead among these currencies as suggested by the indicators presented in Table 1.1 A relatively new entrant in this group of currencies is the renminbi, which the government of China has been promoting as a reserve currency since the time of the global financial crisis. This effort was given important international recognition with the decision of the IMF to include the renminbi as one of the five constituent currencies of the SDR in October 2016, along with the dollar, euro, yen and pound.

Among these five currencies, the dollar is clearly dominant across a number of indicators, as reported in Table 1.1 dealing with the relative currency shares of foreign exchange trading, official global reserves and global payments. In the case of foreign exchange trading, for example, the US dollar is on one side or the other of close to 90% of foreign exchange transactions for trade and financial operations and accounts for around 60% of official foreign reserve holdings, even though this share has fallen somewhat in recent years. As noted earlier in Chapter 3, the dominance of the dollar is also particularly strong in terms of the denomination of international securities and credit operations.

The rising shares of the euro since its creation in 1999 and of the renminbi since 2008 in international currency operations suggest, nevertheless, that an evolutionary process of transition from a dollar-centered reserve currency system to a multipolar one has been under way since the beginning of the new century. However, it has been a very uneven process and not one guided by any international agreement or cooperative understanding. The roles of the pound and the yen in this analysis have been ignored, largely because their status as reserve currencies have been declining for a period of time, even though they continue to factor in the calculation of the SDR.

The changing status of the dollar, euro and renminbi also reflects very different attitudes on the part of their national authorities. In the case of the dollar, while government leaders have traditionally emphasized the importance of a "strong dollar", the US government has adopted a largely passive attitude about the status of the dollar leaving it to market forces, the impact of private international trading and financial transactions, and the strength of US financial markets to maintain its dominant position. The government does not intervene in any systematic way in the determination of the foreign exchange value of the dollar and maintains relatively small amounts of official foreign currency reserves by comparison with other countries. Nevertheless, the United States has sought to maintain its unique power and influence within international institutions such as the IMF in order to play a leading role in its decisions and operations and the work of the international financial architecture, which has a bearing on the central role played by the dollar.

In the case of the euro, the European authorities have not played an active role in promoting its internationalization, even though they are keenly interested in having the euro play a more important role in the international monetary system. Some of this interest has strong historical roots dating back to the mid-1960s, when the French authorities were the first to complain about the "exorbitant privilege" of the United States and its currency. However, the main focus of the European authorities since its inception has been on improving the economic and financial operations of the European Economic and Monetary Union (EMU) among its 19 member states and the viability of the euro as its common regional currency. Since the creation of the euro in 1999, the European Central Bank (ECB) has published an annual report on the international status of the euro, in which it has monitored the evolution of the euro as a reserve currency and its relative status vis-a-vis other reserve currencies that show a clear ascendance to its number 2 ranking at the present time, as reflected in Table 1.1.

In the case of the renminbi, the government of China has adopted a much more aggressive stance than that of the United States and the EMU as regards its status as a reserve currency. The internationalization of the renminbi has been a clearly stated goal of government policy and the objective of a number of initiatives that the government has taken to promote this goal. One of these, for example, has been the effort by the People's Bank of China (PBOC) to develop bilateral currency swaps with other national central banks. Currently, the PBOC has established bilateral currency swaps with 38 other central banks of varying amounts that come to a total of nearly US$500 billion in dollar terms. This is the largest network of central bank currency swaps that currently exist. By comparison, the Federal Reserve has established currency swaps with 14 other central banks, of which only 5 are permanent. In the case of the Bank of Japan, the ECB and the Swiss National Bank, the number of their bilateral currency swaps are 12, 11 and 8, respectively.

In establishing its currency swaps, the PBOC has been guided by two objectives. One is to make available short-term lines of credit with its partner central banks to utilize in periods of financial stress, which is the traditional purpose of such operations. The other is to promote the use of the renminbi as a unit of account for the settlement and clearance of bilateral trade relations between China and its partner countries. This objective is served by allowing a partner central bank to use the RMB funds available in its swap arrangement with the PBOC to lend to banks in its country in order for them to provide trade credit to local trading firms. Since 2010, shortly after the PBOC began to establish its swap network, one can see a clear increase in the use of RMB in global payments for trade and other transactions from near zero to a peak of around 4% in 2015, followed by a decline to a share of around 2% more recently.[2] This share would rank the RMB as number 5 in currency usage, not far behind the pound and yen, but significantly below the dominant shares of the dollar and euro at 42% and 38%, respectively. In addition, the share of Chinese trade denominated in RMB has increased to around 30%, still well below the corresponding shares for the dollar and euro in the external trade of the United States and the EMU.[3] It has been argued that the swap program of the PBOC is similar to the trade acceptance discount facility that the Federal Reserve established in the 1920s as part of a deliberate attempt on the part of the Fed to jumpstart the internationalization of the dollar and compete with the UK pound, which dominated global payments for foreign trade operations at that time.[4] As noted in Chapter 2, that attempt was largely successful.

The primary benefit of a fully developed multi-reserve currency system for purposes of international monetary reform is that it would alleviate the problems associated with the shortage of global safe assets, which is now concentrated on the availability of dollar assets. By implication, an expansion in the supply of safe assets would reduce the "exorbitant privilege" and the problem of the "new Triffin Dilemma" associated with the dollar and the excess reliance on the Federal Reserve as an international lender of last resort. The United States would share its seigniorage revenue with two other countries and pay a higher rate of interest on its treasury debt than it does now.

Conceptually as a design experiment, there could be clear advantages in the creation of a balanced multi-reserve currency system, as compared with a primary reserve currency system, if the conditions for such a system existed. However, in the current unbalanced arrangement among the dollar, euro and renminbi, there are clear risks and impediments that have to be overcome in making a transition to a multi-reserve currency system. It is also far from clear what the likely time period would be for such a transition to be completed, as this would depend upon many unknown factors and contingencies. This transition process itself could be the source of financial instability in the absence of coordination and cooperation in policy-making among the governments involved.

In this context, it is useful to compare the dollar, euro and renminbi across a number of dimensions that are essential features of reserve currency status. These are economic size, shares in global trade, macroeconomic performance and financial market development. On the first dimension, the GDP of the United States measured in dollars at current exchange rates clearly dominates that of China and the EMU (or Eurozone) at an amount of US$21.4 trillion in 2019 (Table 7.1). The GDP of China, while somewhat larger than that of the United States when measured on a purchasing-power-parity (PPP) basis, is around two-thirds

Table 7.1 Global indicators for major economic zones 2019

	GDP at market prices (US$T)	*Share of global economy (in per cent)*	*Total trade (X + M) (US$T)*	*Share of global trade (in per cent)*	*International investment position (IIP) (A + L) (US$T)*	*Bond and stock mkt. value as ratio to GDP (in per cent)*
United States	21.4	24.4	4.2	10.9	69.4	368
Eurozone	13.3	15.2	5.0	13.0	66.3	235
China	14.3	16.3	4.6	12.0	13.4	162

Sources ECB, IMF, SIFMA, World Bank and WTO

the size of the US GDP at current market exchange rates (US$ 14.3 trillion), although it is rapidly converging with that of the United States according to this latter measure. On current trends, they could be equivalent by 2030. In the case of the Eurozone, its GDP measured in US dollars at current exchange rates amounted to US$13.3 trillion in 2019, around 6% less than that of China. By these measures, the United States, China and the Eurozone are the three largest economic units within the global economy, apart from the European Union which includes the EMU along with eight other countries that do not participate in the EMU.

On a geographic basis, each of these three economies dominates a particular region of the world that could evolve into a regional currency zone: China for the Asian region, the United States for the Western Hemisphere, and the Eurozone for Europe and parts of Africa and the Middle East. At present, each of these zones is very different in size. In Chapter 3, it was noted that the dollar currency zone represented around two-thirds of the global economy on the basis of a weighted average of the size (measured by current GDP) of the countries included in that zone. This measure was based on data through 2015 and included China, as its currency had been pegged or managed within a narrow band with respect to the dollar. It also included certain countries that used the RMB as their anchor or reference currency. However, since 2015, the PBOC has modified its rule for determining the value of the RMB by moving to a basket of currencies that includes the dollar, euro and yen and 21 other currencies weighted by their respective countries' share in trade with China.[5] Nevertheless, the RMB continues to be a managed, flexible currency with a limited range of movement with respect to the dollar. While the dollar and euro are listed as "free floating" exchange rates according to the IMF's Annual Report on Exchange Arrangements and Exchange Restrictions, the RMB is listed in a residual "other managed arrangement" category.

If and when the RMB moves to a freely floating exchange rate like the dollar and euro, which is necessary for it to become a fully-fledged reserve currency and is the stated medium-term goal of the PBOC, there would be a significant shift in the relative size of the currency zones for the dollar and RMB. According to one study by the IMF, the economic size of the RMB zone would rise to around 33%, compared with around 40% for the dollar and 20% for the euro.[6] The significant size of this shift reflects not only the economic size of China itself, but also that of Brazil,

India, Russia and South Africa (the other members of the so-called BRICS Group) that use the RMB as a reference currency for the management of their national currencies as part of a BRICS agreement.

In accordance with the criteria of relative GDP and size of currency zone, one can see that a process of convergence has been under way among the dollar, euro and renminbi consistent with a shift to a multi-reserve currency system, even though there is still a significant difference in China's exchange rate policy with respect to that of the EMU and the United States. A similar conclusion is warranted on the basis of the relative weights of China, the EMU and the United States in international trade. Foreign trade of the EMU and China has increased rapidly during the past decade and as of 2019 exceeded the value of foreign trade of the United States. The value of merchandise trade of the EMU in 2019 amounted to US$5 trillion, compared with US$4.6 trillion for China and US$4.2 trillion for the United States.[7] On this basis, there has been a fairly strong convergence among the three economic blocks, consistent with their playing a roughly similar role as reserve currencies.

The third measure against which to gauge the effectiveness of reserve currencies is their macroeconomic performance. A record of low inflation and sustained economic growth for the country of the reserve currency is essential for it to provide an anchor of relative stability for other currencies that would use it as a reference currency and guide for monetary policy. As noted in Chapter 4, the United States has a long history of relative stability in its macroeconomic performance, notwithstanding deviations such as the high inflation period of the 1970s and the major dislocations of the global financial crisis that originated in the United States. During the ten-year period ending 2019, the average rate of inflation on an end of year basis amounted to 1.7%, close to the Federal Reserve's target of 2%, while the average rate of real economic growth was 2.3%.[8] The Federal Reserve has established a strong reputation for independence in its monetary policy decisions free of political interference, while the US government has maintained a generally sound fiscal policy that has allowed it to play an important countercyclical role in macroeconomic policy and maintain its Treasury debt as a domestic and global safe asset.

The macroeconomic record of the EMU provides a more mixed picture. It has sustained a history of low inflation, but in recent years, its inflation performance has been well below the 2% maximum limit set by the ECB, notwithstanding the expansionary effects of its policies and stated goal of reaching its specified target for inflation of "below but close to 2 per cent". During the 10-year period ending 2019, average inflation was 1.3%, while the average rate of economic growth was only 1.4%. In part, the weaker growth in output than that of the United States has been the result of monetary policy constraints imposed on members of the EMU associated with the common currency and the lack of a centralized fiscal arrangement that prevents it from implementing a regional countercyclical policy. Since the beginning of the EMU experiment, there has been a debate as to whether the common currency zone represents an optimum currency area, similar to that of the United States, which displays sufficient flexibility in the flow of factors of production and intra-regional trade to sustain a strong trend of moderate economic growth.

In the area of fiscal policy, without a unified fiscal authority, governmental tax and expenditure decisions within the EMU have been left to each member state. It is also clear that there is a great variation in the fiscal performance among the constituent members of the EMU and little willingness on the part of those countries in a strong fiscal position to coordinate on an expansionary fiscal policy in order to expand aggregate demand at a time when the growth of the region-wide economy was very weak. The fiscal framework established by the EMU under the Maastricht Treaty set limits on the fiscal performance of each member state that have not been observed in practice, nor has it allowed for the pursuit of countercyclical fiscal policy at the national or regional level. As a result, the record on public debt among the member states of the EMU has been highly uneven, with some states such as Germany and the Netherlands showing debt to GDP ratios well below 100%, but many others such as Greece, Italy and Spain, well above. Nevertheless, in the realm of monetary policy, the ECB has been endowed with a strong degree of independence from political factors and has adopted a monetary policy framework very similar to that of the Federal Reserve.

The macroeconomic record of China represents a very different picture from that of the United States, both as regards its actual results and operational framework. For the recent 10-year period cited above, China's average rate of economic growth was 7.7%, while its average rate of inflation was 2.7%, both rates significantly higher than those of the EMU and the United States. As regards its rate of economic growth, China has been a celebrated case among emerging market economies for its strong performance over the past three decades. However, in recent years there has been some deceleration in output growth that suggests that over the medium term it will continue a process of "regression to the mean" that has been typical of other emerging market economies, whereby its rate of economic growth will converge to that more typical of other EMDEs.[9] Even during the decade ending 2019, this process was in evidence as the annual rate of economic growth decelerated from around 10% on average during 2010–2011 to 6% in 2019. The result for 2019 was broadly in the line the government's growth target of 6–6½% that was set by the State Council, which is China's executive committee with authority for macroeconomic policy management.

At the operational level, the PBOC has been shifting over time from a policy of interest rate targeting to an informal price targeting approach in its monetary policy similar to that of the EMU and the United States. However, the inflation target, currently set at around 3% per year, is determined by the State Council. Nor does the PBOC have instrument independence or full autonomy in its policy decisions, which are subject to quarterly review by a Monetary Policy Committee, chaired by the PBOC and including 11 external members from other agencies of the government represented on the State Council.[10] Nevertheless, despite its institutional differences with respect to the EMU and the United States, China has been successful in achieving its inflation and growth objectives and in maintaining a sound macroeconomic policy environment in recent years. In this regard, a broad convergence can be observed among the three economic groups in regard to the effects of their macroeconomic policy, although China will continue to maintain a significant advantage in its economic growth performance vis-à-vis that of the EMU and the United States for the medium term. However, the PBOC has less operational independence than the Federal Reserve or the ECB.

By contrast, a significant difference exists between the United States, on the one hand, and China and the EMU, on the other, in the last of the four dimensions of reserve currency status listed earlier, namely capital market development. The United States has clearly dominated this feature of global financial status for a number of decades, given the depth, breadth and liquidity of its capital markets which are clearly superior to those of any other country. In terms of market valuation, the United States represented close to 40% of the market capitalization of global equity markets and the outstanding value of global bond markets in 2019. As regards global equity shares, China and the EMU each represented around 10%, while in regard to global bonds outstanding, China represented around 14% and the EMU 21%.[11] These differences are similarly striking when market values are measured with represent to domestic GDP. The combined bond and stock market values for the United States amounted to US$78.7 trillion, or the equivalent of 368% of its GDP, whereas the comparable ratios for the EMU and China were 235% and 162% (see Table 7.1). While the stock and bond markets represent a substantial share of the capital market activity of the United States, they still exclude significant financial market activity in derivatives and foreign exchange related to that primary activity. Measures of the International Investment Position also show a leading position for the United States.

In the case of the EMU, it has operated under a severe limitation in its government bond market activity in that it has been highly fragmented by operating mainly at the national level with very little borrowing at the regional level. Among its national governments, only Germany (which has the largest stock of government debt outstanding) and the Netherlands have been awarded AAA ratings. Accordingly, as an issuer of safe assets, the EMU has been very limited by comparison with the United States. As of the end of 2019, total EMU official debt amounted to US$6.2 trillion, compared with US Treasury debt of US$20 trillion, which represents the largest global stock of safe assets. Most of the euro-level debt of around US$1 trillion was for specialized institutions such as the European Investment Bank, and three financial assistance mechanisms for member states. This situation will now change as a result of a decision of the Eurogroup in July 2020 to authorize the European Commission to issue new bonded debt beginning later that year equivalent to US$840 billion for a covid-19 recovery fund and US$112 billion for social programs, both of which will carry AAA ratings. It is likely that these operations will be followed by others, as there seems to be a recognition that the issue of global safe assets is a key feature of an enhanced role of the euro as a reserve currency in the global economy. These operations will be greatly facilitated by completion of the plans for an EU banking union and capital markets union.[12]

The situation of China is quite different from that of the EMU and the United States. Not only does China not issue what could be classified as a global safe asset, until recently it has maintained significant restrictions on a broad range of inward and outward capital flows that limited the access of non-residents to its capital markets. Nevertheless, its bond market activity has grown rapidly during the last two decades and is now the third largest national financial market after that of the United States and the EMU. At the same time, foreign holdings of onshore RMB financial assets (bonds and equities) have more than doubled since the end of 2015 from around RMB 2 trillion to around RMB 5 trillion as of May 2020. Even with this growth, foreign holdings still represent less than 3% of the bonds outstanding in the Chinese market.[13] This growth has been prompted by recent actions of the Chinese government to liberalize foreign access to its domestic financial markets. For example, in June 2018, the existing limits on the repatriation of foreign investment funds were removed and those on their inflows were eliminated in October 2019.[14] Foreign participation in China's government bond market has also been attracted by a favorable yield differential of 200–250 basis points vis-à-vis US government bonds during the second half of 2020, when the RMB was appreciating against the dollar.

Further foreign interest in Chinese bonds is very likely to occur as a result of recent decisions to include 10-year Chinese government bonds in two global indices: in April 2019 these bonds began to be included in the Bloomberg Barclays Global Aggregate index and in September 2020 a decision was made to include them in the FTSE Russell World Government Bond index beginning in October 2021. In the first case, Chinese participation will be phased in over a 20-month period, after which it will be the fourth largest component of the index following bonds denominated in dollars, euros and yen. Part of the attraction of these bonds is the relatively high yield they offer of 2.7% (as of late 2020), compared with rates between zero and 1% in the United States and minus 0.5% in the case of the EMU.

In summary, what conclusions can be drawn from this comparison of the dollar, euro and renminbi across these four dimensions of reserve currency status? Each of these three currencies is backed by one of the three largest economic units in the global economy, measured in both GDP and the value of their foreign trade. They also have the potential to represent large currency zones within the global economy, notwithstanding significant differences at the present time. While both the dollar and euro are freely floating currencies, this is not the case for the renminbi, although it has been on an evolutionary path towards that status in the future. In terms of macroeconomic management, each of the three currencies has been supported by relatively low and stable rates of inflation and sustained rates of economic growth. Some concerns, however, can be raised about the growth record and prospects for the EMU given the limitations imposed by a common currency and the lack of a regional fiscal policy. The government debt crisis of 2010–2012 also weakened external confidence in the euro. Finally, in the area of capital market development, there are major differences among the United States, China and the EMU. The United States clearly dominates this dimension of reserve currency status, both in terms of the breadth and depth of its capital markets and ease of access to a large supply of safe assets. The EMU has effectively only begun the process of issuing regional, euro-denominated debt that could be considered a global safe asset, while in the case of China, non-resident investors have only recently had freer access to its government bond market, while a range of capital account restrictions continue to exist. These restrictions, the absence of a strong rule of law, and the lack of transparency in the management of its exchange rate represent the most important impediments that China faces in its advance towards full reserve currency status.

On balance, the dollar has economic advantages and characteristics that are clearly superior to those of the euro and renminbi. In addition, it is backed by a government with enormous geopolitical reach as suggested by its worldwide navy and the presence of its military forces in 170 countries (counting military bases and attachments to US foreign embassies), which are matched by a foreign aid presence and vast array of diplomatic postings. The EMU/EU as a supranational organization is relatively weak in its geopolitical reach and depends upon the initiatives of its constituent members. China, by contrast, is clearly expanding its geopolitical reach, first militarily on a regional basis, but more widely as a result of programs such as the Belt and Road Initiative through which development projects have been designed with 138 countries. Over time, one can easily foresee growing competition between China and the United States in their geopolitical presence.

The considerations raised in the preceding paragraphs suggest a very unbalanced and gradual process of evolution to a multipolar or a multi-reserve currency system, which itself could be the source of financial instability. For example, without clear lines of coordination and cooperation among the three currency systems, significant changes in monetary or fiscal policy in one system could be the stimulus for substantial shifts in capital flows from one system to another with adverse spillover effects on economic policy management not only within the three currency systems, but also for other countries as well, leading to increased exchange rate and capital flow volatility. The shift to a multi-reserve currency system makes the realization of the “new Triffin Dilemma” less likely as the supply of global safe assets expands. However, an unbalanced, uncoordinated process of evolution, as is likely to take place, will create many opportunities for testing the dilemma, especially if the United States fails to deal with its medium-term fiscal problems. These considerations suggest the need for a stronger presence of an inter-governmental organization such as the IMF, especially if the process of evolution towards a multi-reserve currency system is accompanied by a greater degree of economic and financial globalization. The potential role of the IMF in both the formal and informal approaches to international monetary reform are examined in the next chapter.

Notes

1. A number of private groups have also been formed to make recommendations for the reform of the international monetary system; see, for example, the Palais-Royal Initiative "Reform of the International Monetary System: A Cooperative Approach for the Twenty First Century" (February 8, 2011), which comprised former Finance Ministers, Central Bank Governors and officials of national and international institutions.
2. The data on currency shares of global payments and other financial indicators are published monthly in the "RMB tracker" of SWIFT (the Society for Worldwide Interbank Financial Telecommunication), which is available at www.swift.com.
3. The 30% share is cited in Ilzetzki et al. (2019, p. 625).
4. This thesis has been advanced and examined empirically by Bahaj and Reis (2020).
5. This basket is called the CFETS Index (China Foreign Exchange Trade System) which can be followed at chinamoney.com.cn/RMBindex.
6. These calculations are presented in Tovar and Nor (2018).
7. The data for China and the United States are drawn from reports of the WTO (www.wto.org), while those for the EMU are reported by the European Central Bank (ecb.europa.eu).
8. The data for inflation and economic growth reported here for the United States, the EMU and China are drawn from the IMF's World Economic Outlook database, which is available at www.imf.org.
9. This thesis has been advanced by Pritchett and Summers (2014). A significant change in demographic factors through an aging of the population is likely to reinforce their thesis.
10. A good review of China's monetary policy framework can be found in Jones and Bowman (2019).

11. These data on global equities and bonds are drawn from the 2020 Fact Book of the Securities Industry and Financial Markets Association (www.sifma.org).
12. For a recent assessment of the European Commission's capital markets union action plan, see Demertzis et al. (2021).
13. The data on foreign holdings of Chinese government bonds were reported in the Financial Times ("Booming Demand for Chinese Assets Boosts Renminbi's Global Role") on October 7, 2020.
14. These and other recent actions to liberalize foreign access to China's financial markets are examined in Lardy and Huang (2020).

References

Bahaj, Saleem and Ricardo Reis (2020) "Jumpstarting an International Currency" Bank of England Staff Working Paper #874 (June 12).

Demertzis, Maria et al (2021) "Europe Should Not Neglect its Capital Market Union" Bruegel Policy Contribution #13/21 (June).

Ilzetzki, Ethan, Carmen Reinhart, and Ken Rogoff (2019) "Exchange Rate Arrangements Entering the Twenty-First Century: Which Anchor Will Hold?" *Quarterly Journal of Economics,* 134(2), pp. 599–646.

Jones, Bradley and Joel Bowman (2019) "China's Evolving Monetary Policy Framework in International Context" Reserve Bank of Australia Research Discussion Paper #RDP 2019–2011 (December).

Lardy, Nicholas and Tian lei Huang (2020) "China's Financial Opening Accelerates" PIIE Policy Brief #20–17 (December 2020).

Pritchett, Lant and Lawrence Summers (2014) "Asiaphoria Meets Regression to the Mean" NBER Working Paper #20573 (October).

Tovar, Camilo and Tani Mohd Nor (2018) "Reserve Currency Blocs: A Changing International Monetary System?" IMF Working Paper #18/20 (January).

CHAPTER 8

The IMF and Reform of the Dollar-Centered Reserve System

The IMF plays a unique and indispensable role in the international monetary system through its lending facilities for member countries, its global and country-level surveillance operations, and its research, statistics and technical assistance activities. It also plays an essential role in the global financial safety net (GFSN) and in fostering cooperation among member countries and other agencies within the international financial architecture in promoting global financial stability. The Fund could potentially play a key role in resolving some of the problems with the dollar-centered reserve center noted in the last chapter, if its financial and surveillance capacities could be strengthened.

The Lending Operations of the IMF

As regards its lending function, it is notable that, notwithstanding increases in its lending capacity, its relative position within the GFSN has sharply diminished since the turn of the century with the major expansion in the size of dollar-denominated reserves of the EMDEs. Gross official external reserves on a global basis rose from around US$2 trillion in 2000 to US$7 trillion in 2007 and to a peak of US$15 trillion in 2015, two-thirds of which were in the possession of the EMDEs, in particular China and other East Asian exporters. The total financial resources of the IMF, including quotas or financial subscriptions of its

A. Elson, *The Global Currency Power of the US Dollar*,
https://doi.org/10.1007/978-3-030-83519-4_8

members and special supplementary credit lines from some of its large quota members, amounted to less than 10% of the gross reserve level of 2015 or US$1.4 trillion. Its total lending capacity at that time was actually around US$1 trillion, as three-fourths of quota subscriptions are made in the domestic currencies of member countries, many of which are not convertible or usable for international transactions. The Fund's total resources have remained roughly the same since 2015.

Prior to the global financial crisis (2008–2009), the IMF represented the second largest component of the GFSN, even though its resources were dwarfed by official reserves of member countries. But since then, its relative position has fallen further behind with the development of central banks swap facilities and the expansion of regional financing arrangements.[1] As a result, the GFSN has become very fragmented and unevenly distributed in terms of access and available financing. Nevertheless, the IMF is the only universal component within the GFSN and should play a coordinating role within the GFSN given its central position in the international monetary system.

One obvious question that arises in examining the GFSN is why the EMDEs have become so heavily reliant on self-insurance with their acquisition of official reserves, instead of relying on the various other components of the GFSN, in particular the IMF. One problem is the scale of resources. Given the enormous difference between the lending capacity of the IMF and the size of official reserves, one would need to double or triple the financing capacity of the Fund in order for countries to reduce their reliance on self-insurance. The IMF would also need to establish a rapid disbursement facility that countries could access quickly at times of financial stress due, for example, to a "sudden stop" in capital flows. These two changes would enable the Fund to play much more fully the role of an international lender of last resort.

On the scale of IMF financial resources, there is a regular procedure in place for the review of Fund quotas that determine not only the size of its financial resources, but also the relative voting power and borrowing capacity of each member country. The EMDEs have complained that these reviews have been too slow in increasing the lending capacity of the Fund and have not adequately reflected their growing share of global economy activity. As a result, they argue that they are under-represented in the voting power of the Fund vis-à-vis the advanced countries of North America and Europe. This is a valid concern and represents one reason why they have not viewed the Fund as an alternative to self-insurance.

The next to last (or 14th) Review of Quotas was agreed within the Fund after two years of discussion between 2008 and 2010, but was not finally approved and put into effect until January 2016 because of long delays in obtaining governmental approvals, in particular by the United States whose approval requires congressional action. This review doubled the size of Fund quotas to roughly US$660 billion and made possible a shift in the relative share in total quotas of countries that had been over-represented (e.g., in the European Union) of 6% in favor of the large emerging market economies, such as China. While this shift in voting power was significant, it did not eliminate the problem of under-representation. No further increase in quotas was agreed in the 15th Review of quotas that was concluded in early 2020.

The IMF has made various attempts to establish a rapid credit facility for its members, most recently with the establishment of its Flexible Credit Line (FCL) and Precautionary and Liquidity Line (PLL). Access to these facilities is granted on a pre-qualification basis, i.e., if member countries are judged to have "very strong" macroeconomic fundamentals and policy frameworks in the case of the PCL and "sound" fundamentals and frameworks, a somewhat less stringent policy requirement, in the case of the PLL. These ex ante requirements, in lieu of conditions attached to individual drawings as is typical of other IMF loans, have proven to be a fairly high bar for countries to meet and only a few countries have applied or been approved for access. During the global financial crisis, only five countries were granted access to the FCL (Colombia, Mexico and Poland) and PLL (Macedonia and Morocco), while only four have been given access during the Covid-19 crisis (Colombia, Chile and Peru for the FCL and Panama for the PLL).

During the Covid-19 crisis, however, the Fund sharply expanded its lending under two emergency facilities, the Rapid Credit Facility (RCF) for low-income countries eligible for concessional financing and the Rapid Financing Instrument (RFI) for other EMDEs. These facilities had been put in place to assist member countries meet an external financing requirement in the face of urgent needs, such as a commodity price shock or natural disaster, without a full-fledged economic adjustment program in place, as is required for access to the Fund's regular lending facilities (i.e., stand-by and extended arrangements). The ex-ante conditionality associated with those arrangements has represented a stigma on borrowing from the Fund for many countries in the past and became part of the motivation for self-insurance.

Under the RCF/RFI, annual access was raised from 50 to 100% of a member's quota in response to the Covid crisis until the end of 2021, with cumulative limits raised from 100 to 150% of quota. During the 12-month period ending March 2021, assistance to 75 member countries in the amount of US$31 billion had been approved under these two facilities.[2] (This compares with around US$78 billion that had been committed to 10 other member countries under its regular lending arrangements, most of which under the FCL/PLL for the four Latin American countries noted above.) Notwithstanding the large number of member countries that have taken advantage of the RCF/RFI emergency facilities, the total amount of resources made available was a relatively small share of the Fund's lending capacity at the end of March 2021, which was around US$1 trillion, including regular quota resources of US$478 billion, as well as bilateral credit lines of around US$542 billion that are available from member countries, but have not been activated. As of end-March 2021, the Fund had only committed around one-quarter of its total lending capacity in all of its existing lending operations (including those approved prior to the Covid crisis), prompting some outside observers to complain that it had been too restrained in its lending activities during the Covid-19 crisis.[3] However, it should be noted that the amount of new financing during the recent crisis was roughly similar to the amount of assistance provided by the Fund during the first year of the global financial crisis, but with many more countries receiving very quick support during the recent crisis and substantially more of it on concessional terms. In addition, the Fund's lending activity through March 2021 had already brought its total credit outstanding above the peak level that resulted from the global financial crisis during 2009–2010.

In mid-April 2020, the IMF established a new, quick disbursing facility, the Short-term Liquidity Line (SLL), for emerging market economies with capital market access facing a balance of payments need due to a sudden change in their capital account or reserve positions. Access to this facility was to be granted on the basis of the same criteria as the FCL, i.e., for countries with very strong macroeconomic fundamentals and policy frameworks, in amounts of up to 145% of quota in drawings of a very short-term nature of a few months. Those countries that had access to regular central bank swap facilities or were members of a regional currency arrangement such as the euro would not be allowed to use the facility, leaving a group of perhaps 10–20 countries that could be seen as potentially eligible.[4] In this sense, the IMF was attempting to create the equivalent of a swap line of credit for such countries. As of end-December 2020, however, no member country had requested access to the SLL or accepted the Fund's offer to use the facility. This facility potentially would be of value to the high-reserve EMDEs as a partial substitute for their self-insurance policy, but was undoubtedly viewed as fairly restrictive, both as regards the conditions for access and the amounts available.

One way of enhancing the lending capacity of the IMF would be to establish formal cooperative agreements with each of the regional financial arrangements noted earlier in the event of a financial crisis affecting one or more of the members of that arrangement. This has been done to a limited extent in the case of the Chiang Mai Initiative—Multilateralization (CMIM) arrangement in the sense that drawings above a certain share of a member's access require that a Fund financial assistance program be in place. Unfortunately, this cooperative arrangement between the IMF and the CMIM has not been tested, as the CMIM has not yet approved any lending operation for any of its members, even after more than 10 years of existence. Another more important example of a formal cooperating agreement between the IMF and a regional financial arrangement was the European "Troika" in which the IMF coordinated with the European Central Bank and the European Union (representing the European Stabilization Mechanism) in their assistance to Greece following the outbreak of the European debt crisis in 2010.

In the light of this brief review of the Fund's lending facilities, it is clear that more needs to be done to expand and enlarge the institutional components of the GFSN in order to reduce the reliance of EMDEs on official reserves and self-insurance. Another possibility within the IMF is to increase significantly the role of the Fund's Special Drawing Rights or SDRs in the international monetary system, which is discussed in the next section of this chapter.

The Role of SDRs in the Dollar-Centered Reserve System

Briefly put, it is clear that the role of SDRs in the international monetary system has been vastly under-utilized given the expectations that were created more than 40 years ago when it was agreed in the revised Articles of Agreement that IMF members would collaborate in making the SDR the principal reserve asset of the international monetary system, as noted at the beginning of Chapter 3. The remainder of this chapter focuses on three questions: what problems in the dollar-centered reserve system could an expanded use of SDRs resolve? why have the expectations for the SDR not been fulfilled? and what conditions would need to be in place for the SDR to play a more important role in the international monetary system?[5]

It is useful at first to review briefly some of the key features of the SDR, elaborating on what was noted in Chapter 2. The SDR is an official reserve asset administered by the Fund that is distributed among member countries and used for balance of payments needs, as well as in transactions with the Fund and certain designated holders such as the BIS and World Bank. SDRs cannot be used in transactions involving private parties. SDRs are distributed or "allocated" to member countries in proportion to their quotas, which means those countries with the largest quotas receive the largest shares of SDRs. The value of the SDR is determined on the basis of five constituent currencies (the dollar, euro, yen, pound and renminbi), which are deemed to be "freely usable" or widely used in global payments and traded in foreign exchange markets. The SDR has characteristics of both an asset and liability in that interest is earned on holdings and paid on total receipts or allocations, both at the same rate. If a country maintains its total allocations at an unchanged level, then its interest paid and received cancel out; if a country's holdings exceed its allocations, then it earns interest on that excess, whereas if its holdings are less than its allocations, then it will pay interest on that shortfall.

The SDR cannot be used directly in financial transactions, and needs to be converted into one of its constituent currencies with another holder in order to be used. In practice, all the conversions of SDRs have been made by voluntary agreement among members, even though the IMF is authorized to "designate" certain members with a strong payments position for these conversions, if needed. In this sense, SDRs serve essentially as the mechanism for a reserve pooling device, in that they are used as a means of transferring official reserves from countries that do not have an immediate need for their use to those countries that do. Initially, there had been a "reconstitution requirement" attached to SDRs that required countries to re-establish their neutral position in the use of SDRs after a certain period of use so that their holdings would be equal to their allocations, but this requirement was removed in order to eliminate the connotation that SDRs were similar to a line of credit.

In the operations of the Fund, the global need for SDR allocations is assessed every five years according to certain criteria specified in the Fund Agreement, along with the composition of its currency basket, but in practice there have been very few allocations.[6] During the period 1970–1972, there was an initial allocation of SDR 9 billion, which was followed by one of SDR 12 billion during the period 1979–1981. With the first allocation, SDRs reached a peak of only 8½% of global official reserves, but their share then fell sharply until August 2009 when there was a third general SDR allocation of SDR 161.2 billion, along with a special one of 21.5 billion for those new members of the Fund since the previous allocation had been made in order to bring them to full participation. This most recent allocation was viewed as a key measure of global cooperation in dealing with the effects of the global financial crisis and revived interest in the potential role of the SDR as an official reserve asset. Nevertheless, with the allocations of 2009, the share of SDRs in global official reserves rose to only around 4%. In the early stages of the Covid-19 crisis, there were strong advocates for a similar or larger allocation of SDRs than that of 2009 to assist the EMDEs in dealing with the payments and liquidity problems associated with the crisis, but there was insufficient support within the G20 for such action and resistance to the proposal on the part of the United States. However, in April 2021 a decision was made to allocate SDR 450 billion (around US$650 billion) to help countries deal with the continuing adverse financial effects of the Covid pandemic, which is expected to be disbursed in August 2021.

Despite the relatively limited role that the SDR has played in the international monetary system, it is clear that it has the potential to assist in the resolution of a number of problems in the dollar-centered reserve system to the benefit of global financial stability. The issue of SDRs and the substitution of SDRs for dollars has the potential to diversify the composition of official reserves and satisfy the demand for future reserves, thus relieving pressure on dollar-based safe assets and the downward drift of long-term interest rates on US government securities because of excess demand for those assets. In addition to the use of the SDR as an official reserve asset, it can be used as a store of value by serving as a basis for denominating public or private bonds thus diversifying the risk of such assets, notwithstanding limitations on its use by private parties.

If issued in sufficient amounts, the SDR could relieve pressure on the "up-hill" flow of capital from the EMDEs to reserve currency countries such as the United States in search of safe assets. In this regard, the greater availability and use of the SDR would help to reduce the size of global imbalances. Over the long term, by diversifying the composition of reserve assets, wider use of the SDR would have the potential of reducing the risk and danger of the "new Triffin Dilemma".

The larger issue and use of SDRs would also allow the IMF to play a more important role as an international lender of last resort. For example, the Fund could sell bonds denominated in SDRs to member countries in exchange for freely usable currencies as a means of enlarging its financial resources and lending capacity on a temporary basis at a time of financial stress without full reliance on the cumbersome and time-consuming procedures of quota increases. Quota increases would still be needed to determine the relative voting power, access to Fund lending resources and SDR allocations of member countries. The SDR could also be used as a unit of account in international trade that would lower the volatility of using a single currency in the pricing of commodity trade. Similarly, it could also be used for the pricing of international trade or as a reference rate for determining the value of a country's exchange rate for international transactions.

These possible uses for the SDR suggest that it has a potentially very important role to play in the international monetary system, some of which will be discussed further in the paragraphs below. Why then has its use not fulfilled expectations?

One obvious reason is that there has not been enough official support within the membership of the Fund to expand its use. A decision in support of an allocation of SDRs requires a voting majority of 85% of the membership which, in effect, gives a veto power to the United States, the largest quota member of the Fund with a share of 16.5%. In general, the United States has relatively little use for SDRs in its official transactions, even though it is the largest recipient. Given the central role that the dollar has played in the international monetary system, the United States has simply not viewed a wider role for the SDR as an official reserve asset, competing with the dollar, to be in its own national interest. The United States has used SDRs to a limited extent in the past, but mainly acts as a recipient for countries wishing to convert their SDRs into dollars or other reserve currencies.

The allocation decision of 2009 was a unique event in that it represented a trans-Atlantic act of cooperation spear-headed by the British government to deal with some of the spillover effects of the global financial crisis. When another emergency allocation was proposed in April 2020 for the Covid-19 crisis, the support from the United States was absent, ostensibly on the grounds that there had been a sufficient expansion in global liquidity through other means. Fortunately, with a new Presidential administration, US support for a new SDR allocation in April 2021 was forthcoming. Nevertheless, in view of the very high voting requirement for SDR allocations, it would be important if members could agree to reduce the voting majority for an SDR allocation, say, to 70–75% of the membership.

Another factor that has diminished some of the appeal of the SDR is the limitation on its use and the somewhat complicated procedure involved in its activation. The decision to make an allocation of SDRs may take several months to implement given the near universal requirement for membership approval. Then, following allocation, it can take a few days for a country wanting to use its SDRs to identify another country willing to exchange them for a freely usable currency and to make that conversion. It would be far simpler and more useful if allocation decisions for the SDR could be initiated on the recommendation of the Fund's Managing Director at a time of systemic financial stress, subject to the approval of its in-house Executive Board, instead of residing exclusively with the highest authority of the Fund, its ministerial level Board of Directors (representing the full membership).

As regards the use of SDRs, it would be important that SDRs be allowed to be traded in private markets and used in private financial transactions. Such a change would make SDRs negotiable in their own right and usable without needing to be converted into one of its constituent currencies. The SDR as an international reserve asset would have obvious appeal to private investors given its diversified currency composition, compared with a single currency reserve asset. The linkage of its value to the renminbi would also be attractive to investors seeking to diversify their portfolios with the inclusion of yuan-denominated assets.

A further consideration that has limited interest in expanding the issue of SDRs is the view among some advanced country members of the Fund that the availability of SDRs may carry a moral hazard in that countries with balance of payments problems could delay or postpone making policy adjustments to help rectify those problems. In these circumstances, the use of one of the conditional lending facilities of the Fund would be viewed as more appropriate. While technically this moral hazard concern could arise, it is also true that SDRs provide countries with additional official reserves and access to international liquidity to use in the event of an emergency due, for example, at a time of exchange rate volatility or a sudden change in commodity prices. The allocation decision of early 2009, soon after the peak of the global financial crisis, shows that the membership of the IMF sees SDRs as playing a critically important role in expanding international liquidity at a time of stress in the global financial system in order to limit the damage that countries could experience from extreme variation in capital flows that is unrelated to their macroeconomic policy framework. The experience of the 2009 allocation decision showed that the SDR can play a very useful role as a countercyclical tool in increasing global liquidity at a time of stress in the international financial system. Similar considerations were present in the deliberations that led to an allocation decision in April 2021. If the moral hazard concern became a significant stumbling block in the expansion of SDRs, consideration could be given to re-instating the re-constitution requirement for all or a portion of SDR allocations.

In the light of the considerations discussed above, it seems that a strong case can be made for expanding the use of SDRs in the international monetary system. What are some of the actions that could be taken to further promote its use? The actions discussed below are organized according to the three dimensions of its use that have been alluded to in the preceding paragraphs: one is as an official reserve asset or medium of exchange (the so-called O-SDR); a second is the use of the SDR for the denomination of bonds issued by public or private institutions or as a store of value (the so-called M-SDR); and a third is the use of the SDR as a unit of account in the denomination of international trade and services (the so-called U-SDR).[7] Ideally, it would be useful to have a plan endorsed by the G-20 to move forward in each of these three dimensions as part of an international effort to promote wider use of the SDR for purposes of reforming the international monetary system. Moving simultaneously along each of these dimensions would help to reinforce the status of the SDR and familiarize both public and private institutions with its potential uses in international trade and finance. Developing such a plan would, of course, represent a major accomplishment in international collaboration and would need to be based on a widely held view within the IMF membership (including the United States) that the current dollar-centered reserve system needed to be reformed. Alternatively, some of the actions listed below could be viewed as steps to enhance the role of the SDR as an international reserve asset in keeping with the objectives set out in Articles VIII and XXII of the Fund Agreement, as noted at the beginning of Chapter 3. A number of the actions listed below would require an amendment to the Fund Agreement, and where that is the case, a note is made.

As regards the O-SDR, an effort should be made to have a more regular pattern of allocations, both in their timing and amounts, in order to increase the relative share of SDRs within the total assets of the GFSN over time. One suggestion that has been made is that the Fund membership could agree to a medium-term program of allocations of around SDR 200 billion per year, which is a number that has been estimated by IMF staff to represent the incremental demand for official reserves on the part of the EMDEs. Such a move would have a marginal effect on reducing the size of current account surpluses that these countries have registered in the past and their contribution to the problem of global imbalances. At a time of global financial stress, it should also be established that the IMF would increase its SDR allocations beyond the annual amounts suggested above in order to provide a countercyclical increase in global liquidity that could be reversed once the crisis had been resolved.

At the same time, it would be important to resurrect the idea of a Substitution Account that had been the focus of discussions within the IMF Committee of 20 in the early-1970s that preceded the second reform of the Fund Agreement, as discussed in Chapter 2. The purpose of such an account would be the same today as it was envisaged then, namely to allow countries to exchange some of their dollar reserves for SDRs as a means of reducing the stock of dollar reserves and increasing the stock of SDRs within the GFSN in a more substantial way than would be possible with a plan of annual allocations.

The stumbling block for such a proposal within the Committee of 20 was that there was no agreement among the advanced countries on how the IMF would be reimbursed for any losses it might suffer from a possible decline in the value of the dollar assets that it acquired vis-a-vis the value of the SDRs that it issued. The European countries argued that the United States should cover any value at risk in such an exchange, but the United States maintained that such an open-ended commitment would not be acceptable to the US Congress which would have to approve it. In this regard, it is interesting to note that according to one study, if the substitution account had been in existence between 1980s and 2008, the costs to the United States arising from differences between the interest rate for SDRs and interest rates on US government debt and from changes in the dollar-SDR exchange rate would have amounted to

US$9 billion a year, on average, a relatively small cost.[8] As an alternative arrangement, consideration could be given to sharing this cost among all the countries that chose to take advantage of the Substitution Account or among the Fund membership at large on the grounds that such an Account had direct or indirect benefits for all members. In any event, these two proposals on allocations and a Substitution Account could increase significantly the share of SDRs in the total assets of the GFSN.

A more radical step that could be taken to increase the role of SDRs in Fund operations and as an official reserve asset would be to merge the General Resources Account or General Department of the IMF that now handles Fund lending operations on the basis of quota resources with its other SDR Department that handles SDR transactions, thus converting all its lending activities into SDR transactions.[9] Even today, all financial operations of the Fund are denominated in SDRs even if they are based on the foreign exchange component of quota resources subscribed by member countries. Under such a reform, all the resources that the Fund would use in its lending operations would be generated by decisions of the membership to increase its capital and reserve assets by new allocations of SDRs. These increases would replace the increase in loanable resources that the Fund now obtains from country quotas and bilateral borrowing arrangements. Such a reform would move the Fund to operate more like a national central bank. Country quotas would still need to be established, and increased over time, in order to determine a member country's borrowing capacity and voting power. Unlike the other proposals noted above, this reform of Fund operations would require amendments of the Fund's Articles of Agreement.

As regards the SDR-M, an effort should be made by national governments to encourage both public and private institutions to issue bonds denominated in SDRs. The attraction of such bonds is that they offer less currency and interest rate risk than bonds issued in a single currency. Multilateral lending institutions, such as the World Bank and the regional Development Banks, that regularly issue bonds in the capital markets of their member countries to increase their loanable resources, could easily adopt such a practice. As an example, the World Bank placed a 3-year bond valued at SDR 3 billion in China's bond market in August 2016, which was well received. But this has been an isolated experience. At the private level, there was some experimentation in the placement of SDR-denominated bonds equivalent to SDR 560 million in the 1970s and 1980s, but this practice was discontinued because of the relatively small size of the market for such bonds and its illiquidity. The lessons from that experience suggest that in order to promote the growth of a market for such bonds, governments would need to play a role in creating the infrastructure for these bonds in the form of clearing and settlement systems and in creating a yield curve through its own issues of SDR-denominated bonds. The corresponding central bank would also need to stand ready to purchase SDR denominated bonds until there were sufficient market-makers in the private sector.

As noted earlier, an important change that would greatly promote the M-SDR and expand its use would be to allow SDRs to be held and transacted by private agents and institutions. Such a change, with the market reforms discussed above, would make it possible that SDR-based safe assets would be created that would add to the global supply of safe assets. A reform of the Fund Agreement would be needed to make this change possible.[10]

As regards the SDR-U, a similar effort should be made by governments to expand on the limited experience that has been gained to date in using the SDR as a unit of account. Suez Canal fees, for example, have been set in terms of SDRs for a number of years, and this practice could be adopted by other agencies of international commerce, such as major international ports and shipping companies. The SDR could also be used for the pricing of international commodities, in which case it would show less volatility than commodities priced in dollars. As noted earlier, the SDR can be used as a reference rate for exchange rate determination, which has been the case for Botswana and Libya. Botswana pegs its currency to a currency basket comprised of the SDR (with a weight of 55%) and the South African Rand (with a weight of 45%), while in the case of Libya, its currency is pegged to the SDR. International financial institutions should also be encouraged to use the SDR as the unit of account for their financial transactions and bookkeeping, as is the case for the IMF and the BIS. Obviously, on the basis of this brief discussion, there is great scope for increasing the role of the U-SDR.

Government action to promote each of these three domains for the SDR, i.e., as a medium of exchange (SDR-O), store of value (SDR-M) and unit of account (SDR-U), would be highly effective in expanding its role in the international monetary system and in resolving many of the problems evident in the dollar-centered reserve system. However, the current state of international relations suggests that developing a consensus for such a broad action plan would be very difficult and that making the SDR the principal reserve asset of the international monetary system still remains an objective that will require more time and effort to achieve. A united alliance of Asian and European members would be needed to pressure the United States into a reform mode, especially if it appears that the prime currency country is not dealing with its prospective debt sustainability problem.

Other Important Reforms of the IMF

In addition to reforming the Fund's SDR operations, an effort needs to be made to strengthen its surveillance activities, especially vis-à-vis its advanced member countries, which is one of its key functions within the international monetary system. As noted earlier, there is a widely held view among the EMDEs that the Fund is not able to exercise the same leverage over the macroeconomic policy framework of the former group as it does over the latter. In part, this is due to the fact that the advanced countries tend to be the creditors (or large quota holders) within the organization, whereas the EMDEs tend to be the borrowers (or smaller quota holders). A strengthened and more even-handed surveillance role for the Fund would help to deal with the problem of global imbalances and the global financial cycle and negative spillover effects of US monetary policy.

The surveillance function of the Fund operates essentially at two levels: one is the global level and the other is the national or country level. In the former case, the Fund prepares and disseminates major studies of global macroeconomic prospects (in its World Economic Outlook), the prospects for global financial stability (in its Global Financial Stability Report) and the fiscal prospects of the major advanced and emerging market economies (in its Fiscal Monitor) on a semi-annual basis. In each case, an analysis is provided of recent developments and key challenges that need to be addressed in the period ahead. These studies are widely discussed within the Fund and by its Executive Board and then in summary form with its main governing body, the International Monetary and Financial Committee, which represents its full Board of Governors. At these semi-annual meetings, the Fund also presents an "early warning exercise" on the main risks to the global financial system that it has developed with the Financial Stability Board, the main inter-governmental authority dealing with international financial regulatory issues that was created after the global financial crisis.

At the global level of surveillance, there is one further annual exercise, centered on its External Sector Report, in which the IMF examines specifically the state of global imbalances and the contributions that specific countries or groups of countries are making to their increase or decrease, recently and for the near future. In particular, as discussed in Chapter 5, an effort is made to identify for each of a group of the larger member countries that play a key role in these imbalances the difference between their actual or prospective current account imbalance and that which could be justified on the basis of their underlying cyclical or structural conditions. This difference then becomes the focus of recommendations for policy adjustment in discussions that take place within the Fund's Executive Board. There may or may not be agreement at that level about the kind of policy action that might be appropriate to deal with a country's current account imbalance, if judged to be excessive. In cases of agreement or consensus, however, the Fund does not have any procedures in place to ensure that policy adjustments are made, except by means of the policy dialogue that takes place during the annual consultation or surveillance exercise, which the Fund carries out once a year with each of its member countries. Each of the four global exercises noted above may provide input for this second level of surveillance that takes place at the country level. The results of the policy dialogue conducted by IMF staff with country officials during the annual consultation exercise are then summarized in a report that is discussed with the Executive Board. Where judged to be appropriate, recommendations for policy adjustment are then presented in a summary of the Board's discussion for the country authorities. The degree of follow-up on those policy recommendations is then assessed in the consultation exercise for the next year. In cases where the country in question is also seeking financial assistance from the Fund, then of course it has some degree of leverage over the policy adjustments that a country is prepared to make.

As a general matter, in order to strengthen the IMF's annual consultation or surveillance exercise, a greater degree of "peer pressure" should be introduced at the level of its Board discussions. Accordingly, once an important policy concern has been identified in an annual consultation exercise with a major advanced or emerging market country that is having negative spillover effects on other countries or creating significant problems in its balance of payments, then there should be an understanding that a more focused or frequent round of discussions would occur with that country in order to work towards a resolution of the problem.[11]

Alternatively, consideration could be given to the idea of introducing a system of penalties, e.g., regarding participation in SDR allocations, as a means of exercising greater institutional pressure over the policy conduct of member countries. The question of how to introduce a greater degree of "peer pressure" into Fund surveillance activities is a delicate issue given the strong cooperative spirit that surrounds these activities and the generally strong technical reputation they have earned, which are valuable assets of the organization.

Two final issues related to the governance of the Fund deserve some commentary in this discussion of reform. One deals with the scope of the Fund's jurisdiction and the other deals with the nature of power-sharing in its decisions. In earlier chapters, it was noted that the Fund has taken a strong interest in issues of capital account liberalization, similar to its mandate regarding the liberalization of current account payments that was central to its work during the Bretton Woods era. In the period since the global financial crisis, for example, the Fund has adopted an informal framework for the analysis of the role of capital controls or "capital flow management policies" in dealing with the problem of capital flow volatility and its negative impact on the domestic financial stability of member countries. The Fund has also been advising countries on the pre-requisites and the steps they should take if they want to pursue capital account liberalization, which is generally viewed as a positive development for countries as their macroeconomic policy framework and financial sector become more sophisticated. However, none of this work was envisaged in the Fund's Articles of Agreement, as was the work on current account liberalization. In fact, under Article VI of the Fund Agreement, a country's practices in the area of capital controls were left to the sole discretion of member countries and liberalization of a member's capital account was not envisaged.

Given this background, as well as the extensive and unique work in the oversight of global financial stability that the Fund carries out, it would be appropriate to amend the Fund Agreement to formally recognize the Fund's responsibility for overseeing the international monetary *and* financial system, instead of only the international monetary system, as is now specified in Article IV. In addition, it would be appropriate in an age of financial globalization and extensive capital mobility for Article VI to be revised to include the goal of capital account liberalization as an objective of Fund membership, with the proviso that member countries will consult with the Fund on the appropriate steps they should take to eliminate those controls over time or to use them on a temporary basis to deal with problems of capital flow volatility once they have been removed.

On the final issue of power-sharing within the Fund, one needs to consider the pace of change in the revision of quotas. In principle, quota reviews for the purpose of determining the overall size of the IMF's financial resources and each member's quota or relative share in the distribution of power within the organization take place every five years. In practice, however, these reviews have often been delayed because of disputes over the statistical formula that is used in determining country quotas or the bargaining that takes place to adjust the results of that formula. The 14th Review of quotas, for example, took more than 6 years to conclude in early 2016 because of major disputes on these issues, as well as an extended time period to secure the congressional approval that is required to conclude the US government's agreement on a quota increase. The 15th review of quotas then proceeded for four years, as it was initiated just prior to the approval of the previous review, but concluded in early 2020 without any agreement because of unresolved debates on the two issues of the total size of quotas and their distribution.

The 14th review of quotas was unique in that it roughly doubled the size of quotas and resulted in a relative shift of voting power of around 6% from the advanced countries to the large emerging market economies. China, in particular, became the third largest quota holder, just behind Japan. Significant as this result was, it was still inadequate in terms of the change in relative voting power within the institution and the newly established dependence of the Fund on borrowed resources to increase its lending power. In 2016, with the implementation of the quota increase, total Fund quotas remained at around 1% of the global economy, which is roughly the same share they reached at the conclusion of previous quota adjustments. In order to increase the lending power of the Fund, it was decided to greatly increase its reliance on borrowed resources, as indicated earlier in this chapter. Fund quotas now represent somewhat less than half of the total lending power of the Fund (at around US$1 trillion), whereas borrowing arrangements with some of the larger member countries make up the rest. This is an inadequate arrangement, as the borrowing agreements are not a permanent feature of the Fund's resources and need to be renewed or re-negotiated on a periodic basis. Once in place, there is no guarantee that they will be continued, as is the case with quotas.

As regards relative voting power, it needs to be recognized that the share of the BRICS (Brazil, Russia, India, China and South Africa), for example, is still significantly under-weighted, whereas that of the European Union or Euro area is over-weighted. With the 14th review of quotas, China's quota share was increased to 6.4%, while that of the BRICS rose to 14.7% and that of the Euro area was reduced to 22%. However, if the calculated quota shares according to the quota formula had been followed, the results would have been much different. China's quota share would have increased to 12.9% and that of the BRICS to 21.2%, while that of the euro area would have declined to 19.3%. The share of the United States also would have declined to 14.7%, which would have eliminated its veto power for major decisions requiring a super-majority of 85%.[12] The political element that enters into the determination of quotas is also reflected in the fact that the 15th review of quotas was concluded in early 2020 without any increase in quotas, mainly because of the objection of the United States to a permanent increase in the Fund's financial resources and a further increase in the relative voting power of China.[13]

These kinds of results give basis to the complaint of the EMDEs that they are under-represented in the voting power of the Fund. It may also help to explain why there continues to be such a strong dependence of these countries on self-insurance, along with their greater reliance on regional financing arrangements since the global financial crisis. As a result, the challenge for the Fund is how it can maintain itself as the centerpiece of the global financial safety net.

Notes

1. There are currently 8 regional financial arrangements (with the number of participating countries and financial resources available in parentheses) as follows: the Arab Monetary Fund (22; US$3.7 billion), the BRICS Contingent Reserve Arrangement (5; US$100 billion), the Chiang Mai Initiative—Multilateralization (15; US$240 billion), the Eurasian Fund for Stabilization and Development (6; US$8.5 billion), the European Balance of Payments Facility (8; US$59 billion), the European Stabilization Mechanism (19; US$590 billion), the Latin American Reserve Fund (8; US$3.9 billion) and the North American Framework Agreement (3; US$9 billion).
2. A broad-based discussion of the IMF's response to the Covid-19 crisis can be found in IMF Independent Evaluation Office (2021).

3. The data on the IMF's lending activities cited in this paragraph have been drawn from the "Weekly Report on its Financial Activities" of January 29, 2021 and the "Quarterly Report on IMF Finances" for January 31, 2021, which are available at www.imf.org.
4. The estimate of 10 to 20 countries was suggested by Fund officials in a press briefing on the SLL on May 8, 2020 (see www.imf.org for the "Transcript of the Background Briefing on the Short-term Liquidity Line of May 8, 2020").
5. The Fund has written several papers on the role of the SDR in the international monetary system since 2009 that provide much useful information on its actual and potential use. The most recent of these papers is IMF (2018).
6. The last adjustment in the currency basket occurred in October 2016 with the inclusion of the renminbi.
7. The classification of the M-SDR, O-SDR and U-SDR was introduced in IMF (2018), which is the source for some of the proposals presented in the following paragraphs.
8. This estimate was calculated by Peter Kenen and published in Kenen (2010).
9. The idea of converting all of the Fund operations to an SDR basis was first examined in Polak (1979), its Economic Counsellor at the time. Interest in this idea has more recently been revived in Ocampo (2017), Chapter 2.
10. A strong case for allowing private agents to hold and exchange SDRs is presented in a report of the Triffin International Foundation (2014).
11. A similar proposal was advanced by Raghuram Rajan, a former Governor of the Reserve Bank of India, in Mishra and Rajan (2016).
12. These results from the 2016 adjustment of quotas were reported in Rakic (2019).
13. The resistance of the United States to a further increase in Fund quotas and China's quota share in the 15th review of quotas was reported in Haellert and Messerlin (2020).

References

Haellert, Jean-Jacques and Patrick Messerlin (2020) "The Tragedy of International Organization in a World Order in Turmoil" European Center for International Political Economy Policy Brief #5/2020.

IMF (2018) "Considerations on the Role of the SDR" IMF Policy Paper (April).

IMF Independent Evaluation Office (2021) "The IMF's Emergency Response to the Covid-19 Pandemic" Draft Issues Paper (May 6).

Kenen, Peter (2010) "The Substitution Account as a First Step Toward Reform of the International Monetary System" Peterson Institute for International Economics Policy Brief PB10–6 (March).

Mishra, Prachi and Raghuram Rajan (2016) "Rules of the Monetary Game" Reserve Bank of India Working Paper #04/2016 (March).

Ocampo, Jose Antonio (2017) *Resetting the International Monetary (Non) System* (New York, NY: Oxford University Press).

Polak, Jacques (1979) "Thoughts on an International Monetary Fund Based Fully on the SDR" IMF Pamphlet Series No. 28.

Rakic, Drazen (2019) "The International Monetary Fund: 15th General Review of Quotas" European Union Briefing #PE 631.059 for the European Parliament (April).

Triffin International Foundation (2014) "Using the SDR as a Lever to Reform the International Monetary System" Report of an SDR Working Party (May), which is available at www.triffininternational.eu.

CHAPTER 9

The Dollar and Digital Currencies

At a conference sponsored by the Federal Reserve in August 2019, Mark Carney, the then Governor of the Bank of England, made an important speech in which he criticized the current dollar-centered international monetary system and proposed that over time the dollar should be replaced by a "synthetic hegemonic currency" (SHC), which would be a composite based on the leading central bank digital currencies of the time. In a critique of the global currency power of the dollar, he pointed to some of the same problems in the operation of the international monetary and financial system that were raised in Chapters 5 and 6 of this book. What was more remarkable about Governor Carney's speech was his call, as a leading public figure in international monetary affairs, for a reform of the dollar-based reserve system.[1] This proposal was in fact the second time since the beginning of the current century in which a central bank governor for one of the leading shareholders of the IMF (China) had recommended a reform of the dollar-centered reserve system.[2]

Governor Carney's speech was also remarkable in that he was implicitly forecasting a future world in which digital currencies, and central bank digital currencies in particular, would be common phenomena. Private digital currencies, or cryptocurrencies, as they are often called, have exploded in number during the past decade, ever since the creation of Bitcoin in 2008, the most prominent one in existence today; but as of yet there are no central bank digital currencies (or CBDCs), except

A. Elson, *The Global Currency Power of the US Dollar*,
https://doi.org/10.1007/978-3-030-83519-4_9

for one in the Bahamas (the so-called digital Sand Dollar). A number of central banks are actively exploring the possible introduction of CBDCs, including the central banks of the major reserve currency countries. The Peoples Bank of China and the Swedish National Bank are well advanced in their development of a national CBDC and are now in a testing phase for their implementation. The SHC that Governor Carney was calling for would be another form of digital currency or "global stablecoin" (GSC) backed by a group of the CBDCs of the major reserve currency countries. Stablecoins, which are designed to be less volatile in value than Bitcoin, have been in existence since 2014 with the creation of Tether, but the idea of a GSC became particularly prominent with the proposal by Facebook in April 2019 to create Libra, which potentially could reach a global scale relatively quickly given the large multinational network of Facebook subscribers.

The purpose of this chapter is to examine the implications of the development of digital currencies for the future status of the US dollar. Over time, CBDCs and GSCs could significantly reduce the global currency power of the dollar, just as the development of a multi-reserve currency system and a reformed IMF and SDR arrangement were envisioned to do in the two previous chapters. In the next section of this chapter, some of the key technical aspects of CBDCs and GSCs are examined that have a bearing on the future operations of the international monetary and financial system. This discussion is followed by an analysis of how Governor Carney's proposal for a SHC could deal with some of the problems associated with the current dollar-centered international reserve system. The chapter closes with an assessment of the likely impact of CBDCs/GSCs on the global currency power of the dollar.

The World of Digital Currencies

Since the creation of the Bitcoin digital currency in 2008, there has been a proliferation of digital currencies that are actively traded in over 150 countries mainly for international transfers, with the largest value of transactions on the order of US$200 billion associated with the East Asian region for transfers within the region and with other regions, based on 2019 data. Bitcoin is the largest digital currency used in these transactions, while Tether is the most important stablecoin used, among some 30 large, widely circulated digital currencies and stablecoins that are actively traded on 10 digital exchanges.[3] Cryptocurrencies, cryptoassets or digital currencies, as they are called in different contexts, can be defined as means of payment and stores of value in digital token format that rely on encryption techniques (cryptography) and distributed ledger technology (DLT) mainly in the form of blockchain, as distinct from an outside central ledger manager, to regulate the generation of units and verification of transfers.[4] A stablecoin is a particular form of cryptoasset that attempts to stabilize the value of the digital coin by linking it to that of a conventional financial asset or pool of assets. In late December 2020, according to the digital currency monitoring agency, CoinMarketCap.com, a global set of more than 4000 cryptocurrencies with a total market capitalization of around US$750 billion were listed for trade on more than 300 digital exchanges with global reach, of which roughly two-thirds was represented by the value of Bitcoin and among which some 30 were actively being bought and sold, as noted above. As of mid-April 2021, total market capitalization had jumped to US$2.2 trillion mainly because of a rapidly escalating valuation of Bitcoin and intense interest in it as a speculative investment.

Bitcoin tokens are subject to sharp variations in value, whereas those of Tether are tied one for one to the value of the US dollar, thus their generic label of stablecoin. During 2020, the value of Bitcoin units varied between US$3000 and US$30,000, and then it rose to a peak of around US$65,000 in mid-April 2021, from which it fell to a range of US$35,000–US$40,000 in late May–early June. With the enormous generation of liquidity resulting from the Federal Reserve's responses to the financial effects of the Covid-19 crisis, Bitcoin has become a speculative asset similar to gold in the minds of many investors. However, unlike gold, it has little or no intrinsic value and has been subject to extreme variation in price during the last 5 years. While Bitcoin has served as a means of payment like fiat money, it has been a highly unstable and illiquid unit of account and store of value compared with major fiat currencies. In the case of stablecoins such as Tether, which in principle is tied to the value of the US dollar and goes under the symbol USDT, there is no guarantee that this fixed relationship will be maintained indefinitely, as Tether has not allowed for any strict audit of its reserves to be performed.

One additional concern with the use of Bitcoin is the large and growing carbon footprint that has come to be associated with its "mining" operations or "proof of work" calculations that are required for the validation of transactions in its decentralized and open (or "permissionless") arrangement for participants. Given that only a fixed amount of Bitcoin tokens was set to be created or "mined" over time, the closer the current amount of tokens comes to that limit, the more difficult will become the computer computations that are required to demonstrate "proof of work". These calculations cannot be performed by individual operators, as was the case early in Bitcoin's history, but rather now can only be conducted by large computer plants involving major amounts of power consumption. It is a stunning fact to realize that recent calculations have shown that Bitcoin's "mining" operations in 2019 consumed an estimated 123 terawatt hours, or more than that consumed by countries such as Argentina, Greece, New Zealand or Pakistan in the same year.[5]

Digital currencies are used for both domestic and international transfers, but mainly the latter. The obvious appeal of digital currencies is their available use for the rapid and efficient transfers of monetary value between individuals and businesses at minimal cost without the need for financial and other intermediaries and a full disclosure of the identities of the parties involved. Digital currencies are commonly used for remittances between individuals in different countries, where the cost of such transfers using traditional mechanisms can be as much as 10% of the value of the transfer.[6] In addition, digital currencies are actively used for illicit purposes (e.g., drug traffic, money laundering and terrorist financing) as they are largely unregulated and anonymous. They are also frequently used for capital flight in countries such as Argentina and China that have strict limits on outward capital transfers by resident individuals and businesses.

The announcement of the Libra GSC project by Facebook in April 2019 fundamentally altered the landscape for digital currencies and the official response to them, given the vast global scope of Facebook's user base (approx. 2.9 billion people) that potentially could serve as a user base for Libra relatively quickly. Simply put, the potentially rapid scalability of the Libra project, backed by the resources of a global technology firm like Facebook, could conceivably create a Libra currency zone that would be as large or larger than the size of the dollar currency zone that was described in Chapter 3. (As of December 1, 2020, Facebook changed the name of its planned stablecoin from Libra to Diem.) Governments in all the active reserve currency countries began to consider the legal, regulatory and oversight challenges of digital currencies, while taking a more active interest in the development of CBDCs. This work at the official level has been coordinated by the G7 and G20 and has involved the Bank for International Settlements (BIS) and its Committee for Payments and

Market Infrastructures (CPMI), the Financial Stability Board (FSB), the IMF and the central banks of the leading advanced countries.

One of the issues that has been given clear prominence in the deliberations of these bodies and groups is the slow, costly and cumbersome process that prevails at present for the payment, clearing and settlement of cross-border retail transactions. This feature of the international monetary system is what has motivated to a large extent the development and expansion in the use of digital currencies since the end of the global financial crisis. While the international dimensions of banking regulation were the main focus of the official institutions listed above for much of the period following the global financial crisis, official attention has now shifted to the need for reform in the international payments arrangements of the international monetary system and the regulation of digital currencies.

Cross-border retail payments cover the purchase of goods and services by consumers and businesses and tend to be relatively low in value, but large in volume, for which payment, clearing and settlement arrangements are operated by both private and public providers.[7] By contrast, wholesale payments relate to transactions between financial institutions, for example, for the settlement of securities and foreign exchange trades and interbank funding transactions. While much larger in value than retail transactions, both individually and in aggregate, they are fewer in number. Wholesale payments systems are usually owned and operated by central banks because of their systemic importance. These payments are largely digital in format already and have been subject to rapid processing through what are called "real time gross settlement" (RTGS) arrangements.

Cross-border retail transactions, by contrast, can be a cumbersome process involving a number of intermediaries, e.g., a payment service provider and local bank at the payer and payee side of the transaction to handle the payment, clearing and settlement of a transaction, matched by two international correspondent banks to manage the actual cross-border transfer and cross-currency aspects of the transaction. It has been estimated that the average cost for a US bank of executing a cross-border transaction could be 7% of the value of the transaction (up to 10 times that for a domestic payment), with time delays of more than a few days.[8] These estimates obviously vary by region and the nature of the transaction.

What is also remarkable about the current state of cross-border retail transactions is that the largest share of them (significantly more than half) are managed by US-based correspondent banks and involve a US-bank-dominated international messaging service for the communications involved in financial transactions known as SWIFT (the Society for Worldwide Interbank Financial Telecommunications). These arrangements in international banking reveal another key feature of the global currency power of the dollar and its dominance in the international financial system. As noted in Chapter 4, US dominance of the international correspondent banking network for the processing of international trade and financial transactions, along with the international messaging service that makes those transactions feasible and secure, are the basis on which international sanctions imposed by the US government are judged to have so much impact.

In this context, digital currencies and global stablecoins offer the prospect of peer-to-peer, direct payment arrangements between payer and payee that would eliminate virtually all of the various intermediaries identified above, as well as the excessive cost and time delays involved. Another advantage is that the easy accessibility of digital, mobile payments arrangements can help to deal with the problem of large, unbanked segments of populations in many emerging and developing economies. The availability of digital payment arrangements can facilitate access to a bank-based transaction account for these population groups, which then can be an opening to the use of other bank services that would support many of their basic development needs.

Central Bank Digital Currencies (CBDCs)

What is the rationale for the development of central bank digital currencies (CBDCs)? In the last couple of years, there has been widespread interest among central banks in the possible development of CBDCs. A major difference between CBDCs and private sector cryptocurrencies is that the value and validity of the former are fully backed by the central bank issuing them, whereas there is no such guarantee for the latter. CBDCs are a form of fiat money in digital form, instead of the normal physical shape of notes and coins. The BIS has been tracking central bank activity in this area and has identified some 80 central banks that are actively engaged in the development of a prototype for their country.[9] As noted earlier, the Peoples Bank of China and the Bank of Sweden are in the testing phase for the introduction of their CBDC. The Bank of

Canada is also well advanced in the development of a CBDC, but only on a contingent basis, as it has not yet decided to introduce it.[10]

There seem to have been a variety of motivations for this surge of interest in CBDCs. One is the declining use of physical cash in many countries and the desire of central banks there to provide a supplementary form of currency to match the shift that has taken place among many individuals and businesses to a digital payments mode. In some sense, this rationale is a defensive one, in that the central banks involved did not want to see a situation develop in which the domestic currency supply was being managed and determined in digital form by private companies. They also did not want to confront a situation in which domestic residents took an interest in the use of a CBDC of another country because one was not available in their own country.

Central banks have also viewed CBDCs as a mechanism to promote financial inclusion in countries where a significant share of the population did not have access to financial services. Another motivation of some central banks is that CBDCs could be seen as a means of promoting the internationalization of a country's currency, in that its availability in digital form could promote its use beyond its national borders. Of course, this would only be possible, if the central bank had an established reputation for technocratic management and the maintenance of price stability. This motivation has been important to China, as it has adopted a number of measures in recent years with the objective of internationalizing the renminbi. A greater internationalization of the euro was cited in the discussion paper on a digital euro distributed by the ECB in October 2020 as one motivation for issuing an electronic version of the euro.[11] More generally, however, central banks have viewed CBDCs mainly as a device to promote the efficiency, reliability and safety of domestic and cross-border payments in order to reduce the high costs that apply now to such transactions.

One important issue that has been the focus of debate is the potential impact of CBDCs on the role of commercial banks in the domestic money supply.[12] The existence of a retail or general purpose CBDC would in effect make it possible for the general public to have individual accounts with the central bank that previously had only been available to commercial banks as a feature of reserve money and the deposits that banks hold with the central bank. Apart from the administrative burden on the central bank of dealing with the substantial increase in deposits and accounts that this change would involve, such a change could pose a risk of disintermediation on the part of the banks. The availability of a CBDC would conceivably make it very easy for deposit holders in commercial banks to shift those deposits to the central bank, if it decided to pay interest on its CBDC as it does now for reserve money, and an increase in that interest rate was not matched fully by the commercial banks or if depositors were concerned about the safety of their deposits at a time of financial stress or economic difficulties. The latter concern would presumably be alleviated by the fact that commercial bank deposits are normally insured by the government. However, if there were a shift of deposits to the central bank, it could make some or all of that outflow available to the banks through its rediscount and credit facilities. Alternatively, the central bank could put a limit on the amount of its CBDC that individuals or businesses could hold. In general, the availability of a CBDC would put pressure on banks to increase the interest rate on their retail deposits and adjust it more flexibly, with likely upward pressure on lending rates.

In view of the uncertain effects of CBDCs on commercial banks, a number of central banks are considering so-called hybrid CBDCs in which they would not be involved in the retail payments associated with the use of CBDCs. While CBDCs would represent a direct claim on the central bank and it would be in charge of their issuance, their distribution and use by individuals and businesses in retail payments would be managed by commercial banks or other private intermediaries. The central bank would maintain oversight of the infrastructure for the CBDC and ensure the safety and soundness of the system. This hybrid model would alleviate the central bank of the administrative burden of managing CBDC accounts for what potentially could be a vast proportion of the population, while diminishing the risk of disintermediation for the banks. Both the Peoples Bank of China and the Bank of Sweden have adopted the hybrid model as the basis for their CBDC project.

More generally, it can be assumed that the existence of CBDCs could help to make monetary policy more effective. Interest-bearing CBDCs would serve to transfer the impact of the central bank's change in policy interest rates more directly to consumers, as they normally do not see much of an effect from changes in central bank policy rates in the interest they earn on their commercial bank deposits. If CBDCs replaced to a large extent the demand for physical cash and banknotes, they would also be more responsive to a central bank's introduction of negative policy rates, if these were deemed useful for monetary policy purposes.

CBDCs could also make possible a special form of monetary stimulus that goes under the label of "helicopter money", but has not been attempted in practice, mainly because of the difficulties in implementing it. The idea behind "helicopter money" is that at a time of severe or sustained weakness in aggregate demand, one means of countering this condition would be for the central bank to increase reserve money by giving each individual in the economy a cash transfer of a certain amount that could be used to purchase goods and services. Such an action on the part of the central bank would be similar to an increase in government expenditure or a rebate of taxes, but with more direct effects on consumers and without any increase in the public debt. The existence of a CBDC with universal participation by consumers would make such an experiment in monetary stimulus much more feasible than it would be without a CBDC. It could also be made to be temporary in that the initial digital transfer could be programmed to expire, if not utilized within a given time period.

The prospect of CBDCs also has implications for the international monetary system.[13] As already noted, the digitization of central bank currencies should make it possible for CBDCs to spread in use beyond national borders more easily that it is now possible, in the case of a highly credible central bank with a strong record of price stability and monetary policy management. For example, the existence of CBDCs could make it more likely that cases of currency substitution would occur in countries with a poor record of policy management and price instability, in the same way that dollarization (i.e., the substitution of dollars for domestic cash) has occurred in many countries in the past with a poor record of inflation control. One can also imagine that credible CBDC issuers, even for a relatively small economy, with a strong record of policy implementation, such as Singapore, could see its currency achieve a level of scalability and market liquidity that would permit it to be used as a reserve currency on a par with some of the existing reserve currencies.

It is similarly conceivable that digital currency areas could develop that transcend national borders in the case of a credible central bank that allowed its CBDC to be used beyond national borders. For example, the Belt and Road initiative of China, along with the elaborate central bank swap network that the Peoples Bank of China has established in recent years, could be one means of promoting a more rapid internationalization of the renminbi when its CBDC (the DCEP or digital currency/electronic payment, as it is called) becomes available for domestic and cross-border use. The digitization of the renminbi does not eliminate the basic requirements for the existence of a global reserve currency that were discussed in Chapter 7, in particular capital account liberalization and a flexible exchange rate, but it would facilitate the rapid internationalization of the renminbi once those requirements were in place.

The widespread use of CBDCs and their interoperability will also have implications for international capital flows by reducing transactions costs and frictions in capital markets. The digitization of money and payments is likely to make the infrastructure for international capital flows more efficient, with a consequent lowering of transactions costs, while making foreign financial markets more accessible. At the same time, the availability of CBDCs that are interoperable among each other could make international capital flows more volatile, thus worsening the international policy trilemma and complicating monetary policy and exchange rate management. The global financial cycle that was discussed in Chapter 5 would likely become more pronounced. (As noted in Chapter 5, the international policy trilemma affirms the idea that if a country wants to pursue an independent monetary policy, it must maintain either a flexible exchange rate and an open capital account or a fixed exchange rate with capital controls. More recently, however, Helene Rey has argued that the existence of a global financial cycle in an age of financial globalization has changed the policy trilemma to a dilemma, such that an independent monetary policy requires not only a flexible exchange rate, but also the use of capital controls or capital flow management policies, as they are often called.[14])

It is striking that the Federal Reserve is the only one of the central banks of the major reserve currencies that has not issued a discussion paper about CBDCs and seems to be on a very slow track in making any decision in regards to a digital dollar. Instead, Governor Lael Brainard, who has been a frequent spokesperson of the Federal Reserve Board on this topic, has given a few speeches about the pros and cons of digital currencies and the issues that have to be addressed in coming to a decision for the US dollar. Unlike many countries, the demand for the Fed's paper dollar cash has not declined, especially in the case of US$100 notes, in part because of their popular use abroad. As of end March 2020, around US$1.8 trillion in Federal Reserve notes were in circulation, of which roughly half was in circulation abroad.[15] To be sure, an important question of debate at both the public and private levels will be the relationship between the Federal Reserve and the commercial banks if the Fed were to introduce its own CBDC, as it would affect certain privileges and benefits that the banks now enjoy under the current system. Initially in the 2015–2018 period, according to Governor Brainard, some thought was being given to the possible advantages of a form of CBDC for wholesale payments as distinct from retail use. In a speech in 2018, she made the following comments:

> There is no demonstrated need for a Fed-issued digital currency...A multiplicity of mechanisms are likely to be available for American consumers to make payments electronically in real time. As such, it is not obvious what additional value a Fed-issued digital currency would provide over and above these options...It is possible at some point in the future that a limited central bank digital instrument that serves as a settlement asset for wholesale payment and settlement activity may hold some promise.[16]

Since that time, the Federal Reserve has been a participant in all the various discussions at the multilateral level noted earlier, while making improvements in its existing digital payments arrangements. In August 2020, it introduced the launch of FEDNow, a new digital platform for sending and receiving payments in real time by businesses and individuals that will be available 24 hours day and 365 days a year. It will not be fully operational until 2023 or 2024. At the same time, the Federal Reserve Bank of Boston announced the launch of Project Hamilton with the Digital Currency Initiative of the MIT Media Lab (dci.mit.edu) to develop over the next 2 years the technological and cryptographic requirements for the prototype of a CBDC for retail use that would satisfy stringent requirements for speed, security, privacy and resiliency. If testing is successful, then extensive discussions with various stakeholders over an additional couple of years would take place to determine its full feasibility and operability.[17] With the launch of Project Hamilton, both Federal Reserve Board Chairman Jerome Powell and Treasury Secretary Yellen have expressed strong interest in exploring the possibility of a CBDC for the dollar, but without setting any time frame for a final decision to be made. In late May 2021, the Fed announced that it would issuing a discussion paper for a digital dollar within a few months to elicit public comment on its future possibility.

Global Stablecoins (GSCs)

Global stablecoins are the other major initiative of private sector digital currencies that have been triggered by the growing popularity of Bitcoin and its rivals. As noted earlier, the proposal of Facebook developers to introduce the Diem stablecoin (formerly called Libra) on a global scale has triggered widespread concern among national regulators and official bodies as to its scope and conformity with international regulatory standards. The LIBRA Association introduced a White Paper in June 2019 for its global payments scheme that was revised in April 2020, in which it said very simply "Diem's goal is to serve billions of people". It also clearly indicated that it had been in consultation with a number of national and international regulatory bodies to ensure that it complied with existing standards for international payments, e.g., as regards anti-money laundering and combatting the financing of terrorism (AML/CFT). In addition, the Diem Association, the current overall governing body for the stablecoin, initially established its headquarters in Geneva, Switzerland and sought regulatory approval from the Swiss Financial Market Regulatory Authority (FINMA). By contrast, Bitcoin has made no pretension of meeting regulatory standards for domestic or international payments, and is likely to remain a high-risk venture mainly for speculative purposes.

Given former Bank of England Governor Carney's proposal for a SHC, which would be an official digital venture similar to the Diem global stablecoin, it is useful to explain some of the major characteristics of the Diem proposal, as explained in the Libra White Paper of April 2020. Notwithstanding the change in the name of the stablecoin proposal from Libra to Diem as of December 1, 2020, the White Paper of April 2020 has remained largely unchanged and is available at www.diem.com.

The main characteristic of Diem is its fixed value with respect to an international reserve currency in order to avoid the volatility and unreliability of digital currencies such as Bitcoin as a means of payment and store of value. The White Paper envisaged that Diem would become available in four different digital formats, namely for the dollar, the euro, the UK pound and the Singapore dollar, in order to facilitate its global use. It also aimed at some point in the future to be issued as a multicurrency token (called XDM) that would be a composite of the four single currency digital coins just mentioned, as well as any other currency coins which could be added over time. In this respect, it is striking that the Diem creators recognized that the XDM they planned to establish would be a global digital financial asset similar in structure to the IMF's SDR, in which each currency would be assigned fixed nominal weights. The currency composition of the XDM and its weights would be adjusted over time subject to the oversight and control of a group of regulators and central bank governors yet to be established. The Diem proposal even cited the possibility of the IMF playing a role in determining its currency composition.

Each of the four digital coins of the Diem proposal would be tied to their counterpart national currency at a fixed rate and backed by a special reserve of assets denominated in each currency for an amount equal to 100% of the value of digital coins "minted" in that currency. Eighty per cent of these reserves would be comprised of local currency, short-term government securities (up to 90 days) and 20% in cash, supplemented by a capital buffer to absorb any credit, market and operational losses arising from the payments arrangement. The reserves would be held in a set of geographically dispersed custodial banks and would be subject to regular audit and disclosure. In this respect, the design of the Diem financial structure seems analogous to the structure of "narrow banking" in which deposit-taking is matched by 100% reserves without any lending or investment activities on the part of the bank. While the merits and demerits of such a plan for banks have been debated for many years, it has never been implemented. In this respect, the proposal raises questions as to whether the payments arrangement for Diem would raise enough revenue to be both popular and profitable.

Over time, the amount of digital coins issued or minted would be determined by the demand for Diem's services and the amount of reserves provided in the purchase of digital coins in each currency. These coins would be issued by certain "designated dealers", which would be well-regulated and well-capitalized financial institutions, or "burned" (i.e., destroyed) in exchange for the full value of their reserves. Any conversion between Diem coins and local fiat currency would be managed by third party financial service providers outside the Diem network.

As in the case of other digital currencies, Diem will operate on the basis of distributed ledger/blockchain technology. However, unlike Bitcoin, which has an open (or "permission-less"), decentralized "proof of work" design in the validation of transactions, Diem will operate with a decentralized and geographically distributed system of pre-assigned or "permissioned" validator nodes. These operators will have been selected among the early members or businesses involved in the Diem Association who have been judged to have a strong stake in its success. Over time, it is envisaged that a move to a more permission-less system could take place that is open to anyone based on their Diem coin holdings, with consensus on the extension of the blockchain achieved by "proof of stake". The Diem designers claim that their technology can rapidly adapt to scale in handling high transaction throughput with low network latency (or delays in the transfer of data) and low energy costs, all features that have been absent in Bitcoin.

Notwithstanding the technological advances that have been made in the development of Diem, there are still a number of features that are unclear in the area of regulatory compliance, e.g., with respect to consumer protection as regards data privacy and use, disclosure of fees and other charges, and the exclusion of fraudulent activities.[18] In this connection, it is interesting to note that in May 2021, Diem announced that it had changed its headquarters from Geneva, Switzerland to Washington, DC and had withdrawn its request for regulatory approval from the Swiss Regulatory Authority (FINMA) in order to do so in the United States for a dollar-based stablecoin. Diem also announced that it had formed a partnership with Silvergate Bank of California, which will become the exclusive issuer of Diem USD stablecoins. Once regulatory approval in the United States is obtained, it is expected that a Diem USD pilot will be launched before the end of 2021.[19] How the Diem USD stablecoin will differ from existing stablecoins linked to the dollar, such as Tether and USD Coin, with market capitalizations (as of mid-April 2021) of US$49 billion and US11 billion, respectively, is not clear. Recent growth in USD Coin has been particularly strong with its market capitalization rising by a factor of 600 during 2020, according to the cryptocurrency monitoring agency cited earlier (coinmarketcap.com).

At the economic level, the ambition and scope of the Diem proposal raise some of the same issues that were touched on in the discussion of CBDCs. One is its potential competition with banks, in particular as regards the handling of payments for both domestic and cross-border transactions. Banks have been the dominant players in the payment, clearing and settlement of domestic and cross-border trade, but these functions have now been challenged by the arrival of digital currencies. In response, the banks have begun to develop their own digital currency payment operations. One example was the launch of JPM coin in late October 2020 by JP Morgan bank, which is a global stablecoin linked 1 for 1 to the US dollar, similar to Diem. Unlike Diem, however, which is planned to be a general coin available for both retail and wholesale payments, JPM coin is restricted to wholesale payments, only among JP Morgan's institutional clients on a global basis. It also has the advantage of having been judged to be compliant with JP Morgan's regulatory requirements.

Another issue with Diem, if it begins to gain scale in global use because of the large size of Facebook's client base, is the possibility for currency substitution to occur in countries with weak monetary systems and poorly managed central banks, in the same way that they may have suffered bouts of dollarization in the past. The loss of monetary sovereignty raises obvious questions as to how a country would be able to function economically based on the Diem digital currency. Such a question would also arise in the event that one of the planned digital currencies or the XDM became a currency zone beyond any strict national borders, covering a number of countries because of strong network effects arising from its use in the invoicing and settlement of trade, the denomination of government securities and other foreign payments transactions.

A more extreme case to consider would be one that might occur in the future after the creation of different Diem currencies, and they have established their credibility and trust and are widely in use. At such a point, one could imagine that the Diem Association could decide that one or all of the digital currencies would be established in and of themselves as a form of fiat currency without the full backing of reserves that they had at the beginning of their existence. Such a change could be seen as analogous to the separation of the US dollar from its ties to gold in the early 1970s at the end of the Bretton Woods era, which marked the beginning of the dollar as a fiat currency. This development would represent a complete loss of monetary sovereignty for the affected countries and the surrender of monetary policy-making to non-official sources in somewhat the same way that the ties of countries to the gold standard limited countries to the vagaries of gold supplies. This arrangement would clearly challenge the primary position of the dollar as a reserve currency and represent the surrender of monetary control to private sources.

Governor Carney's Proposal for a Synthetic Hegemonic Currency (SHC)

Governor Carney's proposal for a SHC, cited at the beginning of this chapter, was based on the idea of a global stablecoin and had some apparent similarities with the DIEM proposal, with its global coin (the XDM) linked to separate digital currencies for some of the major currencies. However, for the SHC, instead of separate digital currencies under DIEM's control, it would be linked to separate CBDCs for the major reserve currencies. In Governor Carney's view, a global stablecoin, given its broad scope and purpose, would be better suited to operate under public administration with public policy objectives, instead of under private sector control with private enterprise objectives.

Such a scheme would represent in effect a shift from a major reserve currency system dominated by the dollar to a multilateral one in which the dollar would share that role with other important reserve currencies to which the SHC was tied. In this regard, it is curious that Governor Carney did not cite the SDR created by the IMF as a precedent for the SHC, as in fact the DIEM inventors did for the XDM in their White Paper. By design, the SHC would seem to be similar to a digital version of the SDR, except for the fact that it would not be limited to official transactions. In fact, it would circulate throughout the economies in which it was accepted for use just as its component CBDCs would. In this regard, the SHC would provide more efficient domestic and cross-border payment services, as it would benefit from the credibility of the CBDCs to which it was connected.

The shift to a multi-reserve currency system inherent in the SHC arrangement proposed by Governor Carney would deal with a number of the problems associated with the dollar-denominated reserve system discussed in previous chapters. One is that it would alleviate the problem of the insufficient supply of safe assets that exists now, as well as the medium to long-term concern about the "new Triffin Dilemma" that was discussed in Chapters 5 and 7. The existence of the SHC and its component CBDCs would promote a diversification in the supply of safe assets away from the dollar and into SHC currencies. In this way, it would help to resolve the problem of what Governor Carney referred to as a "global liquidity trap" and low interest rates in the market for US government bonds. The wide acceptance of the SHC would also reduce the dominating influence of the dollar in global trade with its deflationary bias for countries facing the need for balance of trade adjustment. Finally, the architecture of international financial flows could evolve around the SHC as the main unit of denomination, with less volatility in capital flows vis-a-vis the EMDEs in response to changes in monetary policy in the United States and other advanced countries. In this way, the global financial cycle would become less pronounced.

These changes would represent significant gains for the international monetary and financial system. However, there were a number of critical features of the SHC mechanism left unspecified in Governor Carney's proposal that would need to be defined before it could be fully assessed. One was the institutional arrangement through which it would be issued. By implication from the limited amount of information provided in Governor Carney's speech, the "minting" of the SHC would be determined by the central banks whose CBDCs were used to define the SHC, meeting together in some formal or informal institutional arrangement. The obvious parallels between the SHC and the SDR suggest that the IMF could fulfill this function. By creating a digital version of the SDR, the members of the IMF would have a number of rules and procedures already in place for its currency composition, valuation and use in IMF operations. However, two major reforms of the SDR mechanism would be needed to allow its digital equivalent to fulfill the plan for the SHC. As discussed in Chapter 8, one would be to establish a procedure for the regular issuance of SDRs to meet the demand for global reserves and liquidity, which up until now has been filled by the dollar. The other would be to allow the SDR to be used in private sector transactions.

The association of the SHC with a digital form of the SDR would resolve another unknown in the SHC proposal, namely its governance and regulation. These features could be adapted from the existing arrangements for the SDR, suitably reformed to accommodate the two requirements discussed in the previous paragraph. All these changes would be simplified if the IMF were to unify its General and SDR Departments and manage all of its lending and financial activities in terms of SDRs instead of member country currencies, as also discussed in Chapter 8. This consolidation would make sense, in particular, for purposes of the creation and adjustment of global liquidity.

From the perspective of this comparison between the SHC and a digital format of the SDR, Governor Carney's proposal is clearly an ambitious one to work towards over the long term. The link of the SHC with the SDR would ensure that the dollar would be a significant component of the SHC and would continue to be a major reserve currency, but within a more clearly defined multilateral context. In fact, the United States operating within the IMF would obviously have a major role to play in defining how the SDR was to be reformed to take on the full role of the SHC. However, it is conceivable that a group of other reserve currency countries with their own CBDCs, if credibly established and functioning effectively, could decide to create the SHC outside of the IMF in order to provide a clear alternative to the dollar. If the SHC arrangement were to operate outside the IMF, there are many organizational details and procedures that would need to be specified before its feasibility could be fully evaluated. Some of these aspects have been touched on already in the discussion above, for example, as regards the manner in which the SHC would be issued and allowed to expand to meet growing demand, as well as its governance and regulation. In addition, the manner of how it would be used in a lender of last resort function to meet liquidity needs at a time of financial stress would need to be specified. Again, it seems likely that the reforms associated with the creation of an SHC would require many years of experience with CBDCs before it could be realized.

* * *

The prospect of digital currencies raises many questions about the future of the international monetary system and the role of the dollar. It seems likely that significant improvements in the settlement, clearance and payment for cross-border transactions will occur which could challenge the priority and privilege that US banks and the dollar have enjoyed up until now. The prospective launching of the DIEM dollar during 2021 will represent a major experiment in the operation of a stablecoin. If successful and widely accepted, it could be followed up by the issue of at least three other digital currencies and the XDM as a global stablecoin. Given its potentially rapid scalability, the XDM could pose a significant threat to the global currency power of the dollar. Perhaps in a period of 5–10 years, the extent to which this threat could materialize will become clear.

During 2022, it is likely that the CBDC for the renminbi (DCEP) will be officially launched. This event will be significant given the rapid adoption it is likely to experience within China and its widespread use throughout the country and possibly outside, unless restricted to domestic use by the PBOC authorities. The Chinese government's goals for the internationalization of the renminbi suggest that circulation of the DCEP outside of China may not be restricted. Its use within the Asian region and as an adjunct to the government's Belt and Road Initiative will be two developments that will provide important information about the potential reach of the DCEP. If at the same time, the government continues to take steps to liberalize its capital account restrictions and to establish a flexible exchange rate, the rise of the renminbi as a reserve currency will gain strength. Perhaps also in a period of 5–10 years, the extent of this potential threat to the global currency power of the dollar will become clear.

This time period of 10 years is also important for determining whether or not the US government will be able to put in place and begin to implement a plan to establish public debt sustainability.

Notes

1. The speech given by Governor Carney appeared in Carney (2019).
2. Zhou Xiaochuan, a former Governor of the Peoples Bank of China, recommended shifting to an international monetary system based on the SDR in Zhou (2009).
3. Data on digital currency use have been collected and published by the internet company, Chainanalysis, on its website chainanalysis.com, and were made available in *The 2020 Geography of Cryptocurrency Report: Analysis of Geographic Trends in Cryptocurrency Adoption, Usage and Regulation* (September 2020).
4. Two non-technical explanations of distributed ledge technology and blockchain can be found in World Bank (2017) and Yaga et al. (2018). A more elaborate and highly recommended introduction to digital currencies is available in a course taught by Gary Gensler (the current chairman of the SEC) at the MIT Sloan Business School in the Fall of 2018 (Course #15.S12 "Blockchain and Money"), which can be found at ocw.mit.edu.
5. These calculations come from the Cambridge Bitcoin Electricity Consumption Index, which was developed by the Cambridge Centre for Alternative Finance (CCAF) at the Cambridge University Judge Business School (www.cbeci.org.). For an interesting evaluation of CCAF's estimates of Bitcoin's electricity consumption, see Nick Carter "How Much Energy Does Bitcoin Actually Consume?" *Harvard Business Review* blog (May 5, 2021).
6. The cost of remittances was cited in the Annual Report of the European Central Bank for 2020, Chapter 3.

7. The processes and steps involved in the payment, clearing and settlement of cross-border retail transactions are explained in Bech and Hancock (2020). The issues involved in resolving current problems in cross-border payments are discussed in BIS Committee on Payment and Market Infrastructures (2020), which is a good example of the kind of official analysis that has been sparked by the Libra proposal, as noted earlier in the chapter.
8. The costs and delays for cross-border retail transactions noted here were cited in Bech and Hancock (2020, p. 15).
9. Another source of information on the development of digital currencies and CBDCs is the Digital Monetary Institute of the Official Monetary and Financial Institutions Forum (OMFIF), which can be located at www.omfif.org/dmi.
10. The three cases of Canada, China and Sweden are described in Auer et al. (2020).
11. European Central Bank (2020).
12. These and other effects of introducing a CBDC are discussed in Carapella and Fleming (2020). The practical aspects of establishing CBDCs are also well examined in a report by Citi GPS "The Future of Money: Crypto, CBDCs and 21st Century Cash" (April 2021), which is available at Citi GPS—Global Perspectives and Solutions (www.citivelocity.com).
13. A number of the points discussed in this and the following paragraphs have been elaborated on in IMF (2020).
14. This thesis was laid out in Rey (2013).
15. This estimate is derived from Paul Wong and Jessie Leigh Maniff, "Comparing Means of Payment: What Role for a Central Bank Digital Currency?" FEDS Notes, Board of Governors of the Federal Reserve System (August 13, 2020).
16. These comments were drawn from Governor Brainard's speech on "Cryptocurrencies, Digital Currencies and Distributed Ledger Technology: What Are We Learning?" that was delivered at the Decoding Digital Currency Conference of the Federal Reserve Bank of San Francisco (May 15, 2018), which is available at www.federalreserve.gov.
17. A brief introduction to Project Hamilton can be found in a video interview by Patricia Haas Cleveland of the Official Monetary and Financial Institutions Forum (OMFIF) with Jim Cunha, Senior Vice-President of the Boston Fed, who is in charge of the project (see podcast of January 27, 2021 at www.omfif.org and youtube.org).
18. A review of the regulatory concerns that were raised about the original Libra project is presented in Oliver Read and Stefan Schafer "Regulators Act on Global Stablecoins"*Intereconomics* (December 2020), which is available at www.intereconomics.eu.

19. These changes in the Diem project were announced in a press release of May 12, 2021 ("Diem Announces a Partnership with Silvergate and Strategic Shift to the United States"), which is available on the Diem website (www.diem.com).

References

Auer, Raphael et al (2020) "Rise of the Central Bank Digital Currencies: Drivers, Approaches and Technologies" BIS Working Paper #880 (August).

Bech, Morten and Jenny Hancock (2020) "Innovation in Payments" *BIS Quarterly Review*, March, pp. 21–36.

BIS Committee on Payment and Market Infrastructures (2020) "Enhancing Cross-Border Payments: Building Blocks for a Global Roadmap" Stage 2 Report to the G20 (July).

Carapella, Francesca and Jean Fleming (2020) "Central Bank Digital Currency: A Literature Review," FEDS Notes, Board of Governors of the Federal Reserve System (November 9).

Carney, Mark (2019) "The Growing Challenges for Monetary Policy in the Current International Monetary and Financial System" Jackson Hole Symposium of the Federal Reserve Bank of Kansas City (August 23).

European Central Bank (2020) "Report on a Digital Euro" (October).

IMF (2020) "Digital Money Across Borders: Macro-Financial Implications" A Staff Report (September 22).

Rey, Helene (2013) "Dilemma Not Trilemma: The Global Financial Cycle and Monetary Policy Independence" Paper Presented at the Economic Policy Symposium of the Federal Reserve Bank of Kansas City (August).

Wong, Paul and Jessie Leigh Maniff (2020), "Comparing Means of Payment: What Role for a Central Bank Digital Currency?" FEDS Notes, Board of Governors of the Federal Reserve System (August 13).

World Bank (2017) "Distributed Ledger Technology (DLT) and Blockchain" FinTech Note #1.

Yaga, Dylan et al (2018) "Blockchain Technology Overview" National Institute of Standards and Technology Internal Report NISTIR 8202 (January).

Zhou, Xiaochuan (2009) "Reform the International Monetary System" *BIS Quarterly Review* (April 1).

CHAPTER 10

Conclusions

The purpose of this chapter is to draw together the main highlights and conclusions of previous chapters into a synthetic vision of the global currency power of the dollar, highlighting both its benefits and costs for the international monetary system, its direct links to the hegemonic role of the United States in the global economy, and its growing threats to the stability of that system over the medium to long term. In this light, the chapter attempts to lay out possible scenarios for a reform of the current system.

The period since the end of WW2 has been the age of the global currency power of the US dollar. There are many dimensions to this unique status of the dollar. At one level, it has been reflected in the simple fact that the dollar has been the main reserve currency of the international monetary system that other countries use as a store of value to cover future contingencies, such as an unexpected shortfall in foreign exchange inflows or a temporary excess in cross-border payments, and planned investment requirements. This function of the dollar builds on the fact that it has been the main currency or medium of exchange used in global foreign exchange market operations related to international trade and financial transactions. It has also served as the primary unit of account for the invoicing of foreign trade and the valuation of international banking and debt transactions. At another level, the unique status of the dollar has been reflected in the fact that it is the currency most frequently used in

A. Elson, *The Global Currency Power of the US Dollar*,
https://doi.org/10.1007/978-3-030-83519-4_10

determining the foreign exchange value of non-dollar currencies, either as a peg in a fixed exchange rate system or as an anchor or reference rate in more flexible arrangements. The dollar has also been the currency most frequently used in the pricing of primary commodities and recording the financial accounts of international institutions, both private and official. In all these respects, the dollar has served in effect as the de facto global monetary unit for most countries and organizations in the international economic and financial system.

Throughout the post-WW2 period, there have been other reserve currencies that have served some of the same functions of the dollar, but each to a much more limited extent. The UK pound was early on the most important, given its co-equal status with the dollar in the pre-War period and the UK's coordinating role with the United States in planning for the Bretton Woods era. However, during that era the pound continued to decline in global status, following a pattern that began during the Great Depression. Then came the rise of the German mark and Japanese yen, following the highly successful recoveries of their economies in the 1950s and 1960s. However, their roles as reserve currencies were limited by conscious political choice and thus they did not fill the full range of reserve currency functions as the dollar. With the establishment of the European Economic and Monetary Union in 1992, the euro was created which consolidated some of the reserve currency functions that had been provided by the currencies of some of its European member countries. However, through most of its existence, the economic authorities of the EMU have focused mainly on establishing the foundations and authority of the euro as a regional currency, and its status as a global reserve currency has clearly remained secondary to that of the dollar. Now with the emergence of China as a major global economy, its leaders have been actively promoting the internationalization of the renminbi, but to date it has played a very limited role in the various functions of a global reserve currency, especially in comparison with those of the dollar.

The global currency power of the dollar cannot be divorced from the hegemonic status of the United States in the international economic and financial system. It has been both a manifestation of that dominant economic status and a reinforcement of it. With the end of WW2, the United States was the largest economy in the global system and had suffered less economic damage than any other of the major combatants. As the most important of the victorious allied powers in economic and military terms, it played a key role in all the post-war planning and creation of the UN system and the Bretton Woods institutions. In particular, prior to the war, the United States had become the largest holder of gold under the pre-war gold standard arrangements and had established parity with Great Britain as an economic power and in the international role of its currency. The Bretton Woods Agreement recognized and formalized the post-war hegemonic status of the US economy and the global currency power of the dollar that has existed up to the present day. This arrangement was embodied in the gold exchange standard established by that Agreement, which tied the dollar to a fixed price of gold as an anchor for the international monetary system and linked other currencies to the dollar by means of pegged (but adjustable) exchange rates. The dollar also served as the main source of official reserves and international liquidity under the Bretton Woods system.

Other countries' dependence upon the dollar as the centerpiece of the international monetary system reinforced the hegemonic status of the United States, as they had an important stake in maintaining that system in order to avoid financial instability and damage to their own economies. This tendency became manifest during the Bretton Woods era (1945–1973) as various collaborative efforts were undertaken by the G10 countries during the decade of the 1960s to sustain the system in the face of imbalances created by expansionary fiscal and monetary policy decisions of the US government. Ultimately the system broke down with the decision of the United States in 1971 to sever the link of the dollar to a fixed price of gold. At this point, the international monetary system shifted to a de facto dollar standard under which the dollar maintained its status as the primary reserve currency and countries were free to establish one of a variety of exchange rate arrangements ranging from fixed rate regimes to freely flexible ones, with the dollar often used as the peg for a fixed exchange rate or reference rate for more flexible arrangements. The revised Bretton Woods Agreement of 1978 embodied this de facto dollar standard, without describing the role of the dollar in any specific terms, and gave the IMF responsibility for its oversight by means of a new function of macroeconomic surveillance that it would use to assess the viability of each member country's exchange rate arrangement in the context of its current and prospective economic and financial position.

Under the de facto dollar standard, the global currency power of the dollar has been solidified and expanded, in particular with the breakup of the Soviet Union and with the intensification of economic and financial globalization. Economic globalization has been encouraged by the progressive and sustained reduction in international trade barriers, first among the advanced countries and then among emerging market economies, and by advances in information and communications technology that have fostered the development of global value chains. The opening of the Chinese economy and its entry into the WTO in 2001 reinforced these tendencies and initiated a major period of supply chain trade and off-shoring of production from the United States that intensified the role of the dollar in trade invoicing, payments and settlement. Financial globalization has followed a later, but similar process of liberalization through the reduction of capital account restrictions, first among the advanced countries and then among emerging market economies. The dominant positions of US financial markets in the global financial system and of American banks in international financial flows have given the dollar a major role in the valuation of international financial transactions that has been reinforced by the dollar's prime role in the invoicing of international trade.

The global currency power of the dollar reflects a number of unique features of the United States in the international system consistent with its hegemonic status. As the largest country in military, economic and financial terms, it has played an indispensable role in promoting a liberal international economic order in which US domestic firms dominating its market-based capitalist economic system could thrive externally as a growing number of countries were incorporated during the post-WW2 period. The United States has been the leader in promoting a reduction of tariff barriers among the advanced countries and in liberalizing international capital flows that were essential for the sustained growth of the global economy. It also has played a key role in creating and in sustaining the international financial architecture, i.e., the economic and financial institutional infrastructure supporting the liberal international economic order (e.g., the FSB, IMF, World Bank and WTO).

As a financial super-power, the United States plays a unique role as a global financial intermediary. It has the largest domestic financial markets of any country in terms of their breadth, depth and liquidity, with fewer restrictions on their access for non-residents and no limits on the convertibility of the dollar. An outward manifestation of these conditions is its gross international investment position (i.e., the sum of its foreign assets and liabilities) which is also the largest of any country. Unlike that of other advanced countries, the net international investment position (NIIP) of the United States (or difference between its foreign assets and liabilities) has turned sharply negative in recent decades as other countries have purchased increasing amounts of its government securities because of their "safe haven" status, while US-based firms and individuals have continued to expand their portfolio and direct investments abroad. The increasingly negative value of the NIIP of the United States also reflects a growing current account imbalance associated with a weakening of its domestic savings in relation to domestic investment.

What is remarkable about the US NIIP is that, despite its sharply negative value, it nonetheless generates a net inflow of interest income as the foreign interest paid by the United States on its foreign liabilities is very low on account of the substantial safety or convenience premium carried by its government securities held abroad, while the interest earnings on its foreign assets are substantially larger reflecting the significant returns earned on its portfolio and direct investment abroad. This positive interest differential and the sustained current account deficit of the United States are two measures of the "exorbitant privilege" that the United States has enjoyed from its role as a global financial intermediary throughout the post-WW2 era.

The openness of the United States' financial system, which has been a critically important dimension of the global currency power of the dollar, has been reinforced by its strong rule of law. An independent judiciary and the sound protection of property rights have been key features of the US legal system and have been available to residents and non-residents alike as a safeguard for their trading contracts and financial transactions.

The various dimensions of the global currency power of the dollar described above have provided a number of benefits to individuals and firms resident in the United States. The conduct of foreign trade and financial transactions in dollars, for example, avoids the cost and inconvenience for foreign exchange transactions and the associated problem of exchange risk. The use of the dollar for invoicing trade makes the procedures for the payment and settlement of trade transactions simpler and more convenient for agents based in the United States, as does the dollar pricing of primary commodities and imported inputs from other countries. The widespread use of the dollar in international financial transactions makes it easier for domestic firms to find potential buyers for their debt or portfolio choices for their investments.

The US government has clearly enjoyed a number of benefits from the dominance of the dollar as a reserve currency. One of these is the "exorbitant privilege" associated with the "safe haven" status of US government securities and the apparent lack of restraint on the country's current account deficit, as noted above. Without this privilege, the interest payments on government debt would be much higher and the United States government would not find as large a demand for its securities as it does now. This privilege is not without limit, however, as it depends critically upon other countries' desire to absorb increasing amounts of those securities, even as the US share of the global economy continues to decline. Up until now, this willingness has been based on a favorable judgement that the United States government will continue to maintain the sustainability of its fiscal and debt position over the medium term, as it has in the past.

Another key benefit the US government has drawn from the global currency power of the dollar is the ability to pay in its own currency for the deployment of its armed forces on a global scale. The United States maintains troop deployments of various sizes in more than 70 countries, while its navy maintains freedom of the seas throughout the globe. This extension of military power is unmatched by any other country and is a key manifestation of the US hegemonic role in the international system. It has also served to protect the geographic boundaries of the liberal international economic order as it has expanded over time and the basis for free trade on a global scale. In this connection, it should be noted that the post-war reconstruction and development of Western Europe, Japan and the rest of East Asia (excluding China) would not have occurred without the military umbrella provided by the United States.

A third advantage the US government has gained from the global preeminence of the dollar relates to its use as an instrument of foreign policy in the form of foreign aid and economic sanctions. Grants of foreign aid in dollars have been a key feature of US foreign policy ever since the Marshall Plan of the early post-WW2 period. Since that time, the United States has been a leader among the advanced countries in the size of its foreign aid distributions, even as those amounts as a share of its GDP have been falling. The scope of its foreign aid budget has expanded in terms of the range of objectives it has served, as has the number of recipients. The largest share of this budget is administered on a bilateral basis.

The use of economic and financial sanctions does not have as long a history as foreign aid, but they have been given increasing importance in recent years as an instrument of US foreign policy. Some of these sanctions have been imposed on a multilateral basis, for example in the context of UN-sponsored efforts to limit Iran and North Korea's development of nuclear weapons. Many more sanctions, however, exist on a bilateral basis and currently affect 20 countries. Even though these sanctions may not be coordinated with other countries, they can still have a substantial, near-global impact on the targeted country because of the dominance of American banks in the international arrangements for the payment, clearing and settlement of foreign trade transactions and international financial flows. In some cases, these sanctions have imposed restrictions on non-US firms in countries friendly to the United States in doing business with the targeted country, which have given rise to complaints in those countries about the US government's excessive reliance on financial sanctions as a form of "weaponizing the dollar".

Some of the benefits for the United States of the global currency power of the dollar can also be understood as benefits for the rest of the world. The US government's strong support for the liberal international economic order and the international financial architecture fall into this category, as this international system has fostered a sustained period of economic growth and reduced income inequality for the global economy, especially in comparison with the first half of the twentieth century. While the United States has clearly prospered within the dollar-dominated global economy, its record of economic growth and inflation control has provided a reasonably stable anchor for the macroeconomic policy management of other countries over the long term, as reflected in the size of the dollar currency zone and the number of countries that use the dollar as a peg or reference rate in the management of the exchange rate for their own currency.

The long-term record of relative macroeconomic stability maintained by the United States has also been reflected in the sustained reliance of other countries on the benefit provided by US government securities as the pre-eminent safe asset in the global financial system. This benefit would not exist without the long-term commitment that the US government has demonstrated to the maintenance of a sound fiscal position. The safety and soundness of US government securities also point to the benefits that other countries derive from their free access to US financial markets which have generated other safe assets of various degrees, as well as a variety of sources of financing for their investment requirements. The convenience yield of US government securities as global safe assets and the free access of other countries to the US major financial markets are the main reason why so many foreign firms and governments have valued their foreign financial transactions in dollars.

Finally, it is important to recognize the indispensable role that the Federal Reserve plays as an informal international lender of last resort within the dollar-dominated global financial system. Without the benefit of this function, global financial stability could not be maintained. This reality was demonstrated very clearly in the wake of the global financial crisis of 2008–2009 and the outbreak of the Covid-19 crisis in February–March 2020. This function of the Fed, involving swap lines of credit with other central banks and special lines of credit for private financial institutions, has been essential for keeping cross-border, dollar-based private credit flows available and for maintaining major debt markets in the United States that attract global participants liquid and functioning in the face of sharp adjustments in supply and demand.

The post-WW2 liberal international economic order, which has been dominated by the United States and the international use of the dollar, has provided a certain coherent structure for the growth and development of other countries and for the steady expansion of the global economy. However, a number of costs can be associated with this system that are likely to become more severe as the relative share of the US economy within the global economy continues to decline with the rapid growth of a number of emerging market economies (e.g., China and India). In addition, recent political developments within the United States raise questions about the durability of the hegemonic role in the international system that it has played in the past.

There are a number of costs associated with the dominant reserve currency status of the dollar that have adverse implications for the future stability of the international financial system and need to be addressed. One of these arises from the relative scarcity of global safe assets to satisfy the liquidity needs of an expanding global economy and the exceptional demand placed on US treasury debt in particular. While this arrangement has given rise to an "exorbitant privilege" for the United States, it is also subject to a "new Triffin Dilemma" in the future as countries will begin to question the ability of the United States to satisfy a growing demand for safe assets and maintain a sustainable fiscal and debt position at the same time. At some point, debt service costs will have to rise and the perverse effects of "debt dynamics" will lead to a fiscal crisis of one kind or another. While the "exorbitant privilege" continues, many EMDEs have been required to participate in an "up-hill" flow of capital in order to accumulate large amounts of US government securities for their official reserves as a form of self-insurance against the possibility of financial crises associated with the volatility of capital flows. The generation of a current account surplus by these countries to allow for an increase in their official reserves has entailed a significant cost in terms of foregone investment. The exceptional demand for US treasury securities has also contributed to a sustained decline in the yields on medium and long-term government debt that can have a dampening effect on economic growth, while providing a stimulus to speculative activity and "bubble" phenomena.

The practice of self-insurance by many EMDEs points to a number of other defects inherent in the dollar-dominated global financial system. One is the volatility of capital flows, noted above, and the frequency of financial crises, which can be related to the negative spillover effects, or the "surges" and "sudden stops" in capital flows associated with monetary policy decisions of the Federal Reserve and its impact on the global financial cycle. Given that the Fed is required to focus primarily on the performance of the US economy (rather than the global economy) and that the United States' share of the global economy will continue to decline, at some point another arrangement will be needed to provide an anchor of stability for the system. The problem of global imbalances, which is related to the US "exorbitant privilege", is one area that is not addressed by the Fed's monetary policy focus and requires a stronger international cooperative effort for its management and resolution operating under the guidance of the IMF.

The practice of self-insurance also points to the inadequacy of the global financial safety net (GFSN). Prior to 2000, the IMF represented the main component of the GFSN, but since then as financial globalization has expanded, its financial resources have been supplemented by those of various regional financial arrangements and central bank swap networks. However, the expansion in these three components of the GFSN has been dwarfed by that of countries' own official reserves, which now measure in dollar value more than three times the size of the other institutional components. Ideally, the share of official reserves within the GFSN should be much smaller than that of the three institutional components, with the Fund being in the lead position consistent with its intended role as the official international lender of last resort.

In addition to the existing defects of the dollar-dominated global financial system, one should assess how recent developments and prospects for the United States may have a negative impact on global financial stability over the medium to long term. In this connection, two developments deserve particular attention: one is the rise of a strong right-wing populist political movement within the United States and the other is the government's debt management problem associated with its response to the Covid-19 crisis.

The US election of 2016 signaled the assertion of a vibrant, populist political movement that represented a strong reaction against liberal immigration policies and other pro-globalist policies of the United States. It also embodied popular resistance to the forces of economic globalization grounded in its adverse effects on workers and industries in many sectors and regions of the US economy and income inequality. The rise in US trade with China following its membership in the WTO in 2001 clearly had a negative impact on low-wage US employment in manufacturing, which was exacerbated by an increase in the off-shoring of domestic industries and supply chain trade. While these job losses were offset to a large extent by gains for high-tech-related labor and professional workers in various service sectors, it is clear in retrospect that not enough was done by way of official policy to assist displaced workers in job retraining and relocation programs and to stimulate new investment in regions or cities negatively impacted by the shock of increased trade with China. These kinds of trade effects clearly had negative implications for income inequality that were also not addressed by public policy.

The Trump administration that came to power in 2017 gave voice to various anti-globalist sentiments in US domestic politics and projected a strong shift away from the commitment to international collaboration typical of previous administrations. This shift was reflected in the United States' withdrawal from various international organizations and a reversal of the country's free trade stance. For the first time in the post-WW2 era, the US government took actions that signaled its withdrawal from the traditional hegemonic role it had adopted in promoting the liberal international economic order, while asserting the readiness of its superior military force against any and all potential adversaries.

While the outcome of the presidential elections of 2020 represented a strong reaction against the anti-globalist policies and tendencies of the Trump administration, it is clear that the populist forces it represented will continue to be a significant factor in domestic US politics, along with the white supremacist and anti-immigrant groups that participated in the insurrectionist attempt of January 6, 2021. This fact has created two problems for the United States looking ahead. One is whether the current and future administrations can garner sufficient popular support for policies that are supportive of globalization and the United States' active engagement in the liberal international economic order. The second problem is that the on-going contest between liberal and anti-liberal policies in the United States has created doubts among many of its allies as to whether it can be trusted to maintain its positive commitment to key multilateral campaigns, e.g., in the area of free trade, cooperation with China, and dealing with climate change. These doubts have come on top of concerns created by the United States' primary role in the global financial crisis of 2008–2009 and its gross failure in managing the Covid-19 crisis during 2020. Some of these doubts have spilled over into questions about the durability of the global currency power of the dollar.

These questions and concerns may also be affected by the way in which the United States manages the debt burden it has assumed in dealing with the Covid-19 crisis. The expansionary impact of the US government's fiscal and monetary policy actions during 2020–2021 has been far greater than that of any other advanced country and have put the government debt to GDP ratio on a trajectory that will more than double over the next few decades. While the increase in government debt in the near term can be justified by the severity of the pandemic's effects on public health and economic activity, it is nonetheless clear that once the pandemic is brought under control and the US economy has been restored to a sustainable growth path, a strong debt management program needs to be put into place, presumably before the end of the current decade. If not, the perverse "debt dynamics" of a negative primary balance, together with a growing excess of the interest rate on debt over the growth rate of the economy, will hasten the arrival of the "new Triffin Dilemma" cited earlier and the possibility of a debt crisis for the United States.

It is difficult to know when and how such a debt crisis could erupt, but it is clear that an increase in the interest rate on US government debt demanded by foreign creditors can occur relatively quickly as a result, for example, of a change in market sentiment related to adverse, unexpected developments in the US economy that raise concerns about their expansionary effect on fiscal policy. In such an eventuality, the Fed would be under great pressure from the Treasury Department to increase its purchases of government debt in order to dampen the rise in interest rates, but this action would be inflationary if sustained and would conflict with the Fed's anti-inflationary policy mandate. If the interest rate on government debt were to be maintained below the rate of inflation for a time, this action would moderate the negative debt dynamics associated with the government's debt situation, but it would only hasten the withdrawal of demand by domestic and foreign creditors and the arrival of conditions for a debt default by the US government. Such an outcome would have global ramifications because of the "safe" asset character of US government debt and a global financial crisis would erupt.

Looking ahead, there are clear questions about the durability of the US hegemonic role in the global economy and the global currency power of the dollar related to uncertainties about the strength of domestic political support for such a role and doubts about the government's ability to re-establish a sustainable debt position over the medium term. These considerations, together with the many defects of the existing dollar-dominated reserve currency system, make a reform of that system a key priority. Until the global pandemic is brought under control and the growth path of the global economy has been restored to its pre-pandemic trajectory, there is clearly no basis for multilateral discussions on a reform of the international monetary system. Even then, it is unlikely that serious reform discussions could take place with the existence of other pressing items of international concern, such as dealing with climate change, the proliferation of nuclear weapons, global pandemics, international migration, potential regional conflicts between China and the United States, and international cybersecurity and terrorism.

In this context, it is useful to consider two evolutionary changes that are now under way and their potential implications for a change in the dollar-dominated reserve currency system. One is the set of developments that may represent the beginning of a shift to a multipolar reserve currency system. The other is the development of digital currencies, both private and public. Each of these is considered below.

The possible weakening in the hegemonic role of the United States comes at a time when there are growing regional blocs centered in the strength of the renminbi in East Asia and the euro in Western Europe. Can one imagine an international system in which the dollar, euro and renminbi would co-exist as relatively co-equal reserve currencies? In such a system, other reserve currencies, such as the British pound, the Japanese yen and the Australian dollar, would continue to exist as minor participants in their execution of certain functions of a reserve currency, but without the link to a major economy that the other three currencies have. History also suggests that a multipolar reserve currency system can exist as was the case for the British pound, the French franc and the German mark for three decades prior to WW1 and for the co-existence of pound and dollar as primary reserve currencies during the period between WW1 and WW2. The latter period, however, was far less stable than the earlier one.[1]

Both the euro and the renminbi are linked to major economies that are roughly one-third smaller than that of the United States, and are clearly weaker reserve currencies than the dollar at present in terms of their share of global official reserves, global payments and foreign exchange transactions. The euro and renminbi also do not have a link to major financial markets that can match those of the United States for their breadth, depth and liquidity and ease of access by non-residents. These disparities suggest that the evolution of the current dollar-dominated reserve currency system to a more balanced multilateral one would be very uneven and potentially unstable in terms of the responses of international capital flows to adverse economic or financial developments in one of the three currency zones that are not shared initially in the other two. This possibility suggests that close coordination in the monetary policy for the three currency blocs would be essential, if the shift to a multipolar reserve currency system intensified, in order to maintain global financial stability.

In considering the expansion in the reserve currency status of the euro and renminbi questions have been asked as to whether the renminbi could overtake the dollar's role as the primary reserve currency, especially in view of the Chinese government's strong interest in augmenting the internationalization of the renminbi. At present, the disparities between the global currency power of the dollar and the renminbi are very great in terms of their shares of global reserves, global payments and foreign exchange transactions. However, given the more rapid rise of the Chinese economy and its increasing share of global trade compared with that of the United States, the role of the renminbi as a reserve currency can be expected to expand. In addition, there has been a growing interest of foreign investors in the local currency capital markets in mainland China. Nevertheless, there are three factors that suggest that the accession of the renminbi to equal or superior status vis-s-vis the dollar will only occur after a significant time span.

One is that China has not established full capital account convertibility, as have the United States and the EMU, which is essential for foreign investors to have confidence that any funds they commit to renminbi-based bond and equity markets can be withdrawn and transferred abroad whenever they prefer. This capital market condition is essential for China to create and maintain a global safe asset that can compete and relieve the burden that now exists on US government securities. Over the past 10 years, the Chinese government has been taking steps to liberalize capital account transactions for both residents and non-residents, but significant restrictions, in particular on capital outflows, continue to exist. The pace at which capital account liberalization has taken place to date suggests that it will be some time before full convertibility is established.

The main reason for this slow pace of change relates to the second factor that will determine the full reserve currency status of the renminbi, which is the nature of its exchange rate regime. Unlike the dollar and euro which operate under fully flexible exchange rate regimes, the exchange rate for the renminbi is subject to manipulation and intervention by the Peoples Bank of China, while tracking the movement of a basket of other currencies (including the dollar) within a certain range of fluctuation. Again, as in the case of capital account convertibility, while the PBOC has been gradually shifting over time from a fixed exchange rate regime (fully tied to the dollar at one point) to one of more flexibility, it is still not clear when it will establish full exchange rate flexibility. In part, this decision depends upon the timing of when the government will establish full capital account convertibility. The pace of change to date suggests that the process of establishing full exchange rate flexibility will be a slow, deliberate one over time.

The third factor affecting the reserve currency status of the renminbi is the role of the Chinese government in economic and social affairs. The Chinese legal system (or "rule by law") is still a work in progress and stems essentially from basic reforms introduced at the beginning of its current development era in the early 1980s. Currently, China does not have the same rule of law, with the protection of individual and property rights and an independent judiciary of the kind that exist in Western European countries and the United States. In addition, the government has been increasing its surveillance of the activities of its citizenry as a means of enhancing the power and control of the Communist Party, while it has exercised an unlimited authority to intervene directly in business affairs, as it did, for example, in canceling the initial public offering of equity shares by the Ant Group in early November 2020.

The absence of a clear rule of law and an independent judiciary in these conditions raise questions about how the rights and interests of non-residents would be protected in the light of potential conflicts that may arise with residents in carrying out business transactions in renminbi as China becomes more open to foreign investors. "Inconsistent interpretation of regulations and unclear laws and enforcement" was listed as the top challenge of doing business in China in 2016 by the American Chamber of Commerce in China. Also limited progress has been made in the protection of intellectual property rights.[2] Clearly to date, the progress that has been made in strengthening non-resident rights for doing business in China has come about as a result of pressures from foreign governments and business groups, which will continue.

The existence of these three factors bearing upon China's reserve currency status suggest that it will be a slow process of evolution towards a dual or triple reserve currency system involving the dollar and renminbi or the dollar, euro and renminbi. What is clear is that the dollar will not, and cannot, maintain its primary reserve currency status indefinitely, especially in view of the defects of the current regime and the challenges facing the United States and the dollar over the medium term.

The second change under way that has possible implications for the reserve currency status of the dollar is the expansion of digital currencies, both public and private. Bitcoin has been the subject of major discussion because of the intense interest it has received as a speculative investment since the onset of the Covid-19 crisis. However, it has very limited potential to serve as a widely accepted private means of payment because of its unstable value, its heavy use in illicit trade and money laundering, and the excessively high, computer energy cost associated with an increase in its supply. However, two experiments in digital currencies relating to central bank digital currencies (CBDCs) and stablecoins (such as Diem) do have significant potential for active use in the future, even though both of these are still in the development stage.

CBDCs can be justified as a means of supplementing the use of paper bills and coins, especially in countries where the share of digital payments in consumer outlays has been increasing sharply (as, for example, in China and Sweden). They may also be introduced as a means of promoting greater financial inclusion and enhancing the impact of monetary policy changes. For some countries (such as China and the EMU), they have been viewed as a means of enhancing the reserve currency status of the national currency, if other basic conditions are in place, such as a sound monetary policy framework, exchange rate flexibility and capital account convertibility. A CBDC with these conditions in place, could be adopted or substituted more easily by other countries for their own currency, if they are subject to very unstable monetary conditions. Developments over the next 5–10 years will reveal the extent to which CBDCs become a standard feature of the monetary landscape. It is likely that a digital dollar will have been created within that timeframe.

A stablecoin such as Diem seems to have enormous potential given its link to a stable source of value (i.e., the US dollar) and its association with one of the big Fintech firms (Facebook) with a large global user base. As in the case of CBDCs, it has the potential to reduce substantially the cost, time and processes involved in cross-border payments. Once an appropriate regulatory framework has been established, Diem is expected to be expanded to operate in more than one currency regime, with the possibility of a global composite digital currency at some point in the future. A global version of Diem would clearly have the potential to compete with the dollar, especially if it were adopted for the invoicing of trade and the valuation of international financial flows. Developments over the next 5–10 years will also reveal the potential scope of the Diem stablecoin.

Depending upon the pace at which change takes place in the development of digital currencies and the expansion of the reserve currency status of the euro and renminbi, the possibility of a formal reform of the international monetary system should not be completely ruled out. A debt crisis by the US government, as discussed earlier, could clearly be one triggering event. In the wake of the global financial crisis of 2009–09, major reforms were introduced among the larger member countries of the IMF in creating the Financial Stability Board for greater oversight with the IMF of the global financial system and in strengthening the international standards for bank regulation. In a period of 10–15 years, it may be clearer that the dollar-centered reserve currency system is no longer viable and that a formal shift to a multilateral reserve currency system would be appropriate.

In this connection, it would be important to consider the possible role of the IMF's SDR and the commitment that already exists in the Fund's Articles of Agreement to make it "the principal reserve asset in the international monetary system". Procedures already exist for its valuation, composition, distribution and expansion; what is missing is a plan to have it replace the dollar as the primary reserve currency in the system. A number of changes could be made now to increase its use in the international monetary system. These include promoting its use as the unit of account for the operations of international financial organizations and for the pricing of primary commodities, building on a few practices that already exist. These organizations, along with private firms and financial institutions, should also be encouraged to issue bonds denominated in SDRs in order to promote a private market for their trading, with governmental assistance in creating the infrastructure and liquidity for such trading. A substitution account in the Fund could be created to allow countries to convert their dollar assets into SDRs, while a program is established to increase the circulation of SDRs on a continuing basis to satisfy the growing demand for safe assets in the future. Clearly a plan embracing the kind of changes noted here would require strong support among the membership of the Fund and significant pressure from its large quota countries on the United States.

It is interesting to note that both the Governor of the Peoples Bank of China in 2009 and the Governor of the Bank of England in 2019 have made reform proposals supporting the shift to an SDR-based reserve currency system, the first one directly and the second one indirectly. The more recent proposal was expressed in terms of creating a "Synthetic Hegemonic Currency", or a composite of the future CBDCs of the major central banks, that would share certain characteristics with the SDR, but in digital form. With continued periods of instability in the global financial system in the future, it is likely that other public officials will call attention to the potential role of the SDR in a reform of the dollar-centered reserve currency system.

Notes

1. These two periods of currency history are examined in Barry Eichengreen et al. (2018) *How Global Currencies Work: Past Present and Future* (Princeton, NJ: Princeton Univ. Press).
2. These concerns of the American Chamber of Commerce in China were highlighted in a blog of the National Bureau of Asian Research ("Rule of Law in China: An Essential Component of US–China Relations") on May 16, 2017 (www.nbr.org).

Index

A
active labor market policies (ALMP), 105, 106
Afghanistan, 60, 61
American Rescue Plan, 112, 113, 115
Apple iPhone, 97
Argentina, 62, 162
Australia, 36, 68, 192
Autor, David, 101, 102, 117

B
balance of payments accounting, 49
Bancor, 19
Bank of Canada, 68, 84, 165
Bank of England, 68, 84, 159, 170, 197
Bank of Japan, 68, 84, 127
Belt and Road Initiative, 135, 167, 177
Bitcoin, 13, 123, 159–162, 170–172, 177, 195
Blanchard, Olivier, 114, 118
Bloomberg Barclays Global Aggregate Index, 134
Brainard, Lael, 168, 169, 178
Brazil, Russia, India, China and South Africa (BRICS), 130, 156
Bretton Woods Agreement, 9, 15, 17–19, 23, 31, 41, 45, 56, 121, 122, 183
Bretton Woods Conference, 17, 20, 95, 122
Bretton Woods era, 31, 32, 34, 39, 47, 48, 56, 105, 107, 154, 173, 182, 183
Bretton Woods system, 3, 17, 21–26, 28, 40, 80, 83, 85, 90, 108, 122, 183

C
Cambridge Bitcoin Electricity Consumption Index, 177
Canada, 35, 36, 178
capital account liberalization, 19, 95, 154, 168, 194
Carney, Mark, 159, 160, 170, 174, 175, 177
Cecchetti, Stephen, 92, 117

A. Elson, *The Global Currency Power of the US Dollar*,
https://doi.org/10.1007/978-3-030-83519-4

central bank digital currencies (CBDCs), 13, 159, 160, 162, 164–169, 172, 174–176, 178, 195–197
Chiang Mai Initiative-Multilaterialization, 143, 156
Chicago Board Options Exchange (CBOE), 75
Chile, 61, 103, 141
China, 13, 29, 33, 35, 36, 41, 58, 59, 63, 64, 80, 82, 96–104, 108, 125–137, 139, 141, 150, 155–157, 159, 162, 165, 167, 176–178, 182, 186, 188, 190–195
China Foreign Exchange Trade System (CFETS), 136
Chinn-Ito index, 50
Clearinghouse Int'l Payments System (CHIPS), 63
collateralized debt obligations (CDOs), 45, 46
Colombia, 60, 61, 141
Congressional Budget Office (CBO), 111, 117
Cooper, Richard, 28
Covid-19 crisis, 3, 5, 6, 12, 24, 50, 57, 62, 67–69, 84, 89, 95, 98–100, 107, 111, 141, 142, 145, 147, 156, 161, 188, 190, 191, 195
Cross-border Interbank Payments System (CIPS), 64
cryptoassets/cryptocurrency, 13, 159–161, 164, 172, 177, 178
current account balance, 18, 56, 79
current account convertibility, 19, 22
current account deficit, 10, 29, 48–50, 56–58, 80, 83–85, 90, 108, 185, 186

D

debt dynamics, 66, 67, 108, 112–115, 188, 191, 192
debt sustainability, 43, 66, 67, 83, 87, 89, 106–108, 112–114, 123, 152, 177
digital currency/electronic payment (DCEP), 168, 176, 177
distributed ledger/blockchain technology (DLT), 161, 171, 178
dollar pricing, 54, 185
dollar standard, 24, 26, 32, 34, 183
dominant currency, 1–3, 6, 10, 11, 15, 16, 32, 35, 39, 40, 54, 55, 92, 95
dynamic instability, 21, 23, 25, 26

E

Egypt, 60
Eichengreen, Barry, 28, 29, 51
Emerging Market and Developing Economies (EMDEs), 5–7, 10, 11, 13, 20, 80, 81, 88, 124, 132, 139–141, 143, 145, 149, 152, 156, 175, 188, 189
Euro, 1, 2, 12, 22–25, 31, 34, 40, 50, 54, 123, 125–130, 133–135, 142, 144, 156, 165, 170, 182, 192–196
Euro currency zone, 40, 130
European Central Bank (ECB), 46, 68, 84, 126–128, 130–132, 136, 143, 165, 177, 178
European Economic and Monetary Union (EMU), 85, 126–136, 182, 193, 195
European Payments Union (EPU), 22
Exchange Stabilization Fund (ESF), 61, 62
"exorbitant duty", 18

"exorbitant privilege", 10, 23, 29, 32, 48, 55, 56, 58, 59, 84, 89, 90, 124, 126, 127, 185, 186, 188, 189

F

FARC, 60
Federal Reserve (Fed), 6–8, 10, 11, 24, 38, 41, 42, 46, 62, 63, 67, 75, 76, 81, 83, 89, 110, 111, 114, 116, 118, 124, 127, 130–132, 159, 161, 168, 169, 188, 189
FEDwire, 63
financial account surplus, 49
Financial Committee (league of Nations), 16, 18
"financial repression tax", 110, 117
financial sanctions, 5, 63, 64, 70, 98, 186, 187
Financial Stability Board (FSB), 11, 122, 124, 152, 163, 184, 196
"flights" of capital, 76
foreign aid, 59, 61, 135, 186
Foreign and International Monetary Authorities REPO Facility (FIMA), 68
foreign direct investment (FDI), 21, 25, 29, 47, 55, 57, 64, 75
France, 106
FTSE Russell World Government Bond index, 134
"fundamental disequilibrium", 85

G

General Agreement on Tariffs and Trade (GATT), 17, 18, 32, 41
Gensler, Gary, 177
Georgieva, Kristalina, 28
Germany, 43, 64, 85, 106, 131, 133
GINI coefficient, 102, 103
Ginnie Mae (Government National Mortgage Association), 45
"global banker to the world", 47, 48
global financial crisis, 3, 5, 6, 9–11, 24, 29, 34, 36, 37, 43, 45, 46, 48, 58, 66–70, 74–78, 82, 84, 89, 90, 103, 104, 107, 111, 122, 124, 125, 130, 140–142, 145, 146, 148, 152, 154, 156, 163, 188, 191, 192, 196
global financial cycle, 11, 76–78, 88, 91, 124, 152, 168, 175, 189
global financial safety net (GFSN), 11, 81, 90, 124, 139, 140, 143, 149, 150, 156, 189
global financial system, 2–6, 9–12, 35, 36, 38, 43, 45, 47, 48, 51, 56, 65–67, 70, 73, 75, 77, 79, 80, 82–84, 87, 88, 91, 116, 124, 148, 152, 184, 187–189, 196, 197
global imbalances, 11, 29, 57, 58, 79, 86, 87, 90, 124, 146, 149, 152, 153, 189
global stablecoins (GSC), 13, 160, 162, 164, 170, 172, 174, 176, 178
global value chains (GVCs), 33, 34, 41, 55, 184
global "venture capitalist", 48
gold exchange standard, 16, 17, 28
gold pool, 23, 24, 29
Gopinath, Gita, 50, 51, 70, 92
Gourinchas, Pierre-Olivier, 51, 117
Govillot, Nicholas, 51
"Great Moderation", 67, 70
"Great Replacement", 106, 107, 117
G7 (Group of 7), 5, 65, 98, 162
G10 (Group of 10), 23–26, 183
G20 (Group of 20), 5, 11, 98, 145, 162

H

hegemonic power, 6, 11, 48, 56
"helicopter money", 167

I

Ilzetzki, Ethan, 51, 92, 136
impossible trinity/international policy trilemma, 77, 78, 168
Instrument in Support of Trade Exchanges (INSTEX), 63
interest equalization tax, 24
International Clearing Union (ICU), 19, 26
international investment position (IIP), 6, 34, 35, 45, 74, 128, 133, 184
international lender of last resort (ILOLR), 6, 8–10, 13, 67, 69, 81, 83, 88–90, 123, 124, 128, 140, 146, 188, 189
International Monetary Fund (IMF), 2, 15
  Annual Report on Exchange Arrangements and Exchange Restrictions (AREAER), 86, 92, 129
  Articles of Agreement, 20, 78, 124, 143, 150, 154, 196
  Article IV, 27, 154
  Article VI, 19, 154
  Article VIII, 86
  Article XXII, 31
  C20 (Committee of 20), 26, 27
  External Sector Report, 87, 153
  Flexible Credit Line (FCL), 61, 70, 141, 142
  International Monetary and Financial Committee (IMFC), 122, 152
  par values, 17, 26
  Precautionary and Liquidity Line (PLL), 141, 142
  Quotas, 20, 139–141, 144, 150, 155–157
  Rapid Credit Facility (RCF)/Rapid Financing Instrument (RFI), 141, 142
International Monetary Fund (IMF)
  Special Drawing Rights (SDR), 9, 196
  Short-term Liquidity Line (SLL), 142, 143, 157
  Substitution Account, 13, 27, 149, 150
international monetary system, 2, 3, 7, 9, 11–16, 18–20, 26–29, 31, 53, 56, 59, 81, 88, 90, 95, 99, 121–124, 126, 136, 139, 140, 143–146, 148, 151, 152, 154, 157, 159, 163, 167, 176, 177, 181, 183, 192, 196
Iraq, 60
"irreconcilable duo", 78
Israel, 60

J

Japan, 35–37, 43, 79, 155, 186
Japanese yen, 2, 40, 182, 192
Joint Comprehensive Plan of Action (JCPOA), 64, 98
Jordan, 60
JPM coin, 172, 173

K

Kelton, Stephanie, 118
Kenen, Peter, 157
Keynes, J.M., 19, 20, 26, 116
Krishnamurthy, Arvind, 92
Krugman, Paul, 117

L

Lardy, Nicolas, 137

lender of last resort, 9, 69, 176
Libra (Diem), 170
"liquidation effect", 111, 117
Lustig, Haimo, 92

M
macroprudential regulation, 11
"market-maker of last resort", 69
Marshall Plan, 22, 59, 186
Mexico, 61, 62, 68, 103, 106, 141
Modern Monetary Theory (MMT), 115, 118
mortgage-backed securities (MBS), 45, 46
multicurrency digital token (XDM), 170, 171, 173, 174, 176
multi-reserve currency system, 121, 123, 125, 127, 128, 130, 135, 136, 160, 174
"Mundellian Trilemma"/Impossible Trinity, 77

N
"narrow banking", 171
"natural hedges", 37
net international investment position (NIIP), 49, 58, 70, 184, 185
new Triffin Dilemma, 21, 82–84, 89, 107, 108, 111, 114–117, 122, 124, 127, 135, 146, 174, 188, 191
North Korea, 62, 63, 187

O
Obstfeld, Maurice, 87, 92
Official foreign reserves, 2, 4, 39, 40, 51, 65, 79–81, 90, 125
Official Monetary and Financial Institutions Forum (OMFIF), 178
Organization of Economic Cooperation and Development (OECD), 11, 61, 65, 103, 106, 124

P
Peoples Bank of China (PBOC), 126, 127, 129, 132, 160, 164, 166, 167, 176, 177, 194, 197
Peru, 61, 141
Plan Colombia, 60, 61, 70
Polak, J.J., 157
Poland, 61, 141
post-Bretton Woods era, 28, 40, 45, 47, 48, 65, 67, 89
Project Hamilton, 169, 178
"proof of work", 161, 162, 171
protection of property rights, 5, 42, 185
"push" "pull" and "pipe" factors, 75, 76

R
Rajan, Raghuran, 157
real time gross settlement (RTGS), 163
Regional Comprehensive Economic Partnership (RCEP), 96
Reinhart, Carmen, 51, 91, 92, 117, 136
Renminbi, 2, 12, 25, 64, 123, 125–128, 130, 134, 135, 144, 147, 157, 165, 167, 168, 176, 177, 182, 192–196
Renminbi currency zone, 12, 134, 193
repurchase agreements (REPOs), 37, 46, 68, 69
reserve currency, 4, 9, 12, 16, 17, 23, 31, 40, 59, 121, 123–126, 128–130, 132–135, 145, 160, 162, 167, 168, 170, 173, 174,

176, 177, 181–183, 185, 188, 192–197
"retrenchments", 74, 76, 78
Rey, Helene, 51, 91, 168, 178
Rogoff, Kenneth, 51, 70, 91, 92, 136
"Roosa bonds", 24
Russia, 63, 130

S

"safe" assets, 4, 6, 8, 10–12, 14, 45, 47, 48, 50, 54, 56, 57, 66, 69, 73, 79, 80, 82–84, 88, 89, 107, 108, 116, 123, 124, 127, 130, 133, 135, 136, 145, 151, 174, 187, 188, 192, 194, 197
"safe haven" assets, 5, 38, 43, 45, 46, 66, 69, 107, 185, 186
savings-investment gap, 50
Schoenholtz, Kermit, 92
Schott, Jeffrey, 70
seigniorage, 10, 58, 59, 70, 79, 128
"shadow banks", 43
Singapore, 68, 167, 170
Society for Worldwide Interbank Financial Telecommunication (SWIFT), 2, 63, 136, 164
South Korea, 43, 62, 68
"Specially Designated Nationals" (SDN), 63
stablecoins, 13, 160–162, 170, 172, 176, 195, 196
"sudden stops", 6, 7, 74, 76, 81, 88, 140, 189
Summers, Larry, 102, 136
"surges", 74, 76, 78, 88, 165, 189
swaps, 6–8, 11, 24, 29, 36–38, 42, 46, 54, 62, 68–70, 81, 83, 89, 90, 126, 127, 140, 142, 143, 167, 188, 189
Swiss Financial Market Regulatory Authority (FINMA), 170, 172
Swiss National Bank, 68, 84, 127
Synthetic Hegemonic Currency (SHC), 14, 159, 174, 197
Syria, 63

T

Tether stablecoin (USDT), 161
Trade Adjustment Assistance (TAA), 101, 106
Trans Pacific Partnership (TPP), 96, 98
Treasury Department (USA), 7, 19, 20, 24, 61–63, 70, 110, 111, 191
"Triffin Dilemma", 21, 82, 107, 122
Triffin, Robert, 28, 83, 157

U

Ukraine, 63
"up-hill" capital flows, 88, 124, 145, 188
US Agency for International Development (UDSAID), 59

V

Venezuela, 63
VIX indicator, 75, 76

W

World Bank, 5, 20, 22, 65, 70, 98, 128, 144, 150, 177, 184
World Health Organization (WHO), 98, 99
World Trade Organization (WTO), 33, 41, 88, 97, 98, 100, 128, 136, 184, 190

Z

Zhou, Xiaochuan, 177

The manufacturer's authorised representative in the EU is Springer Nature Customer Service Centre GmbH, Europaplatz 3, 69115 Heidelberg, Germany. If you have any concerns regarding our products, please contact ProductSafety@springernature.com

Printed and bound by CPI Group (UK) Ltd, Croydon, CR0 4YY

30/09/2026

02225702-0003